lonely planet

NAOMI ARNOLD, ANDREW BAIN,
PETER DRAGICEVICH, CRAIG MCLACHLAN

Contents

PLAN YOUR TRIP
Welcome to New Zealand 4
My Perfect Hike 6
Our Picks 8
When to Go 16
Get Prepared for
New Zealand 18

BY REGION

THE NORTH 21
Te Paki Coastal Track 24
Kerikeri River 26
Kawerau Track Loop 28
Rangitoto Summit Loop 30
Te Ara Hura Day Walk 32
Coast to Coast Walkway 34
Kauaeranga Kauri Trail 40
Karangahake Gorge 42
Also Try 44

CENTRAL
NORTH ISLAND 47
Tongariro Alpine Crossing 50
Tama Lakes 56
Rainbow Mountain/
Maunga Kākaramea 58
Tarawera Trail 60
Whirinaki Waterfall
Loop Track 62
Ngā Tapuwae o Toi 64
Cooks Cove Walkway 70
Te Mata Peak 72
Also Try 74

SOUTHERN
NORTH ISLAND 77
Pouākai Crossing 80
Wilkies Pools 86

Manawatū Gorge 88
Kāpiti Island Summit 90
Paekākāriki Escarpment 92
Otari-Wilton's Bush Loop 94
Also Try 98

TOP OF THE SOUTH 101
Green Hills &
Wharariki Beach 104
Pupu Hydro Walkway 106
Abel Tasman Day Walk 108
Mt Robert/
Pourangahau Circuit 112
Queen Charlotte Day Walk 114
Also Try 116

CANTERBURY 119
Godley Head/Awaroa 122
Sign of the Packhorse 124
Kaikōura Peninsula Walkway 126
Avalanche Peak 128
Bealey Spur 130
Woolshed Creek Hut 132
Mt John (Ōtehīwai) 136
Hooker Valley 138
Mueller Hut 140
Also Try 142

WEST COAST 145
Charming Creek
North Walkway 148
Punakaiki-Pororari Loop 150
Ōkārito Pack Track &
Coastal Walk 152
Alex Knob 154
Lake Matheson 156
Monro Beach 158
Also Try 160

OTAGO 163
Rob Roy Track 166
Diamond Lake &
Rocky Mountain 168
Roys Peak 170
Ben Lomond 172
Bob's Cove 176
Lake Hayes 178
Routeburn Track Day Walk 180
Sandymount & Sandfly Bay 184
Long Beach 186
Also Try 188

THE SOUTH 191
Milford Track Day Walk 194
Gertrude Saddle 198
Lake Marian 200
Key Summit 202
Mavora Walkway 204
Brod Bay to Te Anau 206
Rainbow Reach
to Shallow Bay 208
Ulva Island - Te Wharawhara
Marine Reserve 210
Port William/Potirepo
to Halfmoon Bay/Oban 212
Also Try 216

BACK MATTER
Arriving 218
Getting Around 219
Accommodation 220
Hiking 221
Health & Safe Travel 222
Responsible Travel 223
Nuts & Bolts 224
By Difficulty 225

Welcome to New Zealand

Nau mai haere mai ki Aotearoa.

Welcome to New Zealand. This friendly, down-to-earth nation moored in the Pacific Ocean has a vast and inspiring range of options for hikers, from popular, well-trodden tracks to backcountry wilderness. Hiking, or 'tramping', is firmly embedded in New Zealand's national psyche, thanks to its large conservation estate, widespread network of tracks and huts, endemic plants and animals, and astonishing landscapes. Hikers here can find themselves ranging along beaches, trekking rims of sulphur-laden volcanoes, and circling blue lakes while admiring rich primeval forest – all of it often within a few hours' drive of each other. A small population of 5.2 million souls (in a country the size of the UK) is concentrated mostly in coastal cities, leaving much of its rumpled rural and wilderness areas refreshingly empty of people. The walks here traverse the best of this grandly beautiful yet neighbourly little hiking paradise.

Hooker Valley (p138)
YUNSUN_KIM/SHUTTERSTOCK

My Perfect Hike

Naomi Arnold

TONGARIRO ALPINE CROSSING

P.50

After I'd walked the one-day Tongariro Alpine Crossing, I told a friend it was the best day I'd had in my life. The feeling of being transported to the smoking throat of the Earth was that powerful. There was light snow that day, and I think the quieter late autumn is a wonderful time to visit; a dusting of snow and a nip in the air makes the bright volcanic colours that much more exciting.

Andrew Bain

MUELLER HUT

P.140

Mueller Hut defies numbers to deliver arguably the greatest tramping high in New Zealand. The little red shed sits only 1800m above sea level – a height at which many world mountains are just getting started – but it delivers views worthy of crampons and an ice axe. Aoraki/Mt Cook is close at hand, the reflections of the Sealy Tarns can be near-perfect and then there's Sir Edmund Hillary's first mountain conquest in its backyard. It's a compelling day out.

Tongariro Alpine Crossing (p50)

Best Scenic Hikes

1 Diamond Lake and Rocky Mountain: Outstanding views of Lake Wānaka and its alpine surrounds.

2 Roys Peak: It's a busy Instagram favourite, but that's for a very good reason: the views.

3 Monro Beach: At this remote West Coast beach you may see tawaki, one of the world's rarest penguins.

4 Green Hills and Wharariki Beach: You won't get high in a physical sense, but the coastal beauty will still send you soaring.

5 Bealey Spur: A gradual climb leads to stunning views. Choose fine weather to make the most of them.

Best Urban Hikes

① **Rangitoto Summit Loop:** Just a short ferry ride from Auckland is a beautiful young volcano with a cloak of forest.

② **Kerikeri River:** Stunning bush and waterfalls abound on this riverside track just out of town.

③ **Coast to Coast Walkway:** Auckland is a beautiful city and this is one of the nicest ways to experience its charms.

④ **Sign of the Packhorse Hut:** A historic stone hut is the destination of this short walk near Christchurch with spectacular views.

⑤ **Ben Lomond:** Climb high above Queenstown on this locals' favourite. At 1438m it's a rewarding slog.

Craig McLachlan

PORT WILLIAM/ POTIREPO TO HALFMOON BAY/OBAN

P.212

I love the walk from Port William/Potirepo back to Halfmoon Bay/Oban on Stewart Island/Rakiura. It feels like a different world down there. Enjoy a coastal boat ride to the now uninhabited, former pioneering settlement of Port William/Potirepo, learn some intriguing local history, then hike back through native bush and along deserted beaches on part of the Rakiura Track, before settling in with a cold beer in a classic Kiwi pub at Oban's South Sea Hotel.

Peter Dragicevich

QUEEN CHARLOTTE DAY WALK

P.114

Of all the tracks I researched for this book, the Queen Charlotte Day Walk is the most memorable. Starting with a boat trip tracing the remotest curlicues of Marlborough Sounds, the whole experience is hard to top for its easy access to lost-in-time wilderness. There were only a handful of other hikers that day, so for most of the track it was just me, a chorus of native birds and a constant succession of extraordinary views.

Best Family Hikes

① **Long Beach:** Let the kids out of the car to run wild across broad sands to a fun sea cave.

② **Brod Bay to Te Anau:** A fun, short boat ride takes you to an easy three- to four-hour bushwalk back to town.

③ **Lake Hayes:** An easy three-hour walk will have the kids racing around this pretty lake loop with good swimming.

④ **Karangahake Gorge:** Fun tunnels and interesting gold-mining history make this walk great for kids.

⑤ **Pupu Hydro Walkway:** Kids and adults alike will be awed by the blue and green beauty of these crystal-clear pools.

Our Picks

BEST MOUNTAIN HIKES

Get high, naturally. New Zealand is on the boundary of the Australian and Pacific plates, making it tectonically active, and that means mountains: alps and volcanoes rearing straight up from flat plains. Though it'll doubtless be a slog, it's easy to get past the tree line into alpine landscapes for views that will quite literally take your breath away. Try tackling these walks to spend a pleasant day among the mountains.

TOP TIP

Summer can still bring snow, hail and ice. Carry enough food, water and clothing to take care of yourself and others.

Avalanche Peak
Head to Arthur's Pass and go straight up, following a poled route to the 1100m summit.
P.128

Tongariro Alpine Crossing
A busy but breathtaking walk among volcanoes. Going in shoulder season will help you avoid crowds.
P.50

Lake Marian
A pretty hike to an alpine lake in a hanging valley. One of Fiordland's best.
P.200

Key Summit
A half-day's walk brings you to panoramic views of mountains and alpine lakes.
P.202

Pouākai Crossing
Admire Taranaki *maunga* (mountain) on a reasonably flat yet challenging full-day mountain hike.
P.80

Left: Mt Taranaki (p81); Right: Lake Marian (p200)

TOP TIP

Mountains are unstable and tracks can become impassable. Always check the Department of Conservation (DOC) website for the latest track conditions *(doc.govt.nz)*.

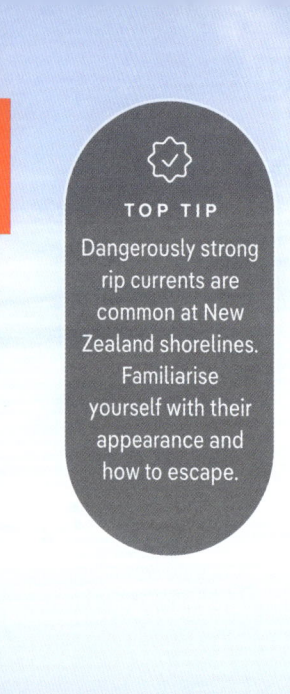

TOP TIP
Dangerously strong rip currents are common at New Zealand shorelines. Familiarise yourself with their appearance and how to escape.

Our Picks

BEST COASTAL HIKES

You're never far from the sea in New Zealand, and its massive, scalloped coastline means you can always find a beach pleasantly bustling with summer crowds, or an empty stretch of sand to run wild on remote dunes, cliffs, headlands and sea caves. The wind and weather in this island nation can be bracing, but that's all part of the fun – and the crowds will stay away.

TOP TIP
Some coastal walks in New Zealand require paying attention to tide times. Check ahead to avoid getting stranded.

1 Abel Tasman Day Walk
Golden sands, blue waters; walk along some of the loveliest beaches in New Zealand.
P.108

2 Te Paki Coastal Track
A sometimes wild, always invigorating trip to a spiritually rich area of New Zealand.
P.24

Queen Charlotte Day Walk (p114)

3 Queen Charlotte Day Walk
Amble along well-formed tracks as beautiful bays reveal themselves in this ocean playground.
P.114

4 Ngā Tapuwae o Toi
Walk headlands to Ōhope, one of New Zealand's best beaches in a quiet seaside town.
P.64

5 Ōkārito Pack Track and Coastal Walk
A wild, remote beach and bush walk in a tiny settlement on the West Coast.
P.152

Cape Reinga (p25)

Our Picks

BEST BIRD-WATCHING HIKES

Though once blessed with rich birdlife that faced no threats from ground mammals, New Zealand's biodiversity is now at severe risk from introduced pests and predators. However, its unique and beautiful endemic birds still thrive in sanctuaries, offshore islands and in some lucky places on the mainland. Bring your binoculars on these walks: here are some of your best chances to spot the tīeke (saddleback), kākā (parrot), kiwi, tītipounamu (rifleman) and more.

TOP TIP

Curious brown weka look cute darting about your picnic spot, but they are devious thieves. Mind your food and gear!

❶ Ulva Island - Te Wharawhara Marine Reserve

Many walkers on Stewart Island/Rakiura are delighted to encounter the elusive kiwi. Good luck!

P.210

❷ Kāpiti Island Summit

A beautiful day out on a bird-filled island sanctuary not far from Wellington.

P.90

❸ Kawerau Track Loop

Just an hour's ferry ride from Auckland is this subtropical, bird-lover's paradise.

P.28

❹ Mt Robert/Pourangahau Circuit

Years of predator trapping in Nelson Lakes National Park has seen birdlife thrive.

P.112

❺ Mavora Walkway

Flitting, friendly toutouwai (South Island robin) abound at this *Lord of the Rings* filming location.

P.204

Left: Tiritiri Matangi Island (p28); Right: Kākā, Kāpiti Island (p90)

TOP TIP
Human food is not for wildlife. As tempting as it may be, don't feed any curious creature eyeing your sandwich.

Our Picks

BEST GLACIAL HIKES

New Zealand's remarkable geology means some of its glaciers and alpine areas are surprisingly accessible to the main state highways. It's not uncommon to pull into a parking bay near the coast and be able to view nearby glaciers. Although glacial extent is now retreating due to climate change, it's still possible to glimpse these mighty, land-shaping forces on a half-day or day walk.

TOP TIP

Resist the temptation to jump into glacial lakes or rivers for that Instagram picture – currents and ice make them dangerous.

❶ Alex Knob
It's a challenging day walk, but the reward is a close encounter with Franz Josef Glacier/Kā Roimata o Hine Hukatere.
P.154

❷ Mueller Hut
A challenging day walk into a jaw-dropping glacier-strewn alpine landscape. Or stay overnight!
P.140

❸ Lake Matheson
A justifiably famous vista of a serene lake reflecting Aoraki/Mt Cook and mountains to mirror perfection.
P.156

❹ Rob Roy Track
A forested track climbs to a dramatic alpine gallery, with splendid views of waterfalls and the Rob Roy Glacier.
P.166

❺ Hooker Valley
Walk among alpine giants to a view of the glacier-fed, iceberg-filled Hooker Lake.
P.138

AUTUMN SKY PHOTOGRAPHY/SHUTTERSTOCK

Mueller Hut (p138)

Our Picks

BEST DRAMATIC HIKES

New Zealand has plenty of calm, serene landscapes, but sometimes a mix of the elements, landscape and tides can provide you with a more invigorating day out. If you're after particular drama, check out some of these walks that get you up close and personal with interesting interactions between coastal or alpine natural processes clashing with wind, weather, oceans and erosion. Be extra cautious and step very carefully in some of them!

TOP TIP
New Zealand has a variable enough climate that the weather can still play havoc with plans. Prepare accordingly!

Cape Brett (p44)

1

Paekākāriki Escarpment
Take a train and reach dizzying heights – literally – on this remarkable, vertiginous one-way track near Wellington.
P.92

2

Punakaiki-Pororari Loop
On a stormy day at high tide, the waves smash into the Pancake Rocks, bringing blowholes to life.
P.150

3

Milford Track Day Walk
Experience a snippet of 'the finest walk in the world' on this trip into New Zealand's best scenery.
P.194

4

Cape Brett Track
Step carefully – this track clings to cliffside trails with steep drop-offs and expansive views.
P.44

5

Te Whara Track
More vertiginous vistas: this steep climb showcases a stunning sweep of ocean and offshore islands.
P.44

When to Go

Summer is for holiday crowds; head to New Zealand in autumn for quieter tracks and more settled weather.

> ### 📍 I LIVE HERE
>
> **ALL THE WEATHER, ALL THE TIME**
>
> **Lauren Fletcher is a marine biologist living in the hiking hub of Nelson, a seaside town surrounded by mountains and national parks. @laurenfletch**
>
> 'I find beauty and joy in the heat of summer as well as short winter days of snow and hoar frost. A 10-day trip to reach Fiordland's remote Ivory Lake one New Year had both; the tiny six-bunk hut is perched on the edge of a cirque, requiring ice travel to reach it. Another trip to Hector Mountains/ Mt Tapuae-o-Uenuku in late summer was a reminder of New Zealand's tempestuous weather; we faced a freak snowstorm, but had prepared for anything.'

Buffeted by sun, wind and sea on all sides, New Zealand lives up to the title of one of its favourite songs, Crowded House's 'Four Seasons in One Day'. Hiking during the Kiwi summer holidays (December to February) means sunburn from the devastatingly clear atmosphere, as well as crowds; avoid Christmas to New Year.

Autumn (March to May) should be the hiker's target, with calm, dry weather and swimmable sea and river temperatures. Winter (June to August) is rewarding for solitude and clear, crisp days, but snow and icy conditions leave some tracks off-limits. Spring (September to November) can mean storms and slips (landslides), but tracks are still quiet.

Mt Taranaki (p81)

Weather Watch (Wellington)

JANUARY	FEBRUARY	MARCH	APRIL	MAY	JUNE
Average daytime max: **17°C**. Days of rainfall: **7**	Average daytime max: **17°C**. Days of rainfall: **7**	Average daytime max: **16°C**. Days of rainfall: **9**	Average daytime max: **14°C**. Days of rainfall: **10**	Average daytime max: **12°C**. Days of rainfall: **13**	Average daytime max: **10°C**. Days of rainfall: **13**

> **TOP TIP**
>
> Because of its position on the International Date Line, New Zealand is one of the first places in the world to see the sunrise. Head to the North Island's East Cape to get a jump on the rest of the world's rays.

Tolaga Bay (p70)

A Bunk for the Night

For a cheaper rest, avoid visiting in the high season (December to February) and try choosing from among New Zealand's large selection of holiday parks. Even small settlements will have one in an excellent location offering basic cabins with shared bathrooms, recreation and kitchen facilities. The holiday parks run by the Top 10 chain are clean and well-maintained, but quirkier independent options abound, too.

> **FROM SUBTROPICAL TO SUBANTARCTIC**
>
> Though a Pacific archipelago, New Zealand has a broad range of temperatures. Overlaying Aotearoa New Zealand on North America would see it stretching from Toronto to Orlando. A cool summer's day in Milford Sound/Piopiotahi will be quite different from that in Kaitaia!

BIG & BOLD FESTIVALS

Rhythm and Alps

A New Year's institution, this multiday international music festival attracts tens of thousands to a picturesque sheep station (farm) near Wānaka. Rhythm and Vines is the North Island equivalent, in the Hawke's Bay. **December/January**

Polyfest

For half a century, talented young performers have been competing across music, dance, speech and costume disciplines over four days at Polyfest. It offers a remarkable glimpse into how Pacific New Zealanders celebrate their heritage. **April**

WOMAD

Brings together the global best of art, dance and music across three days in New Plymouth. **March**

Hokitika Wildfoods Festival

A national icon celebrating the West Coast of the South Island, Wildfoods will see you slurping up huhu grubs, snails, locusts and wild game, as well as tamer options. Dance it all off afterwards. **March**

JULY Average daytime max: **9°C**. Days of rainfall: **13**

AUGUST Average daytime max: **10°C**. Days of rainfall: **12**

SEPTEMBER Average daytime max: **11°C**. Days of rainfall: **11**

OCTOBER Average daytime max: **12°C**. Days of rainfall: **12**

NOVEMBER Average daytime max: **14°C**. Days of rainfall: **10**

DECEMBER Average daytime max: **16°C**. Days of rainfall: **10**

Get Prepared for New Zealand

Useful things to load in your bag, your ears and your brain.

WATCH

After the Party
(Peter Salmon; 2023)
A critically acclaimed six-part drama as tense as a thriller, it will leave you with lingering moral questions.

Hunt for the Wilderpeople
(Taika Waititi; 2016)
Wildly popular family movie featuring Sam Neill and a cast of Kiwi characters against a backdrop of rural New Zealand.

The Piano
(Jane Campion; 1993)
One of New Zealand cinema's first big hits, the 19th-century drama launched the career of Anna Paquin.

Shortland Street
(Various directors; 1992–today) New Zealand's longest-running TV soap opera is a medical drama renowned for highlighting timely Kiwi social issues.

Outrageous Fortune
(Various directors; 2005-10) This popular, critically acclaimed comedy drama follows a working-class crime family trying to go straight.

Clothing

Raincoat: Resurface your rain jacket before getting to New Zealand; you'll need it no matter the season.

Boots/trail runners: Scrub every speck of soil from these before you leave home to ensure they don't carry alien organisms; customs may check.

Wide-brimmed sunhat: New Zealand's blistering sunlight will make your hike a misery in just a few minutes of peak-time exposure. Clouds won't always protect you, either.

Lightweight, long-sleeved pants and shirt: Although fine in town, shorts and tank tops will leave you miserable at New Zealand's remote beauty spots; the biting sandflies are merciless and can really ruin your day. Long sleeves and pants are also helpful for added sun protection.

Merino layers: The weather can turn dangerous on the nicest of days, particularly in the mountains or shoulder seasons. Layer up with warm-when-wet fibres on both torso and legs.

Warm or waterproof gloves: When the weather turns bad, these can make a big difference to your comfort.

Neck gaiter or buff: Don't forget your neck and chest when you put sunblock on your face. A gaiter will protect them from UV exposure. Take a fleece gaiter when tramping in colder months as an extra hat or eye mask, or to tuck your chin into on a cold day.

Arthur's Pass (p128)

Words

Awa: The Māori word for river.

Bush: Forest.

Chilly bin: A cooler.

Dairy: A corner store.

DOC: The Department of Conservation, which administers tracks, huts and campsites.

Hīkoi: A walk.

Hut: A simple name for a complex network of more than 950 basic yet delightful backcountry accommodation spots. You need a hut pass from the DOC to stay overnight.

Hut book: A DOC trip intentions book that you should write in if you encounter one. It's essential for search and rescue efforts.

Kai: The Māori word for food or a meal.

Knackered: You might hear a Kiwi sit down and pronounce themselves this; it means very tired. 'Crook', however, means sick.

Lollies: Candy; you can buy great pick 'n' mix (bulk) lollies to add to your scroggin (trail mix) at all supermarkets and dairies.

Long drop: Outhouse/pit toilet.

Manu: The Māori word for bird.

Maunga: The Māori word for mountain. They are ancestors to local iwi; on significant maunga, the summit, or head, is tapu (taboo), so do not stand on it.

Munted: Broken, often heard in relation to slips (landslides); e.g. 'The track's munted from a slip.'

Tiki tour: A pleasant, roundabout way to your destination.

Ute: Short for utility vehicle, this means a pick-up truck.

Wop wops/boonies/back of beyond/backcountry: The middle of nowhere.

LISTEN

Pure Heroine
(Lorde; 2013) The Auckland 16-year-old's Grammy-nominated debut album encapsulated the ennui of teen life in suburban New Zealand.

Waiata: Anthems
(Various; 2019–today) An ongoing music-documentary project celebrating personal stories of disconnection, reclamation and courage through *waiata reo* Māori (Māori song).

The Aotearoa History Show
(Radio New Zealand; 2022) Learn New Zealand's history on the plane ride over; this accessible podcast takes you from its geological origins to today.

READ

Birnam Wood
(Eleanor Catton; 2023) The Booker Prize–winning author pits a tech king against community environment do-gooders in this Shakespearean thriller.

Auē
(Becky Manawatu; 2020) The West Coast author wowed everyone with her enthralling debut, a literary exploration of grief, family and resilience in a Māori community.

The Whale Rider
(Witi Ihimaera; 1987) A young Māori girl struggles with *whānau* (family), tradition and identity on the way to fulfilling her destiny as a leader.

19

Rainbow Falls (p26)

The North

01 Te Paki Coastal Track
Traverse remote beaches and cliffs at the very top of Aotearoa/New Zealand. **p24**

02 Kerikeri River
History and hiking come together in a riverside amble. **p26**

03 Kawerau Track Loop
Meet some of NZ's rarest birds on their island sanctuary. **p28**

04 Rangitoto Summit Loop
Climb an island that didn't even exist 650 years ago. **p30**

05 Te Ara Hura Day Walk
Explore remote coves and popular beaches on Auckland's island playground. **p32**

06 Coast to Coast Walkway
Visit urban Auckland on a hike right across the country. **p34**

07 Kauaeranga Kauri Trail
Hike through dense forest to a striking tower of rock. **p40**

08 Karangahake Gorge
Delve into gold-mining history along this dramatic Coromandel gorge. **p42**

Explore
The North

Spectacular beaches, deeply indented harbours and myriad islands are the hallmarks of the narrow corridor of land that stretches out to form the tip of the North Island. Auckland – Aotearoa/New Zealand's biggest city by far – is perched on a narrow isthmus to the south. To its east, the rugged Coromandel Peninsula reaches out to form a protective barrier enclosing the glistening, island-studded Hauraki Gulf. At the very top, Northland basks in a steamy subtropical climate and a sense of its own starring role in the country's history.

Kerikeri

The Bay of Islands ranks as one of Aotearoa/New Zealand's top summertime destinations. Lingering shots of its turquoise waters and 150 undeveloped islands feature heavily in the country's tourist promotions, but you won't get much of a sense of that in its main settlement. Kerikeri (population 8000) is a prosperous inland township surrounded by orchards and vineyards with local farm-gate sales of oranges, avocados, kiwifruit and vegetables. It's a great place to stock up on supplies, whether at the large supermarkets, the artisan chocolate shop or the weekend farmers markets. There's also a large camping and outdoors store.

Auckland

It's hard to imagine a more geographically blessed major city than Auckland. It has two harbours that frame a narrow isthmus punctuated by volcanic cones and surrounded by fertile farmland. From numerous vantage points, you'll be surprised how close the Tasman Sea and Pacific Ocean come to kissing and forming a new island.

Within an hour's drive from the city's high-rise heart there are tracts of dense rainforest, thermal springs, wineries and wildlife reserves. No wonder Auckland is regularly rated one of the world's top cities for quality of life and liveability.

To truly get under the skin of the place, base yourself in one of the inner-city suburbs comprised of wooden Victorian and Edwardian cottages (Grey Lynn, Ponsonby, Freemans Bay, Mt Eden, Parnell and Devonport are all great choices). Wherever you

WHEN TO GO

With mild winters and hot and steamy summers, walking in the North is an all-year-round proposition. Northland and Coromandel beaches get crammed with Auckland families during the summer school holidays (Christmas to the end of January) and prices shoot up. February is quieter and enjoys the best of the weather, although it's usually pretty good until early April. Expect colder and less settled weather from May to October. Although warmer, November and December can also be fickle rain-wise.

wind up, you'll never be far from an excellent coffee and good dining options.

Anything you need for your walks can easily be procured from the many malls, supermarkets and outdoors shops.

Thames

Characterful wooden buildings from the 19th-century gold rush still dominate Thames, but grizzly prospectors have long been replaced by alternative lifestylers. It's a good base for hiking in the nearby Kauaeranga Valley. There are also some terrific cafes, bakeries, stores and galleries along Pollen St and a big supermarket at the end of Mary St.

TRANSPORT

Auckland is NZ's major transport hub with direct international flights to and from Asia, the Americas, Australia and the South Pacific. Domestic flights head all over the country, including Northland (Whangārei, Kerikeri and Kaitāia all have airports). All of the major North Island towns are connected by bus, and there's also a train service from Auckland to Wellington. Ferries depart from central Auckland to all of the main islands of the Hauraki Gulf and to Coromandel Town.

WHAT'S ON

Lantern Festival *(aucklandnz.com/lantern)*, timed around the Lunar New Year.

Polyfest *(facebook.com/asbpolyfestnz)*, a massive secondary schools Māori and Pacific Islands cultural festival held in March.

NZ International Comedy Festival *(comedyfestival.co.nz)*, held in April and May.

Resources

Bay of Islands i-SITE
(northlandnz.com)

Princes Wharf i-SITE
(aucklandnz.com)
Incorporates the DOC Auckland Visitor Centre.

Cornwall Park Information Centre
(cornwallpark.co.nz)
On the Coast to Coast Walkway route.

Thames i-SITE
(thecoromandel.com/thames)
Excellent source of information for the entire Coromandel Peninsula.

DOC Kauaeranga Visitor Centre
(doc.govt.nz)
Department of Conservation advice and maps for Coromandel walks.

WHERE TO STAY

Auckland has a good range of accommodation of all kinds. If you're after a boutique hotel, try the central city's **Hotel DeBrett** *(hoteldebrett.com)*, or if you'd prefer an upmarket B&B, there's **Ascot Parnell** *(ascotparnell.com)*. Waiheke Island also has excellent options, including top-notch rental houses such as **Waiheke Dreams** *(waihekedreams.co.nz)*. Thames and Kerikeri both have good motels and B&Bs. If you'd rather stay closer to the very top of the North, **Kahoe Farms Hostel** *(kahoefarms.co.nz)* is one of the country's very best hostels. Further north in Mangōnui, the **Old Oak** *(theoldoak.co.nz)* is a historic hotel that's been converted into a stylish boutique property.

01

Te Paki Coastal Track

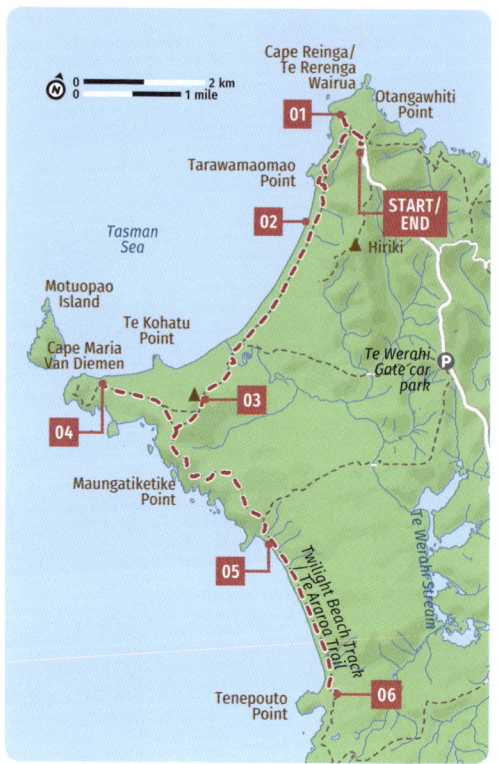

DURATION	DIFFICULTY	DISTANCE	START/END
7–8hrs	Moderate	21km	Cape Reinga /Te Rerenga Wairua car park

TERRAIN	Beach, slopes, low coastal forest

Explore an extraordinarily beautiful and eerily empty strip of coast at the very tip of the country on part of the Te Paki Coastal Track. The track passes through coastal forest, red rock landscapes and the sands of semitropical beaches.

Getting Here

The trailhead is at Cape Reinga/Te Rerenga Wairua lighthouse car park, which is the very end of State Hwy 1 (SH1). There's no public transport to these parts and the nearest large town, Kaitaia, is 80 minutes' drive away.

Starting Point

Aside from plenty of parking and some very spiffy public toilets, there's nothing at the start of the track.

01 After parking, amble down the wide, attractive and well-formed path to take in the famed squat, **Cape Reinga/Te Rerenga Wairua lighthouse** and many-pronged yellow sign pointing out directions all over the world. Return to the car park and follow signs south to the Te Paki Coastal Track.

02 Head south down a steep clifftop path and admire the gorgeous sweeping sea views before descending a zigzag track to reach **Te Werahi Beach**. Check tide times ahead of arriving to avoid having to wade; it takes about 20 minutes

Best for

COASTAL SCENERY

Cape Reinga /Te Rerenga Wairua

Cape Reinga /Te Rerenga Wairua

SH1 terminates at this dramatic headland where the waters of the Tasman Sea and Pacific Ocean meet, breaking together into waves up to 10m high in stormy weather.

Cape Reinga /Te Rerenga Wairua is the end of the road both literally and figuratively: in Māori tradition the spirits of the dead depart the world from here, making it the most sacred site in all of Aotearoa/New Zealand. Out of respect, you're requested to refrain from eating or drinking in the vicinity.

The actual departure point is believed to be the 800-year-old pōhutukawa tree clinging to the rocks on the small promontory of Cape Reinga/Te Rerenga Wairua (Leaping Place of the Spirits) far below; access is forbidden to those in corporeal form.

to reach the beach from Cape Reinga/Te Rerenga Wairua. Clustered flocks of oystercatchers and other coastal birds will scuttle out of your way as you traverse the sands.

03 Walk along the sand edging the sinuous loops of Te Werahi Stream, then wade across and climb to the signpost on the headland. Around the next bend, pretty Cape Maria van Diemen comes into view and you'll enter an unusual landscape of artfully eroded gullies and colourful patches of pink, peach and orange clay-coated stone. Some of this section is quite steep and it can be difficult to spot the orange markers against the peach-coloured slopes of **Herangi Hill**.

04 Around 2km after Te Werahi Beach, you'll reach the junction with a side track leading to **Cape Maria van Diemen**, the North Island's westernmost point. If you've got 90 minutes to spare, it's worth the 2km (each way) detour to what look like rocky islets, anchored to the shore by sand dunes. If not, content yourself with the gorgeous views from just up the next hill.

05 The next 3km of track is rough and steep before it eases into a smooth stretch through low scrub heading for the northwestern end of remote **Twilight Beach/ Paengarēhia**. Stop to watch the breakers rolling in along the empty beach before starting your return journey. Feral dogs have been sighted near here; do not walk alone or leave food scraps.

06 Continue another 3km along the beach and climb a set of steps to **Twilight Campsite** if you're of a mind for a longer day and a rest in the open-sided octagonal shelter. Return along the same route to Cape Reinga/Te Rerenga Wairua.

☕ Take a Break

The **Kāuri Unearthed** food truck serves burgers, nachos and fish and chips from the trailhead car park, operating from roughly 11am to 3pm in summer. Hours are sporadic in winter.

02

Kerikeri River

DURATION	DIFFICULTY	DISTANCE	START/END
3hrs	Moderate	10km	Landing Rd car park

TERRAIN	Bush track, rough in places

Combine beautiful native bush with some of the most important historic sites in the country on this riverside walk. In 1819 the powerful Ngāpuhi chief Hongi Hika allowed Rev Samuel Marsden to start Aotearoa/New Zealand's first Christian mission here, under the shadow of his *pā* (fortified village). The route takes in gorgeous waterfalls, swimming holes and the country's oldest building.

Getting Here
Take the Heritage Bypass from central Kerikeri and follow the signs to the Stone Store.

Starting Point
The car park at the bottom of Landing Rd is adjacent to toilets and picnic areas, and close to a cafe and bistro.

01 Cross the lawn to the popular **Kerikeri River Track**, which follows the river upstream through a lush corridor of native bush. Despite passing right through Kerikeri, there are long stretches where you feel like you're deep in the bush. After 1km you'll reach **Wharepuke Falls**. What they lack in height they make up for in breadth, descending into a large swimmable basin.

02 About an hour into your walk, you'll pass the **Fairy Pools**, another potential place for a dip. Twenty minutes later you'll come to the impressive **Rainbow Falls**, where even on dim days

The Stone Store

Kerikeri Mission Station

Two of the nation's most significant buildings nestle side by side on the banks of Kerikeri Basin. **The Stone Store** *(historic.org.nz)* is NZ's oldest stone building (1836). Upstairs there's an interesting little museum, while downstairs the shop sells Kiwiana gifts as well as the type of goods that used to be stocked here in the 19th century. Tours of neighbouring **Kemp House** depart from here. Built by the missionaries in 1822, this humble yet pretty wooden Georgian-style house, encircled by well-kept heritage gardens, is Aotearoa/New Zealand's oldest building.

the 27m drop conjures dancing rainbows. Continue up to the viewpoint at the top.

03 Rather than retracing your steps all the way to the beginning, backtrack only as far as the **Heritage Bypass** and take the side track up to the road. Cross the bridge and take the concrete path on the other side, labelled **Southside Track**. At the river, it becomes a dirt track skirting the backs of houses before winding through some lovely native bush. In places it's a little rough; if you're ever unclear where to go, look for the colourful ribbons in the trees.

04 After 45 minutes the track terminates on Kerikeri Rd. Continue down the footpath as far as pretty little **St James Church**. The original mission church was built on this site in 1823 but this incarnation dates from 1878. It's worth poking your head inside to admire the fine stained-glass windows incorporating NZ flora and fauna.

05 Take the gate beside the church and, at the bottom of the path, turn right. Head up through the *pou* (carved wooden poles) and up onto the *kāinga* (village) site. Nothing remains, but the large grassy expanse gives you an idea of its former size. Turn left and cross the lawn to the palisade at the far end, facing the once mighty **Koropiro Pā**. Information boards effectively make sense of the terraces and pits that remain.

06 Head back along the gravel path to the site of the **Kerikeri Mission Station**, passing the Plough & Feather bistro, the Stone Store and Kemp House – all of which are worthy of further examination. Complete your walk by crossing the footbridge and wandering through the orchard.

☕ Take a Break

In summertime, a cafe operates from a cottage beside Kemp House. However, we strongly recommend the **Plough & Feather** *(ploughandfeather.co.nz)*, which serves Kiwi-inflected bistro-style food from a house right on the basin.

03

Kawerau Track Loop

DURATION	DIFFICULTY	DISTANCE	START/END
3hrs	Easy	5km	Tiritiri Wharf

TERRAIN	Well-formed bush tracks, boardwalk

Encounter some of the world's rarest birds on a magical island eco-sanctuary. Over the decades, hundreds of volunteers have worked to eradicate pests, restore the forests and reintroduce birds onto Tiritiri Matangi. It's one of Aotearoa/New Zealand's great conservation success stories.

Getting Here
Fullers360 *(fullers.co.nz)* ferries depart for Tiritiri Matangi Island at 8.30am or 9am depending on the day, leaving the island at 4pm. The journey takes 75 minutes from Auckland's ferry terminal. Check the Fullers360 website for the latest timetable.

Top Tip
When you book your ticket we highly recommend you pay the additional $10 for the guided tour along the first part of this route, on which enthusiastic volunteers spot, identify and provide information about the birds as you go.

Whether you take the tour or go it alone, start by heading along the coast for 10 minutes to Little Hobbs Beach and then **Hobbs Beach**. If you're with a guide, they're likely to show you nesting penguins along the way. After the beach, a stepped boardwalk climbs through the oldest patch of forest on the island, full of huge puriri and pōhutukawa trees and a multitude of rare birds.

Turn right at the junction with the **Totora Track**, which leads up to the Ridge Rd. Walk along the grass track that shadows the road through the edge of the bush. Eventually you'll reach a grass-covered **hill** with wonderful views over the Hauraki Gulf.

Tours end at the **visitors centre** near the **lighthouse**, where there are lots of information panels and an excellent souvenir shop. Slowly meander back to the wharf via the **Wattle Track**, looking out for tūī, tīeke (saddleback), korimako (bellbird) and the highly endangered kōkako along the way.

Best for

SPOTTING WILDLIFE

THE NORTH 03 KAWERAU TRACK LOOP

Tūī, Tiritiri Matangi

04

Rangitoto Summit Loop

DURATION	DIFFICULTY	DISTANCE	START/END
4½hrs	Moderate	14km	Rangitoto Wharf

TERRAIN	Scoria track, road, rough in parts

Experience a unique terrain of scoria and pōhutukawa forest on a climb up Auckland's youngest and largest volcano. Rangitoto Island is only 25 minutes by ferry from central Auckland, yet a world apart. It slopes elegantly to its 260m-high summit, offering magnificent views over the metropolis and surrounding islands. In 2011, after an extensive eradication program, it was officially declared predator-free and it now teems with birdlife, including several endangered species.

Getting Here
Ferries run by **Fullers360** *(fullers.co.nz)* depart from Piers 13 and 14 at the Auckland Ferry Terminal; bookings are essential.

Starting Point
There's a shelter, seating, information boards and toilets at Rangitoto Wharf, but no food or drinkable water on the island, so stock up beforehand. Don't miss the return boats, or you'll be faced with an expensive water-taxi ride back.

01 From the wharf, pass through the carved **Māori gateway** and follow the signs marked 'Rangitoto Summit'. A well-formed gravel track leads to the top, sloping gently at first but eventually reaching some stepped sections. Pōhutukawa trees and low scrub rise tenaciously from the dark volcanic stone, although you'll also cross barren lava flows where they've yet to take hold. After 30 minutes there's a clearing where you can take a 15-minute (each way) detour to some **lava caves**.

Best for

ESCAPING THE CITY

Rangitoto Island

Auckland Volcanic Field

Some cities think they're tough just by living in the shadow of a volcano; Auckland's built on more than 50 of them. The last one to erupt was Rangitoto, about 600 years ago, and no one can predict when the next eruption will occur. Auckland's quite literally a hot spot – with a reservoir of magma 100km below, waiting to bubble to the surface. But relax: this has only happened 19 times in the last 20,000 years.

Some of the volcanoes around are cones, some are filled with water and some have been completely quarried away. Moves are afoot to register the field as a World Heritage Site and protect what remains.

02 Continue on the main track for a further 15 minutes and you'll reach the 60m-deep and 200m-wide crater, filled with lush native bush. Follow the **Crater Rim Track** clockwise to the **summit**. Here, there's a viewing platform facing out to the Hauraki Gulf islands and another offering exhilarating views of Auckland.

03 Complete the crater circuit and, at the junction, follow the signs to Islington Bay Wharf along the stepped **boardwalk**. After 10 minutes you'll pop out on a dirt road; the only traffic you're likely to encounter is the Volcanic Explorer 4WD road train. Turn right and head down the road for 45 minutes, following the signs to Islington Bay Wharf at every junction until you see a sign pointing towards **Motutapu Island**. After 500m you'll reach the causeway over the narrow channel separating the two islands. There's a cute little beach on the Motutapu side.

04 Pick up the track by the bridge to **Islington Bay Wharf**, which skirts the edge of a gorgeous estuary. After the wharf, keep following the **Islington Bay Track** along the coast. Turn left when you hit the road, which terminates shortly afterwards, at **Yankee Wharf**. From here, follow the signs reading 'Rangitoto Wharf via Coastal Track'. It follows the coast before cutting across the volcanic rock on a rough track through the bush. Eventually, it comes out alongside the water for the final leg to the jetty.

☕ Take a Break

There are no shops or eateries on the island, but the ferries have cafes serving pastries and drinks. If you're looking for a pre- or post-walk fuel stop on the city side, try the nearby Britomart precinct. Options include **The Store** (thestorebritomart.nz) and **Amano** (amano.nz).

05

Te Ara Hura Day Walk

DURATION	DIFFICULTY	DISTANCE	START/END
3hrs	Moderate	11km	Mātiatia/Palm Beach

TERRAIN	Headlands, bush, beach, roads

Get a taste of Auckland's favourite island playground. Waiheke is loved for its warm weather, glorious beaches and acclaimed wineries. Te Ara Hura is a large loop route that traverses the island on a combination of bush tracks and local streets. We've chosen a section that's simple to access via public transport and takes in tucked-away bays that most day trippers never see, along with two popular beaches.

Getting Here

Ferries depart from central Auckland for Mātiatia every every 30 to 60 minutes depending on the day; the journey takes 40 to 50 minutes.

Starting Point

The ferry terminal at Mātiatia has a cafe, toilets and an information stand stocking free walk maps.

01 Check the tides before heading out as the first section, along the beach, can only be walked 1½ hours either side of low tide. Otherwise you'll have to scramble over the steep, gorse-covered bank. The route then undulates around headlands, with views back to the city and other Hauraki Gulf islands. Along the way, you'll pass some of Waiheke's most exclusive houses. Eventually, it winds down to pebbly Cable Bay and then steps steeply up again before continuing on to **Owhanake Bay**. Beyond here, erosion has closed the coastal route, so cut across the lawn and continue along Kororā Rd until you reach Oneroa.

Little Oneroa beach

> ## Waiheke Wine
>
> Waiheke's warm, dry microclimate mimics the Mediterranean, lending itself to the production of excellent olive oil and wine. The reds, in particular, have achieved international attention, with Bordeaux-style blends near the top of the heap. There are also some excellent chardonnays and rosés produced on the island. It would be remiss to visit Waiheke and not stop for a tasting. Waiheke's most famous vineyard, **Stonyridge** (stonyridge.com), is home to world-famous reds and an atmospheric cafe. Impressive architecture, interesting sculpture and beautiful views set the scene at **Cable Bay** (cablebay.co.nz), where you can follow up a tasting with a meal.

02 In **Oneroa** (meaning 'long beach'), take the steps down to the beach and walk along the sand. Oneroa is the island's main commercial hub, with shops, cafes, restaurants and bars.

03 At low tide, continue around the next headland to pretty **Little Oneroa Beach** – alternatively, follow the road. Pick up the track at the far end of the beach. This shady section heads through some lovely native bush. Turn right at the 'Track to Queens Drive' sign.

04 After following the road for a brief spell, look for the 'Access to Hekerua Bay' sign. Wind down to pebbly little **Hekerua** and pick up the path on the opposite side. Next up is self-explanatory **Sandy Bay**, and then **Enclosure Bay** where a natural rocky barrier forms a lagoon.

05 Turn up Empire Ave, the dirt road opposite the beach. A set of black *pou* marks the beginning of **McKenzie Reserve**, where a team of volunteers is working to regenerate native forest. Wind your way up through the bush and turn right onto Coromandel Rd. Turn left onto Hauraki Rd, which becomes Cory Rd and offers wonderful views towards **Great Barrier Island** and, in the distance, Little Barrier Island.

06 Take the track down to the naturist section of **Māwhitipana Bay**, or continue along the road to the clothed section. Universally known as **Palm Beach**, Māwhitipana is one of the island's best beaches, with strikingly clear water. After a refreshing dip, catch the bus back to Mātiatia from outside the shop.

 **Take a Break**

Specialising in 'artisan wood-fired food', the **Dragonfired** (dragonfired.co.nz) food truck at Little Oneroa Beach is one of Waiheke's best. It's open daily in summer and Friday to Sunday in winter. For a sit-down cafe meal, try **Wai Kitchen** in Oneroa.

06

Coast to Coast Walkway

One Tree Hill/Maungakiekie

DURATION	DIFFICULTY	DISTANCE	START/END
5hrs	Moderate	16km	Onehunga/ Viaduct Harbour

TERRAIN	City streets and parks

Cross from one side of the country to the other on this brilliant introduction to urban Auckland. Start with a leisurely wander through the suburbs and wind up at the popular Viaduct Harbour drinking and dining precinct for a celebratory beverage. Along the way, you'll pass important sites from Auckland's Māori and colonial history and climb three small volcanoes.

Getting Here

Catch a train to Onehunga station and take a 10-minute walk west along Princes St to the Onehunga Bay Reserve at its end.

Starting Point

Cross the footbridge to Taumanu Reserve, the little waterfront park sandwiched between Manukau Harbour and a busy motorway. On the city side of the footbridge, there are toilets and a skate ramp.

01 Look for the **wooden plinth** cleverly carved with Māori deities and the view in front of you, from each angle, including volcanic Māngere Mountain and the jagged heads of the Manukau Harbour. Sadly, the vista is somewhat marred by the snarling motorway and the light industry around the old port. Signage for the Coast to Coast is sketchy, at best, but, in theory, there are blue disks pointing towards the city and yellow disks pointing in the opposite direction. The walkway is also part of the nationwide trail Te Araroa, so look out for those markers too as you progress.

One Tree Hill/ Maungakiekie

Looking at One Tree Hill, your first thought will probably be 'Where's the tree?' Up until 2000 a Monterey pine stood at the top. This was a replacement for a sacred tōtara that was chopped down by British settlers in 1852. Māori activists first attacked the foreign usurper in 1994, finishing the job in 2000. After much consultation, a grove of native trees was planted on Maungakiekie's summit in mid-2016. In an arboreal version of the *X-Factor*, the weaker performing trees will be eliminated, with only one tree left standing.

U2 named a song for the landmark on its 1987 album *The Joshua Tree*, remembering their Kiwi roadie Greg Carroll, who died in a motorcycle accident in 1986.

Head back over the footbridge and take some time to read the display boards illustrating the shoreline as it once looked. Skirt around the edge of the little **estuary beach**, cross Beechcroft Ave and head up Normans Hill Rd past the row of pretty Victorian and Edwardian **cottages**. Turn right when you reach Grey St.

02 Enter **Jellicoe Park** and cut through the cluster of historic buildings, including the Block House (built in 1860 to withstand potential Māori attack during the New Zealand Wars) and the grand-on-a-shrunken-scale Lashley House (1856). Pass under the **Arch of Remembrance**, constructed from Auckland's ubiquitous volcanic stone and dedicated to the fallen from WWI. From here the route takes Quadrant Rd, turns left on Trafalgar St and then right onto Symonds St. As you pass the school, take note of the row of giant pōhutukawa trees. Native to the North Island coast, this beloved species is known as the 'New Zealand Christmas tree' because of its propensity to erupt in crimson flowers in December. Cross the busy Royal Oak intersection over to Manukau Rd, and follow it for around 500m to the entrance of One Tree Hill/Maungakiekie Domain.

03 One of Auckland's most beautiful parks encircles **One Tree Hill/Maungakiekie**, the 182m-high volcano which was the isthmus's key pā in precolonial times and arguably the greatest fortress in the country. Head along the avenue of oaks and up to the summit, noticing the complex system of terraces, pits and defensive ditches as you go. At the top is the grave of John Logan Campbell, who gifted the land to the city in 1901 and requested that a **memorial** to the Māori people be built on the summit. This grand structure was unveiled in 1948, taking the form of a bronze Māori warrior standing regally in front of a large obelisk. Nearby are the young contenders for the title of One Tree, partly sheltered behind a hedge.

Take in the view and then head back down and through the little gate just left of the fork in the road. Look out for shell middens in the banks as you follow the dirt track until it comes out by the scoria gate to Cornwall Park.

04 **Cornwall Park** is well known for its beautiful mature trees, both native and introduced. While you're here, call into Campbell's pretty **Acacia Cottage** (1841), Auckland's oldest house. Neighbouring **Huia Lodge** houses an information centre, which has fascinating interactive displays illustrating what the Maungakiekie *pā* would have looked like when 5000 people lived there. Head down the grand stone stairway and follow the shady lane to the busy main road. Cross over to the northern section of the park and follow the avenue of puriri trees.

05 A large **fountain** surmounted by a bronze statue of Campbell astride a rocky islet marks the end of Cornwall Park. Cross busy Manukau Rd carefully and walk to the end of Kimberley Rd. Cross Gillies Ave, head up the short cul-de-sac directly opposite and cut across the **Melville Park** cricket ground. After the playground, turn right into the grounds of the University of Auckland's Faculty of Education. Here, it gets a bit tricky as the walkway markers disappear and you're left to stumble up some steps and around buildings until you come out on Epsom Ave. Cross, take Cecil Rd to its end, turn left onto Owens Rd and look for the footpath to the right, heading up the mountain.

06 At 196m, **Mt Eden/ Maungawhau** is Auckland's highest volcanic cone. From the top, the entire isthmus and both harbours are laid bare. The remains of *pā* terraces and food-storage pits are clearly visible on its slopes. The symmetrical crater (50m deep) is known as Te Ipu Kai a Mataaho (the Food Bowl of Mataaho, the god of things hidden in the ground) and is considered *tapu* (sacred), and hence off-limits.

Descend the north side of the mountain and take Clive Rd.

Take a Break

The advantage of an urban walk such as this is the myriad opportunities for pit stops en route. There are good snack options on Manukau Rd and within each of the major parks. At the finish line, call into **Dr Rudi's** for an ice-cold craft beer or **Soul Bar & Bistro** *(soulbar.co.nz)* for a glass of bubbly.

View from Maungawhau/Mt Eden

Auckland Museum

This imposing neoclassical **temple** (1929), capped with a copper-and-glass dome (2007), dominates the Auckland Domain and is a prominent part of the Auckland skyline when viewed from the harbour.

The displays of Pacific Island and Māori artefacts on the museum's ground floor are essential viewing. Highlights include a 25m war canoe and an extant carved meeting house (remove your shoes before entering). There's also a fascinating display on Auckland's volcanic field, including an eruption simulation.

The upper floors showcase military displays, fulfilling the building's dual role as a war memorial.

Auckland Museum

Turn left onto Mountain Rd, where you'll pass the distinctive Spanish Mission–style buildings of prestigious Auckland Grammar School. Cross over the motorway and busy Khyber Pass, and continue up Park Rd to the Auckland Domain.

07 **Auckland Domain** covers about 80 hectares, incorporating expansive lawns, formal gardens and native bush. Capping it all is the impressive **Auckland Museum**. The walk cuts across the sports fields and up and over a small hill, which is actually the remains of a volcanic cone. It then heads past the wonderful **Wintergarden**, with its fernery, tropical house, cool house, cute cat statue, coffee kiosk and neighbouring cafe; both the garden and the museum are well worth a visit. Opposite the duck pond, take the **Centennial Walkway** down through the trees to the tangle of motorways and feeder roads filling the gully. Cross over and head up Grafton Rd, under the shade of the plane trees.

08 At the top, you'll enter the main campus of the **University of Auckland**. Cross towards the grand Old Choral Hall and duck around behind it, past the university library. Look for the old stone wall that is all that remains of the Albert Barracks, which stood on this site during the New Zealand Wars. Further on is one of Auckland's most interesting pieces of architecture, the **University Clock Tower** (1926), which displays the influence of both art nouveau and the Chicago School. It's usually open, so feel free to wander inside. Pop out onto Princes St, lined with grand **Victorian-era merchants' houses**. The attractive building on the corner of Princes St and Bowen Ave was once the city's main synagogue.

09 Princes St culminates in tiny **Emily Place Reserve**. Under the boughs of a giant pōhutukawa is an obelisk dedicated to an early churchman. Imagine the frustration of the stonemason who had almost finished the long inscription before making a spelling mistake in the fourth to last word. Proceed down Emily Pl and turn left into Customs St. Turn right onto the tail end of Queen St, Auckland's main drag, passing the elegant old **Central Post Office** building (now Britomart Station). Queen St ends at the Edwardian-era **Ferry Building**; turn left and wander down to the **Viaduct Harbour**. Stop for a triumphant photo by the information panel outlining the route before hitting one of the bars to toast your accomplishment.

07

Kauaeranga Kauri Trail

DURATION	DIFFICULTY	DISTANCE	START/END
7½hrs	Hard	17km	End of Kauaeranga Valley Rd

TERRAIN	Steep bush track, rough in places

Climb through verdant rainforest to the top of a castle-like crag of layered limestone. Better known as the Pinnacles Walk, this popular track leads into the heart of the Coromandel Forest Park, a wild expanse of native bush. The easier route goes straight up and down the Webb Creek Track but we've outlined a more challenging loop, descending on the rough-and-tumble Billygoat Track.

Getting Here

From Thames, it's 12km to the DOC Kauaeranga Visitor Centre and a further 9km along unsealed Kauaeranga Valley Rd to the trailhead.

Starting Point

Drop into the DOC centre for track conditions before setting out as the end of the Billygoat Track crosses the Kauaeranga River, which can be extremely hazardous in wet weather – although at the end of a dry summer, you're unlikely to get your boots wet. The visitor centre toilets are better than those at the trailhead.

01 From the trailhead car park, follow the signs to the start of the **Webb Creek Track**. It almost immediately crosses a swing bridge (suspension bridge) over the Kauaeranga River, then skirts the river for 20 minutes, going through an impressive forest of rātā, ferns and nīkau palms.

02 The track then crosses the rocky **Webb Creek** several times, first via a swing bridge, then over the rocks, then on a little wooden bridge, and then on another wobbly swing bridge. At the junction, turn right to follow the signs to the Pinnacles Hut.

Coromandel Forest Park

Coromandel Peninsula

The Coromandel Peninsula juts into the Pacific east of Auckland, forming the eastern boundary of the Hauraki Gulf. Although relatively close to the metropolis, the Coromandel offers easy access to splendid isolation. Its dramatic, mountainous spine bisects it into two very distinct parts.

The east coast has some of the North Island's best white-sand beaches. When Auckland shuts up shop for Christmas and New Year, this is where it heads.

The cutesy historic gold-mining towns on the western side escape the worst of the influx, their muddy wetlands and picturesque stony bays holding less appeal for the masses.

03 The **Hydro Camp**, reached 1½ hours from the trailhead, is a clearing built in the late 1940s by workers erecting power lines. It is also the major junction for the Billygoat Track.

04 Continue to follow the signs towards the Pinnacles. The track quickly climbs to an open ridge, where there are superb views of jagged peaks and rugged valleys. Take the right fork towards the Pinnacles to arrive at **Pinnacles Hut** (80 bunks).

05 From the hut, follow the steeply stepped route to the jagged summit of the **Pinnacles** (773m). The final ascent is via two ladders and then a set of iron rungs bolted into the rock face. It's a little scary when the wind's gusting, but otherwise not as bad as it sounds. The views from the summit are spectacular, stretching to the peninsula's east coast.

06 Backtrack to the Hydro Camp and at the signposted junction take the left fork to follow the **Billygoat Track**. The rocky track undulates up and down (although mainly down) and parts of it are in a rough state. It begins with a 30-minute climb to a saddle, where there are excellent views down the Kauaeranga Valley. Drop down into Billygoat Basin and cross **Billygoat Stream** before passing through a clearing with basic camping facilities. The track ends with a steep descent to the **Kauaeranga River**, which must be crossed to reach Kauaeranga Valley Rd. The main car park is 300m to the right.

Take a Break

Nearby Thames has good cafes, bakeries, ethnic restaurants and pubs. Try spacious **Cafe Melbourne** or chic little **Coco Coffee Bar**, both of which are on Pollen St.

08

Karangahake Gorge

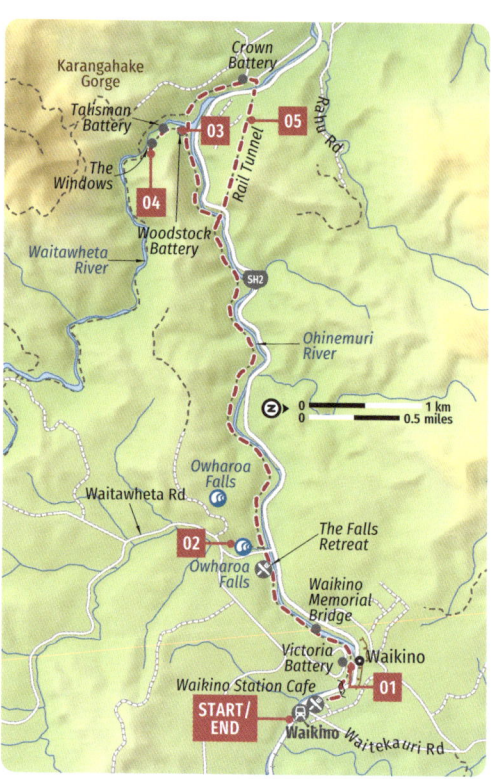

DURATION	DIFFICULTY	DISTANCE	START/END
4hrs	Easy	13km	Waikino Station

TERRAIN	Well-formed track, tunnels, bush

On this walk, gold-mining detritus adds extra glister to an already beautiful landscape. The section of SH2 through this gorge is one of the most dramatic roads on the North Island. This walk follows a shared walking/cycling trail along the most spectacular stretch of the gorge, branching off onto trails that burrow through tunnels carved by miners.

Getting Here

Waikino is 6km west of Waihi. The **Goldfields Railway** (waihirail.co.nz) runs vintage trains between the two, although the schedule is limited.

Starting Point

Waikino Station has a large parking area and a decent cafe (with a toilet, of course). The trail starts just across the side street.

 The track passes under the busy highway and takes a metal rail bridge over the Ohinemuri River before entering the **Victoria Battery**, the most extensive of the gorge's gold-mining relics. If you're here on a weekend, you might stumble into the scheduled tours and tramway rides around the site.

 On leaving the battery, the route follows an unsealed road past the **Waikino Memorial Bridge** before reaching Waitawheta Rd. Turn left to take a 100m detour to the base of the **Owharoa Falls**. Consider cooling off in the idyllic swimming hole on your return leg.

Owharoa Falls

Coromandel Gold

Gold was first discovered in Aotearoa/New Zealand near Coromandel Town in 1852. Although this first rush was short-lived, more gold was discovered around Thames in 1867 and later in other places. In Māori spirituality, the Karangahake Gorge is said to be protected by a taniwha (supernatural creature). The local *iwi* (tribe) managed to keep the area closed to miners until 1875, aligning themselves with the militant Te Kooti.

Gold and silver have been dragged out of Waihi's Martha Mine, Aotearoa/New Zealand's richest, since 1878. After closing down in 1952, open-cast mining restarted in 1988 and, in late 2019, Australia-based OceanaGold was given approval to continue mining until 2028.

03 Head back to the main track along the river. After 45 minutes you'll come to a steel bridge popping out of an old rail tunnel. Rather than crossing, keep following this side of the river until you reach the remains of the **Woodstock Battery** and a suspension bridge. Stay on this side of the Waitawheta River and follow the signs for the 'Windows Walk'.

04 Keep straight ahead at the next junction on the route marked 'via Talisman Battery Remains'. The track switches back on itself a couple of times as it climbs the various layers of the **battery**, with information panels explaining the gold-extraction process. At the next junction, turn right towards the **Windows**, a series of tunnels carved into the cliffs, with 'windows' so miners could toss waste rock into the river below. This is just a small part of 12km of mining tunnels that puncture the area. Things get dark in one stretch, so bring a torch (flashlight); the one on your phone will do the trick.

05 You can cross the river on the swing bridge, but a gate at the other end signals the track on the opposite side is closed due to a slip.

Return back through the Windows and cross another swing bridge to walk the **Rail Tunnel Loop**. This goes through a 1km-long former rail **tunnel**. Claustrophobes needn't worry; it's large, well-lit and completely straight, so you can always see daylight at the other end.

Back on the main walkway, head 4.3km back to Waikino.

☕ Take a Break

The **Waikino Station Cafe** *(facebook.com/waikinostationcafe)* serves good burgers and counter food. However, the best dining hereabouts is the bistro at the **Falls Retreat** *(fallsretreat.co.nz)*, near the Owharoa Falls.

Also Try...

Cape Brett Track

JANICE CHEN/SHUTTERSTOCK

Te Whara Track

DURATION	DIFFICULTY	DISTANCE
5–6 hrs one-way	Hard	9.6km

A challenging, very steep forested climb between beautiful Northland beaches, rewarded by lofty sea and island views.

An area with strong local Māori history, Te Whara Track features some of the best coastal forest in Northland and absolutely spectacular, panoramic views. Starting at Urquharts Bay near Whangarei, you'll climb to a top elevation of 476m before descending past historic WWII relics to pretty Ocean Beach. Get picked up here or create a strenuous loop by returning via the Peach Cove Track for a whopping 1365m in total elevation.

Cape Brett Track

DURATION	DIFFICULTY	DISTANCE
2 days	Moderate	33km

A scenic underscore to the Bay of Islands, Cape Brett is a thin strip of land that ends beside the Hole in the Rock, the most popular tourist attraction in the area. While boats and helicopters hurry to the famous island rock arch, this track winds slowly along the tops of the cape where the land plummets away into the Pacific Ocean and the full cliff-lined drama of Cape Brett is revealed.

If you're willing to shell out for a water taxi, it can be undertaken as an eight-hour day walk, but then you'll miss the opportunity to stay a night inside a former lighthouse keeper's cottage, in one of the finest coastal regions in New Zealand. The track crosses private land for which a track-maintenance fee of $40 is charged, payable when you book your stay at the Cape Brett Hut.

Mangawhai Cliffs Walkway

Six Foot Track

DURATION	DIFFICULTY	DISTANCE
3hrs	Moderate	7km

Leading from the end of a country road to a remote six-bunk DOC hut, this short hike takes in native bush, small waterfalls and views over the Hokianga district.

You'll walk in and out on the same track, which follows an offshoot of the Whirinaki River and climbs into the Waima Ranges on a gentle gradient. View it as a teaser for the longer, more difficult walks that start from the hut and explore the Waima Forest. The track trailhead is at the end of Mountain Rd, 9km east of Opononi.

Mangawhai Cliffs Walkway

DURATION	DIFFICULTY	DISTANCE
2–3hrs	Easy	9km

Part of Te Araroa, the national walking track, this short walk affords extensive views of sea and land on the beautiful coast heading north from the spectacular surf beach at Mangawhai Heads.

Suitable for the whole family, it can be walked as a loop with a return along the beach at low tide – otherwise, you'll come and go via the cliffs. Along the way, you'll pass plenty of unusual rock formations and, if you're lucky, you might even spot whales and sharks passing by below.

Crater lake, Rainbow Mountain/Maunga Kākaramea (p58)

Central North Island

09 Tongariro Alpine Crossing
The colourful volcanic traverse lauded as Aotearoa/New Zealand's best day walk. **p50**

10 Tama Lakes
Twin crater lakes pinched between striking volcanoes. **p56**

11 Rainbow Mountain/Maunga Kākaramea
Climb the Rotorua mountain as colourful as its name. **p58**

12 Tarawera Trail
End a lakeside walk with a hot lake swim. **p60**

13 Whirinaki Waterfall Loop Track
Head deep into dinosaur forest to find a hidden waterfall. **p62**

14 Ngā Tapuwae o Toi
A coastal loop through glorious beaches and kiwi-filled forest. **p64**

15 Cooks Cove Walkway
Hike past an enormous sea cave to Captain Cook's landing site. **p70**

16 Te Mata Peak
Discover a little hill with very big views. **p72**

Explore

Central North Island

The North Island's finest and most dramatic walking comes across its midriff, where a trio of volcanoes rises spectacularly from just beyond the country's largest lake in Tongariro National Park, painting dazzling colours into an otherwise barren landscape. Walkers often come purely for the much-hyped Tongariro Alpine Crossing, but, for many, it becomes a case of not being able to see the forest for the volcanoes. There are so many magnificent walking opportunities here – radiate out from Tongariro's compelling volcanic spectacular and you'll find yourself among forest-tangled rivers, waterfalls and brochure-worthy beaches.

Rotorua

Rotorua is a sensory experience as much as a place, and there's a fair chance you'll smell its pungent, sulphur-rich (OK, farty) air before you even see the city. The Māori revered Aotearoa/New Zealand's most dynamic geothermal area, naming one of the most spectacular springs Wai-O-Tapu (Sacred Waters). Today 37% of the population is Māori, with cultural performances and traditional *hāngi* (earth-cooked banquets) as big an attraction as the landscape itself.

Taupō

Sitting inside a caldera formed by one of the most violent volcanic eruptions on record, Taupō's existence should feel precarious and edgy. But when the lake wakes to a new day as flat as a windowpane, with the snowcapped peaks of Tongariro National Park rising beyond its southern shores, it feels almost paradisiacal. With an abundance of adrenaline-pumping activities, thermally heated waters, lakeside strolls and some wonderful places to eat, Taupō is a magnet for lovers of the outdoors.

WHEN TO GO

With plenty of mountains in their midst, the walking areas around Tongariro National Park and the central North Island are prone to unpredictable weather patterns. What is predictable is heavy rain appearing at some point. The same weather patterns can leave alpine areas snowbound even through to the start of summer. Tongariro's substantial alpine areas mean its walks are best attempted from November to March. This is also the most pleasant time to be on other tracks in this region, though they can be walked at any time of year in favourable conditions.

Napier

The Napier of today – a charismatic, sunny, composed city with the air of an affluent English seaside resort – is the silver lining of the dark cloud that was the deadly 1931 earthquake. Rebuilt in the prevailing architectural style of the time, the city retains a unique concentration of art-deco buildings. Don't expect the Chrysler Building – Napier is resolutely low-rise – but you will find amazingly intact 1930s facades and streetscapes, which can provoke a *Great Gatsby*–esque swagger in the least romantic soul.

TRANSPORT

The central North Island is a large area – it's a four-hour drive from Rotorua to Gisborne – and it's serviced by domestic airports in Rotorua, Taupō, Tauranga, Whakatāne, Gisborne and Napier. They're all linked to Auckland, and a few to Wellington and Christchurch. Hiring a car is the only way to reach most trails, though shuttle services are a better option in Tongariro National Park, where driving to the start of the Tongariro Alpine Crossing is actively discouraged. InterCity (intercity.co.nz) buses connect most of the towns near the walking trails.

 ## WHERE TO STAY

There's a wide spread of towns and an even wider spread of accommodation options across this region. In almost every town of note, you'll find hotels and at least one campground and hostel. In Taupō, the historic **Wairakei Resort** (wairakei.co.nz) is nestled in a thermal valley and features a golf course, tennis and squash courts, and spa treatments, along with swimming and geothermally-heated hot pools. Nearby are the famous Huka Falls and Huka Jet, as well as mountain biking and walking trails.

On walks such as the Tongariro Alpine Crossing, Tama Lakes and Whirinaki Waterfall, Loop Track, there's also the possibility of branching away for a night in a tramping hut.

 **WHAT'S ON**

Rotorua Walking Festival
(rotoruawalkingfestival.org.nz)
Two days of walks ranging from 10km to 42km; held in March.

Lake Taupō Cycle Challenge
(cyclechallenge.com)
Join 6000 people pedalling around Aotearoa/New Zealand's largest lake on the last Saturday in November.

Rhythm & Vines
(rhythmandvines.co.nz)
Three-day Gisborne music festival, held in late December, featuring big-time local and international bands and DJs and boundless East Coast wine.

Resources

Tongariro National Park Visitor Centre
(doc.govt.nz/tongarirovisitorcentre)
Sells the *Walks in and around Tongariro National Park* brochure.

Destination Great Lake Taupō
(lovetaupo.com)
Information for Taupō, Tūrangi and around.

Visit Ruapehu
(visitruapehu.com)
Official tourism body around Tongariro National Park.

Rotorua
(rotoruanz.com)

Whakatāne
(whakatane.com)

Gisborne
(tairawhitigisborne.co.nz)

Napier
(napiernz.com)

09

Tongariro Alpine Crossing

DURATION	DIFFICULTY	DISTANCE	START/END
6–8hrs	Moderate	19.4km	Mangatepopo Rd/Ketetahi Rd
TERRAIN	Exposed alpine ground; steep and loose near the highest points		

Tongariro Alpine Crossing

You don't get to be routinely called Aotearoa/New Zealand's best day walk without being pretty special. The Tongariro Alpine Crossing is like a full almanac of volcanic features laid out for all to see. It funnels between two volcanoes – Mts Tongariro and Ngauruhoe – passing through desert-like landscapes with neon-bright lakes, hissing steam vents and craters like gashes in the earth. With big raps come big crowds – there can be up to 2000 people a day on the track in summer – so don't expect isolation, but do expect to be wowed.

Getting Here

The Mangatepopo Rd car park, 20km from Waimarino (formerly National Park Village) and 45km from Tūrangi, has a four-hour parking limit, so unless you're having someone drop you off, it's almost compulsory to use one of the many early-morning shuttle services that converge on Mangatepopo Rd from Taupō, Tūrangi, Waimarino, Whakapapa and Ōhakune. One shuttle service from Waimarino sets out at 4am, but 6am and 7am shuttles are more common. Bookings include afternoon pick-up from Ketetahi Rd.

Starting Point

Things get so busy at the Mangatepopo Rd car park that there's a three-lane drop-off system in place for shuttle buses. The car park has toilets (there are also six toilets along the track) and a shelter with information boards that include the day's weather forecast.

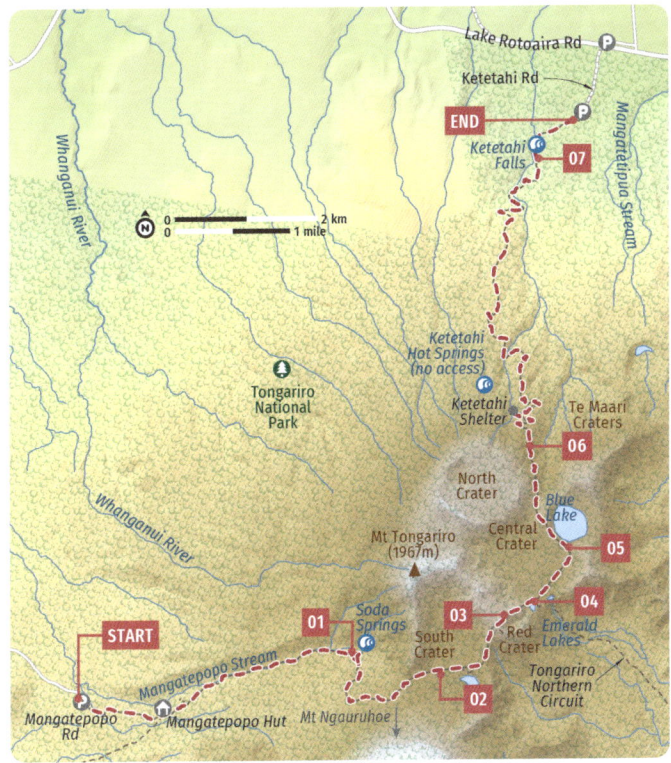

The Greatest Gift of All

In the late 19th century, when Pākehā (white people) were eyeing the tussock grassland of what is now Tongariro National Park for grazing, chief Horonuku Te Heuheu Tukino IV saw only one solution that would ensure the area's everlasting preservation.

Before the Native Land Court, on 23 September 1887, Horonuku presented the area to the crown for the purpose of a national park, the first in Aotearoa/New Zealand and only the fourth in the world. With incredible vision, the chief realised that Tongariro's value lay in its priceless beauty and heritage, not as another sheep paddock.

An Act of Parliament created Tongariro National Park in 1894.

01 From the car park, the track starts out fairly flat along a partly boardwalked section, skirting **Mangatepopo Hut** (an overnight hut used by hikers on the multiday Tongariro Northern Circuit). If you want to check out the hut, which has 20 bunks and has to be booked ahead, it's just a few minutes' walk off the track. From here, you ascend through the Mangatepopo Valley, crossing a succession of old lava flows to reach a side track to **Soda Springs**, a cold spring that adds a bright spark of colour to the landscape as it pours over a low rock face five minutes' walk away.

02 Settle in for the first of the big climbs, which rises towards a saddle strung between **Mt Ngauruhoe** and Mt Tongariro. In fine weather, look for **Mt Taranaki**, the fourth of NZ's big volcanoes, on the horizon behind you. Immediately below the perfectly conical summit of Mt Ngauruhoe, which starred as Mt Doom in the *Lord of the Rings* movie trilogy, the track crests the saddle – expect the climb to the saddle to take around 45 minutes to one hour. Atop the saddle, the track enters the vast walled amphitheatre of **South Crater**, looking like a dry lake bed backed by an enormous encirclement of rock.

03 The really good stuff begins here. The walk crosses the ruler-flat, desert-like floor of South Crater – Mt Ngauruhoe rises to one side and Mt Tongariro to the other – and, at its far end, the trail forks. If you take the right-hand trail, it comes to a vantage point over

☕ Take a Break

For food with a local fly-fishing theme – and to pick up your fishing licence, tackle and flies, of course – visit the **Creel Tackle House** *(creeltackle.com),* next to NZ's oldest tackle shop and the mighty Tongariro River itself. The all-day menu features burgers, brioche and breakfast favourites, including scrambled egg croissants, vegan stack and bacon butties.

a lake beneath Mt Ngauruhoe. The two trails merge again just a few hundred metres ahead, where you make a short climb to the lip of the crater. Here a view opens out directly ahead over the **Oturere Valley**, studded with volcanic rock. The area around the Oturere Valley is often called Aotearoa/New Zealand's only desert, though it's a desert only in appearance, not in rainfall reality. Soak in the view for a while because the climb now steepens, rising up a ridge along the lip of Red Crater.

When you reach the top of this climb, furnished with a rock cairn, you've arrived at the highest point of the Tongariro Alpine Crossing – 1886m above sea level. Plunging away below you are the shiraz-coloured walls of **Red Crater**, with Mt Ngauruhoe standing tall and pyramid-like behind. If you're lucky enough to be here on a clear day, you will enjoy stupendous views that include Mt Taranaki to the west and Mt Tauhara, Mt Putauaki and Mt Tarawera to the north.

04 Within a few steps, you'll be looking down onto **Blue Lake** and the dazzling Emerald Lakes far below.

The descent along this side of the angry-looking Red Crater is steep and loose – it's a bit like roller skating off a mountain – so take great care. The ever-narrowing ridge eventually reaches the shores of the highest two of the three **Emerald Lakes**.

This trio of brilliantly coloured lakes are explosion pits that draw their amazing hues from minerals washed down from Red Crater. Walking past them is usually a full sensory experience – visually vibrant, pungent with the whiff of sulphur, and with steam hissing from the walls around them. For many walkers, they are the highlight of the day.

05 The track continues down, passing the third of the Emerald Lakes before turning its back on the lakes and briefly flattening out across Central Crater.

If you want a closer look at the third of the Emerald Lakes, turn right at the track junction where the Tongariro Northern Circuit departs the Alpine Crossing and it's a short walk to the shores of the lake. **Central Crater** is similar in size to South Crater and is magnificently split by a large

Emerald Lakes

The Night it Rained Rocks

Before 2012 the Te Maari craters were barely noticed by hikers as they descended from Blue Lake, already satisfied with the volcanic wonders behind them. Then, on 6 August 2012, the craters erupted, spitting rocks that came thudding down around the track above Ketetahi Hut. Rocks also crashed onto the hut, smashing through the roof and crushing a bunk bed. By good fortune, it was the middle of winter and nobody was sleeping in the hut. Ketetahi was immediately closed as a sleeping hut, and for almost seven years served as just a day shelter – you could even peer in through a door to see the spot where the rocks crushed the bunk.

In March 2019, the shelter was pulled down by park authorities because of the risk of ongoing eruption from Te Maari.

tongue of black lava – you'll appreciate this lava flow best when seeing it from beside the elevated shores of **Blue Lake**.

It's a short climb out of Central Crater to reach Blue Lake, aka Te Wai-whakaata-o-te-Rangihiroa (Rangihiroa's Mirror), a cold, acidic lake that's up to 16m deep. The large lake is *tapu* (sacred), so you shouldn't eat here, even though some days there are so many people lunching at its edge that it resembles a picnic ground.

06 After rounding the lake and skirting the flanks of **North Crater**, the Alpine Crossing begins its long descent, with views opening out ahead over 1326m-high Pihanga and Lakes Rotoaira and Taupō. Away to the right as you descend is the ominous steaming wound of the **Te Maari craters**. The most recent volcanic eruption in Tongariro National Park was from these craters in 2012. About an hour from Blue Lake, you'll come to a flat bench of land where the Ketetahi Shelter stood until it was removed in March 2019.

07 The track descends quickly, cutting across a ridge beneath **Ketetahi Hot Springs** – these are also *tapu* and access is strictly forbidden. Around 3km from the finish, as the track rolls off the ridge, you descend into forest cover for the first time. It's a moment of high contrast after so many hours spent in alpine terrain.

The final section of the walk follows a fast-flowing stream on sections of boardwalk. Do not drink from this stream, as it's naturally polluted by the thermal activity higher up the slopes, and take heed of the signs asking you not to stop along here because of the small risk of a lahar (volcanic mudflow) if an eruption were to occur. Past the lahar zone, look for a short side track that descends to the base of pretty **Ketetahi Falls**. Very soon you cut away from the stream and make a short crossing to the car park at the end of Ketetahi Rd, where shuttle buses make their pick-ups.

Te Maari craters

10

Tama Lakes

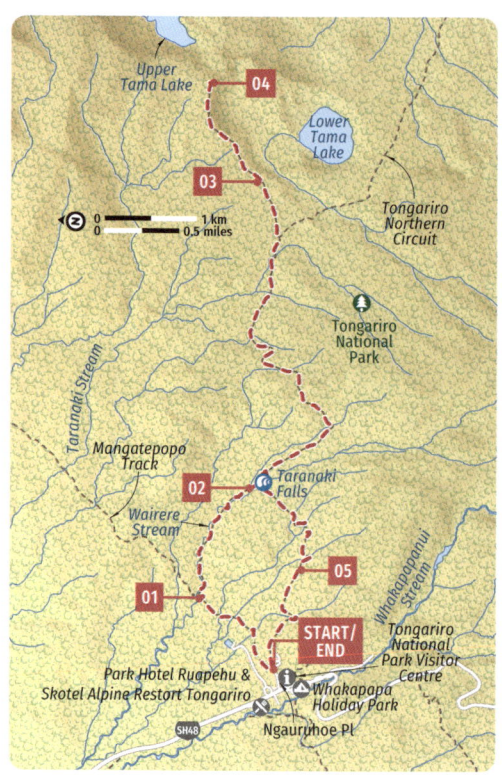

DURATION	DIFFICULTY	DISTANCE	START/END
5 (or 2½) hrs	Moderate	17.4km	Whakapapa Village
TERRAIN	Wide, smooth track; steep and loose above Lower Tama Lake		

Pooled in a line of volcanic craters dotted between Mt Ngauruhoe and Mt Ruapehu, the Tama Lakes add a stark shot of colour to Tongariro National Park's barren landscape. The track gets just a fraction of the walker numbers of the Tongariro Alpine Crossing, and yet the two lakes are every bit as spectacular as any along the Crossing. Along the way, you'll pass powerful Taranaki Falls – if time is pressing, the loop walk just out to the falls and back takes around two hours.

Getting Here
The walk begins in Whakapapa Village at the foot of Mt Ruapehu. You can get here by bus from Tūrangi and nearby Waimarino.

Starting Point
The trailhead is near the end of Ngauruhoe Pl – look for the big green 'Taranaki Falls Track' sign on the left. There's limited parking on Ngauruhoe Pl, with more parking available along Bruce Rd (SH48) below Chateau Tongariro.

 Draped between Mt Ruapehu and Mt Ngauruhoe, **Tama Saddle** is dimpled with six volcanic craters. Three have filled with water, creating two spectacularly blue lakes (Upper Tama Lake covers two craters). The walk to the lakes begins on the Taranaki Falls lower track, crossing several streams before entering a thick strip of mountain beech forest and descending quickly to **Wairere Stream**.

 Ignore the bridge crossing and continue straight ahead beside the stream. When the track pops out of the forest again, it crosses

Best for

OFF THE BEATEN PATH

Tongariro Northern Circuit

The bulk of the Tama Lakes walk, from Whakapapa Village to Tama Saddle, follows the course of the Tongariro Northern Circuit, a three- to four-day, 43km hike that is one of Aotearoa/New Zealand's 10 designated Great Walks.

The Circuit loops around Mt Ngauruhoe, combining the Tama Lakes and the Tongariro Alpine Crossing with a stunning section through the rock-plugged Oturere Valley along the eastern flank of the mountain.

Between November and April, huts along the Circuit must be booked ahead through the DOC website *(doc.govt.nz)*.

Tama Lakes

Wairere Stream on another bridge above a narrow gorge and small waterfall. A few minutes upstream, you come to **Taranaki Falls**, plunging 20m over the cliffs of an old lava flow.

03 From here, the track ascends 133 steps to the top of the lava flow and a track junction. Turn left and set out across the tussock grasslands. There are good views of Mt Ruapehu along this stretch. Soon after, the track squeezes through a dry ravine and comes to **Tama Saddle**. Here, you leave the Tongariro Northern Circuit and cross quickly to the edge of a crater and a view over **Lower Tama Lake**.

04 The best views are still ahead, but they have to be earned. The track scribbles up a steep ridge, flattening out towards the top, before a final rise to the ridge's high point, which looks down onto Lower Tama Lake to one side and **Upper Tama Lake** to the other.

05 Retrace your steps to the top of Taranaki Falls and swing left to join the falls' upper track (if it's cold and windy, the lower track affords more protection). You'll immediately cross Wairere Stream just above the waterfall and continue through **tussock grassland**, returning to Whakapapa just a few metres up the road from where you started.

 Take a Break

Stay at the popular three-star **Park Hotel Ruapehu** in Waimarino, or simply drop in to its **Spiral Restaurant & Bar** to cosy up on the fireside sofas and enjoy a snack or meal *(the-park.co.nz)*.

In Whakapapa Village, the **Skotel Alpine Resort Tongariro** features a ski-inspired, welcoming bar and restaurant with rooms available from backpacker bunks to a cabin *(skotel.co.nz)*.

11

Rainbow Mountain/ Maunga Kākaramea

DURATION	DIFFICULTY	DISTANCE	START/END
2½–3hrs	Moderate	7km	Rainbow Mountain/ Maunga Kākaramea Scenic Reserve car park

TERRAIN	Open hilltops with some steep and exposed climbs

Pinched between popular Wai-o-Tapu Thermal Wonderland and the Waimangu Volcanic Valley, evocatively named Rainbow Mountain/Maunga Kākaramea (Mountain of Coloured Earth) – rises above a section of the country that seems to boil and melt with geothermal activity. It is sacred to the local Ngati Tahu-Ngati Whaoa people and its summit has one of the finest views in the Rotorua area. The short climb passes the vivid Crater Lakes and cliffs coloured true to the mountain's name. The trails are shared with mountain bikers, so be alert to their possible presence.

Getting Here

Rainbow Mountain/ Maunga Kākaramea Scenic Reserve is beside SH5, 26km south of Rotorua. There's no public transport, but if you want a big day of activity, it's a 35km ride along the Te Ara Ahi cycle trail from Rotorua.

Starting Point

The trail begins at a large gravel car park directly across SH5 from Lake Ngahewa. There's a grassed picnic area, toilet and a shelter with information about the area's Māori and forestry history.

01 From the car park, the walk sets out gently, contouring across the lower slopes through tall forest and towering ferns. A 30m detour to the left leads to a platform overlooking the **Crater Lakes**, where the etymology of Rainbow Mountain/ Maunga Kākaramea's name becomes obvious – the lakes are like blue eyes in the face of the mountain, with the cliffs above them streaked with colour.

Waimangu Volcanic Valley

The Cooling Rainbow

As you walk, note the unusual combination of geothermal landscape and lush forest – none of that barren, battling bush here. Across the last century, geothermal activity on Rainbow Mountain/Maunga Kākaramea has declined and soil temperatures have cooled, creating conditions that have allowed the forest to grow and thrive. Before that, the scene here would have been very different.

The mountain was used by the Ngati Tahu-Ngati Whaoa people as a place of refuge during battle. Women and children would shelter on the summit, known as the Owl's Perch, and warriors would take up defensive posts across the slopes, from where they could see oncoming invaders.

02 Return to the main track and turn left, ascending the **narrow ridge** that encloses the lakes before reaching the base of the summit track, marked by a pair of wooden barriers.

03 Cross through the barriers, where the track turns up the mountain. As the track bends back on itself to begin the summit push, there's a **wooden seat** looking across to pine-covered Maungaongaonga. Sit. Pause. You're just over halfway to the summit.

04 The climb begins to steepen at about the point the summit tower comes into sight. The views also open up here, first south towards Taupō and the distinctive Mt Tauhara, and then down onto the well-named Green Lake/Rotowhero. At a side trail, head the few steps downhill to a **lookout** peering directly across to a colourful set of cliffs.

05 Through a corridor of forest, the walk rises to meet a vehicle track; turn left and branch left again onto another walking trail to rise onto the **summit**. The view from here, 743m above sea level, is a highlights reel of Rotorua: the coloured lakes of Wai-o-tapu in one direction, the deep gash of Waimangu Volcanic Valley to the other, with Lake Tarawera and Mt Tarawera away to the north. When you've had your fill, turn around and return to the car park along the same route.

☕ Take a Break

The **Pukeko in a Ponga Tree Cafe** at the **Waikite Valley Thermal Pools** *(hotpools.co.nz)* is a good stop for burgers, garlic mussels, nachos or just an ice cream or beer, but the real treat here is a post-walk soak in one of the geothermally heated pools.

12

Tarawera Trail

DURATION	DIFFICULTY	DISTANCE	START/END
4hrs	Moderate	15km	Tarawera Rd/ Hot Water Beach

TERRAIN	Undulating lakeside path with one sustained climb near the end

Few walks in the world end with such reward as the Tarawera Trail. After following Lake Tarawera's southern shores, this fine walk finishes on Hot Water Beach, where you can soak away the effort of the past few hours in geothermally heated waters. Not all the trail's delights are reserved for the end, however, with the walk passing cold springs and lake swimming opportunities, with views of one of Aotearoa/New Zealand's most storied volcanoes. Hot Water Beach is simply the piece de résistance.

Getting Here

The trailhead is on Tarawera Rd, 15km from Rotorua and 2.5km before Lake Tarawera. **Totally Tarawera (totallytarawera.com)** runs a water taxi to and from Hot Water Beach; pick-up includes a return shuttle to the car park. Bookings required.

Starting Point

The trail's large car park has toilets and a rainwater tank beside a Māori *pou* (ancestral carving).

01 The trail to Lake Tarawera sets out through the Te Wairoa valley. To your left as you cross the bridge over the gin-clear Te Wairoa Stream is the **former village of Te Wairoa**, buried beneath ash in Mt Tarawera's 1886 eruption. From the stream, the trail ascends gently to the **Te Wairoa Valley Lookout**, which offers a peep down into the valley and the buried village.

02 As you descend from the ridge, you'll be accompanied by the sound of unseen Wairere Falls, before the trail follows the valley to the shores of **Lake Tarawera**.

Best for

ESCAPING THE CITY

Lake Tarawera

Wonder No More

Tourism around Lake Tarawera was at its peak in the 19th century, when visitors came to the village of Te Wairoa to be ferried across the lake to the Pink and White Terraces on Lake Rotomahana. The terraces were considered the eighth natural wonder of the world.

That all came to an end on 10 June 1886, when Mt Tarawera erupted, killing around 120 people, burying Te Wairoa beneath ash, Pompeii style, and destroying the Pink and White Terraces.

03 Soon the trail rounds Karikaria Point and ambles along Kōtukutuku Bay. The first time you come to the water's edge is at **Hawaiki Bay**, where there are picnic tables, a sandy beach and good views of the hulking figure of Mt Tarawera.

04 From here, the trail rises back above the shore and into cool, fern-dominated forest. The trail descends back to the lake on a set of wooden steps and soon crosses the **Twin Streams Cold Springs**, where four cold springs rush out of the earth.

05 The trail runs, set back from the shore, for about 20 minutes, before starting its ascent over the long finger of Mourā Point, rising to **Oneroa Lookout** and a keyhole view across the lake.

06 From the lookout, the trail cuts across the point before descending to **Wairua Stream**, which has picnic tables and a toilet. The stream marks the start of the trail's most significant climb, cutting at first beneath crumbly rock walls and then rising to the overgrown **Rotomahana Lookout**, which peers across to adjoining Lake Rotomahana.

07 The trail continues on the narrow ridge before slowly lowering to Lake Tarawera's edge. At the shore, the trail doubles back on itself, finishing along the water's edge at **Hot Water Beach** – head for the steam at the far end. Sites at the beach's campsite must be pre-booked.

☕ Take a Break

Grab a deck table and ponder the power of Mt Tarawera from across the water at the **Landing Cafe**, a cafe-cum-bar-cum-bistro on the shores of Lake Tarawera.

13

Whirinaki Waterfall Loop Track

DURATION	DIFFICULTY	DISTANCE	START/END
3½hrs	Easy	11km	River Rd car park
TERRAIN	Smooth, mostly flat path with a couple of short climbs		

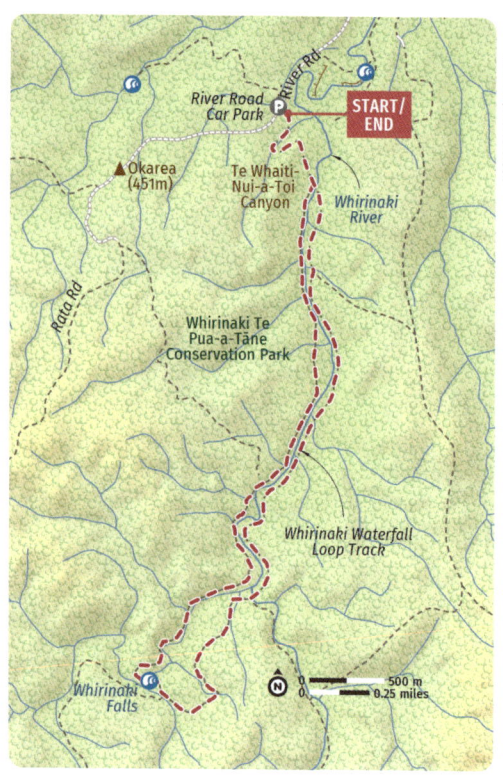

This gorgeous walk through a so-called 'dinosaur forest' of towering kahikatea, tōtara, matai, rimu and miro trees, leads to an 8m-high waterfall on the remote Whirinaki River. Beneath the dense canopy, birdlife can be profuse – look for the aerial dance of the fantails, and listen for the distinctive calls of the tui.

From the River Rd car park, just south of the town of **Minginui**, the Whirinaki Waterfall Loop Track sets straight out into **magnificent forest** – some of the most impressive trees of the whole walk are along the first 1km. Be sure to look up and note the vast number of epiphytes growing high in the rimu and tōtara trees.

After 1km, the trail reaches the **Whirinaki River**, turning upstream. At times, the river is more a sound than a sight and, at other times, there are glimpses into still, clear pools. It's worth pausing by these pools, for this river is considered the region's best for sighting the nationally vulnerable **whio (blue duck)**. There's one steep pinch as you near the waterfall, and then a descent (past a toilet and picnic table) to a bridge that crosses the river just above the **top of the falls** (you can't get to the bottom of the waterfall).

The return walk follows the opposite bank, where the track typically runs closer to the river. As it re-crosses the Whirinaki River, there's a good view from the bridge into the narrow slot of the water-polished **Te Whaiti-Nui-a-Toi Canyon** (a Middle-earth kind of place, if ever there was one), before it rejoins the outward route back to the car park.

Whirinaki forest

14

Ngā Tapuwae o Toi

DURATION	DIFFICULTY	DISTANCE	START/END
5–6hrs	Moderate	17km	Pōhaturoa, Whakatāne

TERRAIN	Sealed footpaths, hard-packed dirt tracks, sandy beaches

View from Kōhī Point (p66)

Imagine a walk that takes you around a wild headland to Aotearoa/New Zealand's 'most loved beach', into forest proclaimed as the kiwi capital of the world, and past views of a steaming island volcano. You've just imagined Ngā Tapuwae o Toi, a walk that has the added benefit of starting and finishing in the very centre of the tourist town of Whakatāne. Be sure to check tide times before setting out – Otarawairere Bay can be inaccessible around high tide.

Getting Here

Pōhaturoa sits in the centre of Whakatāne, which is a 1¼-hour drive from Rotorua, and a 2½-hour drive from Gisborne through the spectacular Waioeka Gorge. **InterCity** *(intercity.co.nz)* has daily coaches to Whakatāne from Auckland, Rotorua and Gisborne. **Air Chathams** *(airchathams.co.nz)* also flies to Whakatāne from Auckland.

Starting Point

The Pōhaturoa rock outcrop is beside a roundabout on The Strand, with a monument beside it to respected Ngāti Awa chief Te Hurinui Apanui (1855–1924).

Footsteps of Toi

Ngā Tapuwae o Toi, or Footsteps of Toi, honours Māori chief Toi, who arrived in the area by *waka* (canoe) around 1150, and established a *pā* (fortified village) atop Whakatāne Heads. You'll pass the *pā* – one of Aotearoa/New Zealand's oldest *pā* sites – along the **Kōhī Point Walkway**, immediately outside of Whakatāne.

All that remains of Toi's stronghold here are the ramparts and a view that makes abundantly clear why this particular spot was such a strategic location.

01 Suitably, this walk named in honour of a Māori chief begins at Pōhaturoa, a large *tapu* rock outcrop capped with pōhutukawa trees, where birth, death, war and *moko* (tattoo) rites were performed. The Treaty of Waitangi was also signed here by Ngāti Awa chiefs in 1840.

Head through the tunnel in Pōhaturoa, which used to be a cave until road builders arrived in town, and straight up the stairway immediately across Canning Pl, ascending the ridge that runs behind Whakatāne. The top 43 steps of the stairway form a tiled **'vertigraph'** – an artwork created on the panels of the steps, with the panels forming a single image when seen from below. Created in 2007, this vertigraph is claimed as the world's first.

02 At the top of the stairway, continue straight ahead on the footpath beside Hillcrest Rd and then turn left into Seaview Rd. In a couple of minutes, turn left again down a set of steps to join the **Kōhī Point Walkway**. The track quickly crosses the top of **Wairere Falls**, which powered Whakatāne's mills and supplied the town's water until 1924. There's a lookout platform peering over the waterfall's edge to the left just before the bridge.

03 The smooth track threads along the top of the ridge until, at the top of a sustained climb, a side track detours up to **Kapu-te-Rangi**, the site of chief Toi's *pā*, with views over the Bay of Plenty and the coastline running north from Whakatāne.

04 Return to the main track, which continues north along the narrow point of the ridge, passing through other *pā* sites, with intermittent views

☕ Take a Break

Cobbled together out of shipping containers and a very flash louvred roof, the mainly open-air **Moxi**, about 150m off the trail in Ōhope, is one of the Bay of Plenty's finest cafes. If you're around in the evening, the burritos, tacos and house-brewed beer at adjoining **Cadera** *(cadera.co.nz)* are muy bueno.

of Whakatāne and Moutohorā (Whale Island), with White Island/Whakaari blowing smoke rings on the horizon. On a fine day, you can see as far along the coast as Mauao, the 232m-high peak that puts the mount in the name of Mt Maunganui. If you look carefully below you, you might see a small statue of a woman standing on one of the boulders at the mouth of the Whakatāne River. This is Wairaka, daughter of the warrior Toroa and part of the first *waka* crew that arrived in the Whakatāne area. With all the men ashore, the tide turned and the *waka* – with all the women on board – drifted out to sea. Wairaka broke the traditional *tapu* on women steering a *waka*, taking up the paddle and bringing the boat safely ashore.

At a fenced barrier, you arrive at **Kōhī Point**, peering down onto the wild tip of Whakatāne Heads.

05 At Kōhī Point, the track turns south, briefly contouring across the headland, around 100m above the jagged shore, before making a long descent on wooden steps to the shell-covered sands of paradisiacal Otarawairere Bay.

Along the way, there are good views of Otarawairere Bay and Ōhope Beach beckoning you forward.

Take your time wandering and exploring the beach at **Otarawairere Bay**. There's a small cave bored through the rocky shores right beside the point at which you arrive on the beach, and the patterned rock platforms at the far end of the beach are well worth exploration if the tide is low enough. Otarawairere Bay is also a great spot for a sneaky swim – you've earned it.

A slip closed the track from Otarawairere Bay to Ōhope Beach in 2023, and while there are plans to repair it, take alternative trails to complete the loop. At Otarawairere's toilet block turn right and follow a track to Otarawairere Rd, then left on Ohope Rd to reach Pohutukawa Rd. Here you can visit 11km **Ōhope Beach**, which likes to promote itself as 'NZ's most loved'. West End, set beautifully beneath the bush-smothered cliffs of Whakatāne Heads, is definitely the best end.

Otarawairere Bay

Tragedy on the Horizon

One of the recurring sights along Ngā Tapuwae o Toi is the steaming White Island/Whakaari, the volcanic island on the eastern horizon, 49km off the White Island/Whakatāne coast. White Island/Whakaari has long been Whakatāne's premier tourist attraction, at least until a sudden and tragic eruption on 9 December 2019. That afternoon, with 47 people on the island, there was a phreatic eruption of scalding steam and gases that killed 21 people.

They were the first deaths on the island for more than a century – in 1914, when the island was being mined for sulphur, 10 men disappeared without a trace following a lahar (volcanic mudflow). The only survivor was Pete the camp cat (subsequently dubbed 'Peter the Great').

White Island/Whakaari

06 To return to Whakatāne, the walk strings together a series of forest trails. Across Pohutukawa Ave a Māori *waharoa* (archway) marks your entry into one of NZ's largest remaining **pōhutukawa forests**. Turn either direction on the **Fairbrother Loop Track** – both arms of the track rise past some magnificent pōhutukawa trees to meet atop the hills. This section of forest is said to be home to around 300 kiwi, a population that has earned Whakatāne the (self-crowned) title of 'kiwi capital of the world', though you won't see any of the nocturnal birds during the day. The **Whakatāne Kiwi Trust** *(whakatanekiwi. org.nz)* does run night tours each Friday in April, May and June. The glowworms that light the evenings in this dense patch of forest will also be switched to dimmer mode during the day.

07 From this track junction, the walk cuts further inland, running along the hills before descending through a ferny patch of forest to cross Burma Rd. Past here, you'll briefly cross private farmland before gently descending on a short section of sloping **boardwalk**. The boardwalk is a good spot to stop and pause, for it runs through what is probably the most beautiful section of forest along the entire walk. The boardwalk bottoms out through a small section of wetlands and then runs along the edges of an unruly pine plantation. At the end of a long descent, turn left at a prominent track junction just above White Horse Dr.

08 This last section of forest trail is known locally as the **Bird Walk**, so expect plenty of birdsong as you burrow through the forest. You will likely see robins and hear the distinctive chatter of tui. The track climbs out of, and then circuits the head of, a valley before following a narrow ridge to a final succession of steps that lead steeply down to a car park on Gorge Rd, the road that connects Whakatāne to Ōhope. Cross the road by the nearby roundabout and return to Whakatāne and Pōhaturoa along the footpath beside Commerce St.

15

Cooks Cove Walkway

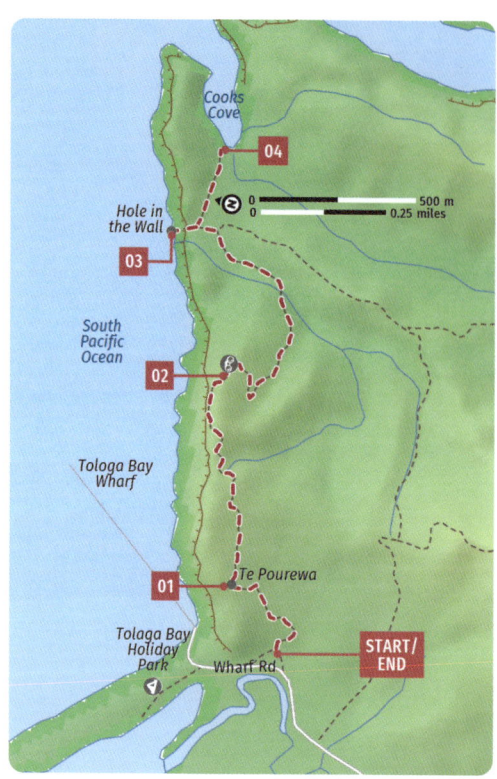

DURATION	DIFFICULTY	DISTANCE	START/END
2–2½hrs	Easy	5.8km	Wharf Rd, Tolaga Bay

TERRAIN	Undulating farm tracks broken by a few steeper climbs

Human history and natural history delightfully intersect on this beautiful coastal walk north of Gisborne. The end goal is one of Captain James Cook's most famous landing sites, though, to get there, you have to traverse a gorgeously eroded section of coast. There's the chance to explore a huge cave naturally burrowed through the cliffs, with a view to Aotearoa/New Zealand's longest wharf. Note that the track is on private land, and is closed for lambing season from August until late October.

Getting Here

The walkway starts near the end of Wharf Rd outside of Tolaga Bay; the turn-off is signposted on SH35, 53km north of Gisborne.

Starting Point

The walkway car park has space for around a dozen cars. If it's full, head about 200m down the road to the car park for the Tolaga Bay Wharf. There are no facilities at the walkway car park, but a few signboards offer some track and history information.

 Through the wooden barrier, the walkway begins an immediate climb, snaking up the slopes through light bush. Near the top, cross a fence on a stile and continue through an open paddock towards the tall arrow-shaped sculpture, **Te Pourewa** – the **Beacon of Light**, which honours ancestors who kept a flame burning here. Wander around the sculpture to get a good view along the Tolaga Bay beach.

 From here the walkway follows farm tracks cut below the lip of the cliffs, stepping across another stile and then rising more steeply.

Best for

COASTAL SCENERY

Cooks Cove

A Cheery Cove

In October 1769, less than three weeks after first making landfall in Aotearoa/New Zealand, Captain Cook's *Endeavour* sailed into the cove that now bears his name but was known to the local Te Aitanga-a-Hauiti tribe as Opoutama.

Cook anchored here for six days, and it was a remarkably harmonious interaction between the crew and the Te Aitanga-a-Hauiti. Goods were traded and the *Endeavour* took on supplies of water, food and wood.

Things went so well that the Te Aitanga-a-Hauiti named a couple of places (and future children) after Tupaea, the Tahitian high priest aboard the *Endeavour*.

Just past the cabbage-tree-topped high point, the walk dips to a **lookout** and your first view into Cooks Cove, nibbled into coast 120m below where you stand. Catch your breath here as most of the climbing is done (at least until the return leg).

03 From the lookout, the track descends rapidly on wooden steps, funnelling through a narrow fern-covered gully and bottoming out across a bridged stream. Just downstream from the bridge, you'll pass a side track that heads a few metres into **Hole in the Wall**. Spend some time exploring this ocean-scoured cave that's like a tunnel through the cliffs. Pop through the hole and you'll find a view of the **Tolaga Bay Wharf** – Aotearoa/New Zealand's longest (660m) – and the high cliffs across the bay.

04 Return through the hole to the main track and turn left, crossing the grassed area to reach **Cooks Cove**, which looks barely wide enough to have sheltered Cook's ship, *Endeavour*. Depending on the tide, you can head out into the sands and shores, where there are good views of the **Mitre Rocks**, which are ranged like sharp teeth across the mouth of the cove. Return to the car park along the same route.

Take a Break

The doughnuts at Gisborne's **Curbside Kitchen** are to die for, but the popular cafe also serves all-day brunch, including slow-roasted tomatoes with the unusual addition of salted buffalo curd. The cafe also sells a range of stylish home goods and preserves to take home with you.

16

Te Mata Peak

DURATION	DIFFICULTY	DISTANCE	START/END
2–2½hrs	Moderate	5.5km	Te Mata Park main gates

TERRAIN	Open hilltops with some steep and exposed climbs

For a hill that tops out at just 399m above sea level, Te Mata Peak offers ridiculously good views. Seeming to bubble up from the Heretaunga Plains behind Havelock North, the peak's open ridges and summit provide 360-degree panoramas across almost the entirety of Hawke's Bay.

Getting Here

Te Mata Park's main gates and car park are on Te Mata Peak Rd, 5km southeast of Havelock Park. There's no public transport to the park.

Starting Point

The car park immediately beyond the park's stone gateway is set beneath tall Californian redwoods. An open-topped shelter above the car park has maps and park information, and there are toilets and tables beside the shelter.

01 The various walks in popular Te Mata Park are colour-coded – the route described here is the **Rongokako Trail**, which is marked with blue triangles and is the most dramatic of the park's walks. It starts at the shelter above the main gates, heading up immediately beside the road. Along the right edge of the trail, you'll notice (and probably smell) the white trunks of yellow-scented eucalypts – imports from Australia. By the Te Aratipi mountain-bike track junction, the walk turns away from the road and descends gently into a large grove of **Californian redwoods**. In their native North America, these redwoods, or sequoias, are the planet's tallest trees.

Redwoods, Te Mata Peak

The Sleeping Giant

Te Mata Peak is known as the Sleeping Giant for the shape of its profile (a likeness that's most obvious when seen from around Hastings) and for its connection to the legend of Waimarama chief Te Mata.

The rival Pakipaki people enticed Te Mata into falling in love with Hinerakau, the daughter of a Pakipaki chief. In order to prove his love, Te Mata was set a series of tasks, including biting his way through the peak that now bears his name. In doing so, he choked on the earth and died. His body become Te Mata Peak – you'll pass the bite, or The Gap, between the summit and Saddle Lookout.

02 The walk zigzags up a slope, weaving through the redwoods. The trail soon seems to overhang a deep, narrow valley and you'll be looking across the tops of the redwoods that grow from it. Turning left by a fence, the trail bottoms out among the most impressive section of **redwoods**, where it crosses a stile and emerges into open grassland.

03 The summit climb begins here, winding onto, and then along, a broad ridge. There are some precipitous sections along the ridge, with steep drop-offs and a short scramble up a well-stepped rock face known as the **Goat Track** (it's better ascended than descended). Crossing a narrow gap in the ridge, the final steep climb awaits, rising to the **summit**, which you'll share with those who drove up the road. The view from the summit stretches along Te Mata's hog's back ridge and takes in Napier, Hastings, the Mahia Peninsula, the Ruahine, Kaweka and Maungaharuru Ranges, and even distant Mt Ruapehu on a fine day.

☕ Take a Break

Around 1km up the road from the park's main gate, with a grand view of its own, **Peak House** *(thepeakhouse.co.nz)* is a lodge-like coffee, beer or wine stop with a breakfast-style menu (avocado on toast, muesli). There are several points on the final descent where you can branch off to the cafe.

04 The blue triangles continue directly across the summit car park, where the track rolls across the lumps and bumps of the ridge to **Saddle Lookout** and a view back to the summit. The walk cuts across the inside corner of the road (past a drinking fountain) and back into the cover of bush. It descends quickly to cross Te Mata Peak Rd just below Peak House, continuing down to the main gates and car park.

Also Try...

Huka Falls

JUERGEN_WALLSTABE/SHUTTERSTOCK

Waitonga Falls

DURATION	DIFFICULTY	DISTANCE
1¼–1½hrs	Easy	4km

Pouring 39m down the southern slopes of Mt Ruapehu, high above the town of Ōhakune, Waitonga Falls is the highest waterfall in Tongariro National Park.

The walk to the base of the falls follows a small section of the Round the Mountain Track, providing a glimpse of the longest of the park's multiday trails (66km) as well as the tall waterfall. The walk is almost entirely through thick native bush, though halfway along it briefly pops out into an alpine clearing dotted with tarns that offers a fine view of Mt Ruapehu's summit. The walk ends (before you turn around and retrace your steps) just downstream from Waitonga Falls – to get any closer, you'll likely have to get your feet wet to cross to the other side of the shallow stream. The walk begins from a car park on Ōhakune Mountain Rd, around 15km from Ōhakune.

Huka Falls to Aratiatia Rapids

DURATION	DIFFICULTY	DISTANCE
2hrs one-way	Easy	7km one-way

Connect Taupō's two premier river sights on a track that showcases the power of Aotearoa/New Zealand's longest waterway.

This shared-use track – walkers and mountain bikers – stretches between the powerful Huka Falls and the dam-controlled Aratiatia Rapids on the Waikato River. At the Huka Falls end, where the river squeezes through a narrow chasm, making a dramatic 11m drop, the trail traverses cliffs before following bush through to Wairakei power station. The Aratiatia Rapids drop 28m in 1km, but only run when the floodgates are opened, which happens at 10am, noon and 2pm (plus 4pm from October to March), releasing 80,000L of water a second for 15 minutes. Time your walk to be here at one of those times. If you're unable to leave a car at both ends of the track, you'll also need to make the return walk.

Blue Lake/Tikitapu

Mt Ruapehu Crater Lake

DURATION	DIFFICULTY	DISTANCE
7hrs	Hard	10km

Climb the barren slopes of Mt Ruapehu, the North Island's highest mountain (2797m), to colourful Crater Lake.

The unmarked ascent begins from the Whakapapa ski field, though it can be shortened by taking the Sky Waka gondola to Knoll Ridge Chalet. From the chalet, there are two options: the most popular route cuts across to Restful Ridge, ascending to narrow Dome Ridge and the lake. In early summer, before the snow has melted, ascend Knoll Ridge to Dome Ridge. Only climb in fine conditions.

Blue Lake/Tikitapu

DURATION	DIFFICULTY	DISTANCE
1½hrs	Easy	5.5km

Circuit one of Rotorua's prettiest lakes, through lovely bush and with views over the palette of the Blue/Tikitapu and Green (Rotokakahi) Lakes.

Starting from the northern end of Tikitapu, around 10km from Rotorua along the road to Lake Tarawera, the trail makes a full lap of the lake, rising at its southern end onto a spit of land separating Tikitapu from Rotokakahi and returning high above Tikitapu's shores through the beautiful Whakarewarewa Forest. There's good swimming back at the walk's starting point if you've worked up a sweat.

Pouākai Crossing (p80)

Southern North Island

17 **Pouākai Crossing**
Traverse a volcanic landscape on a challenging full-day hike. **p80**

18 **Wilkies Pools**
Take an easy stroll through a goblin forest to chilly swimming holes. **p86**

19 **Manawatū Gorge**
Wander through native bush punctuated by views of the gorge below. **p88**

20 **Kāpiti Island Summit**
Walk to the summit of an island bird sanctuary. **p90**

21 **Paekākāriki Escarpment**
Climb the cliff to blissful views of the Kāpiti Coast. **p92**

22 **Otari-Wilton's Bush Loop**
Delve into Wellington's largest remnant of untouched forest. **p94**

Explore
Southern North Island

Two major highlights bookend this part of the North Island: the perfectly proportioned volcanic cone, Taranaki, in the north, and the nation's feisty little capital, Wellington, in the south. Much of what lies between is fertile farmland. Hidden behind the Remutaka and Tararua ranges at the southeast of the island, the Wairarapa District has cute heritage towns, a wonderfully rugged coastline and its own notable wine region, centred on Martinborough. On the other side, the Kāpiti Coast is known for its long, lovely beaches.

New Plymouth

The city of New Plymouth (population 83,100) is the gateway to Egmont National Park. The city has a bubbling arts scene, some fab cafes and craft-beer joints, and a rootsy, outdoorsy vibe. You'll find all your essential supplies and plenty of places to eat and drink in the compact city centre around Devon St.

Martinborough

Laid out in the shape of a Union Jack with a leafy square at its heart, Martinborough (population 1680) is a photogenic town with endearing old buildings, surrounded by a patchwork of pasture and pinstripe grapevines. It's famed for its wineries, which lure visitors to swill some pinot noir, pair it up with fine food and snooze it off at boutique accommodation. There's a small supermarket on the main square.

WHEN TO GO

The oft-repeated cliché about Wellington is that you can't beat it on a good day – which just happens to be true. However, it's often blowing a gale and, some years, its hardy residents complain of missing out on summer altogether. That said, summertime (particularly January and February) is still the best bet for the capital – and, indeed, all parts of the region.

The weather is more settled in Taranaki but it does get crowded during summer school holidays (roughly Christmas to the end of January) and prices increase accordingly. February to April is a better bet. Note, winter snows and spring melts can cause slips and avalanches on the mountain; check with Department of Conservation (DOC) staff before setting out.

Wellington

Wellington sits on a hook-shaped harbour ringed with ranges that wear a snowy cloak in winter. It's not huge (population 424,500), but Welly's compact city centre gives it a bigger-city buzz and, being Aotearoa/New Zealand's capital, it's endowed with museums, galleries and arts organisations completely disproportionate to its size. Wellingtonians are rightly proud of their caffeine and craft-beer scene, but the city is infamous for two things: its frequent tremors and the umbrella-shredding gales that barrel through with regularity.

Accommodation in Wellington is more expensive than in regional areas, but there are plenty of options close to the city centre. The inner city is riddled with restaurants, cafes and bars, with high concentrations around raucous Courtenay Pl, bohemian Cuba St and along the waterfront.

TRANSPORT

Wellington is a major transport hub, with an international airport and the main interisland ferry port for the North Island. There's a limited train service running north to Auckland, but buses radiate out from Wellington to most corners of the island. Local buses and trains will get you most places you wish to go, and there are plenty of taxi and rideshare options.

New Plymouth, Palmerston North and Kāpiti Coast also have airports, offering limited domestic services. Track shuttles are available from New Plymouth to Egmont National Park, which is especially handy for the Pouākai Crossing.

WHERE TO STAY

The best place to stay within close striking distance of Mt Taranaki is **Ngāti Ruanui Stratford Mountain House** (stratfordmountainhouse.co.nz). Otherwise, top options in New Plymouth include the **Ducks & Drakes hostel** (ducksanddrakes.co.nz) and **King & Queen Hotel Suites** (kingandqueen.co.nz). If you're after a hostel in Wellington, try **YHA Wellington City** (yha.co.nz) or **Dwellington** (the dwellington.com). For something self-contained, try **City Cottages** (wellingtoncityaccommodation.co.nz), or for the boutique hotel experience, there's **Ohtel** (ohtel.nz) and **QT Wellington** (qtwellington.com).

 WHAT'S ON

The biggest events on New Plymouth's calendar are the summer-long **Festival of Lights** (festivaloflights.nz) and the **WOMAD** (womad.co.nz) music festival.

Toast Martinborough (toastmartinborough.co.nz) is a hugely popular wine, food and music event held on the third Sunday in November.

Wellington has a jam-packed events calendar, highlights of which include the artsy **New Zealand Festival** (festival.co.nz; held in even years, late February to mid-March) and the kooky **World of Wearable Art show** (worldofwearableart.com; September and October).

Resources

Taranaki/Egmont National Park Visitor Centre (doc.govt.nz)

Visit Taranaki (visit.taranaki.info)

Manawatu (manawatunz.co.nz)

Martinborough i-SITE (wairarapanz.com) Maps and advice.

Kāpiti Coast District Council (kapiticoast.govt.nz)

Wellington Gardens (wellingtongardens.nz)

Wellington i-SITE (wellingtonnz.com) Tourist information centre, with maps and helpful pamphlets.

17

Pouākai Crossing

DURATION	DIFFICULTY	DISTANCE	START/END
9hrs	Hard	19km	North Egmont/ Mangorei Rd

TERRAIN	Mountain, some bush, lots of steps

Mt Taranaki

The major highlights of mighty Mt Taranaki and Egmont National Park are packed into this track. It's a challenging hike but hugely rewarding, traversing a wide variety of terrain and offering expansive views across the region and all the way to the peaks of the Central Plateau. It's a worthy runner-up to Tongariro for the title of Aotearoa/New Zealand's best day walk.

Getting Here

The trailhead is a 30-minute drive from New Plymouth. Consider enlisting **Taranaki Mountain Shuttle** *(taranakishuttle@gmail.com)* to pick you up from the city or the Mangorei Rd car park and drop you at the start.

Starting Point

The Taranaki/Egmont National Park Visitor Centre has a cafe and proper flush toilets. Note: the car park fills up quickly in late December and January, making a shuttle a very sensible idea.

01 From the visitor centre, start by following the signs pointing towards Holly Hut. After about a minute there's a platform showcasing views over New Plymouth and the coast. Get used to it: these kinds of vistas will accompany you for most of the day. The track then heads up Taranaki through low bush, which eventually opens up to views towards the volcanic peaks of the Central Plateau. About half an hour in, another **viewpoint** provides a chance to take a breather and admire the distant mountains.

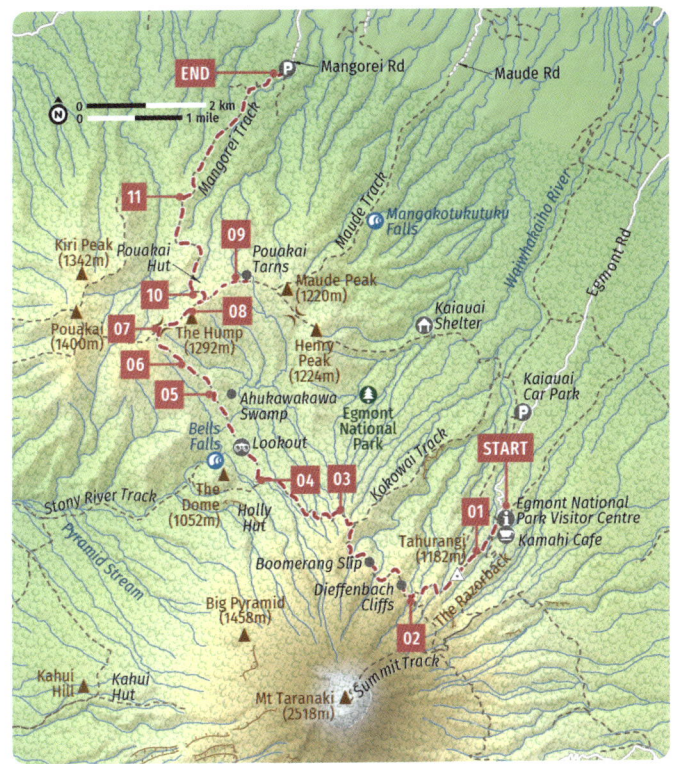

Mt Taranaki

A near-perfect 2518m volcanic cone wearing a cap of snow, even in summer, Taranaki dominates the region that proudly bears its name. It's the youngest of three volcanoes (including Pouākai) that stand along the same fault line. Taranaki is still active, with a major eruption expected every 500 years (the last one was around 375 years ago).

According to legend, Taranaki belonged to a tribe of volcanoes in the middle of the North Island. But after a great battle with Tongariro over Pihanga, the beautiful volcano near Lake Taupō, he was forced to leave. He finally settled in the west and remains here in majestic isolation, often hiding his face behind a cloud of tears.

02 The track then continues up the **Razorback ridge** and, after a short exposed section, it returns to low scrub as it traces a gentle curve around the top of a valley – and then another, and another... Sheer rock faces come into view, becoming more dramatic as you continue. After passing your highest point on **Taranaki** (1357m, which is over half the way up), there's a short scramble over loose rocks across an avalanche zone. Take care and don't tarry, although the track is generally safe outside of heavy rain or snow.

03 About three hours into your walk, **Pouākai** starts to fill the horizon. Although locals know it as the Pouākai Ranges, it's actually a volcano in its own right, having last erupted around 250,000 years ago – around 100,000 years before Taranaki exploded onto the scene. The track continues to skirt around Taranaki before starting a 2.5km stepped downhill section towards the saddle. Look back from time to time for some of the most extraordinary views of Taranaki and the rivers of solidified lava snaking out from its cone.

04 **Holly Hut** sits five minutes off the main track, across the little unbridged Minarapa Stream, 7.3km from your starting point. Here, you'll find a long-drop toilet, drinking water and a 32-bed bunkhouse. It's one of the main stopping points for those undertaking the full two-day Pouākai Circuit. If you have time, consider going the extra distance to the spectacular 31m-high **Bells Falls**, around 30 minutes away, signposted from the hut.

☕ Take a Break

On the northern side of the mountain, **Volcanoview Cafe** *(volcanoview.co.nz)* offers a gorgeous view of the *maunga* (mountain), with nearby cabins and campsite open seven days a week. Otherwise, stock up in New Plymouth or Inglewood before setting out, and carry plenty of water. Drinkable water is available at Holly Hut but it needs to be boiled at Pouākai Hut.

05 From Holly Hut, head back onto the main track, which within 500m reaches a seating platform near the southwest end of **Ahukawakawa Swamp**. It's a great spot to stop for a snack while you read the information panels about the surrounding area's ecology, although there's no shade. The swamp was formed 3500 years ago when debris blocked a stream, forcing it to pass through the porous volcanic rocks beneath.

06 The track crosses the remarkable sphagnum-moss swamp via 1km of boardwalks before reaching a bridge across the very pretty **Stony River**. Take a pic and catch your breath: the hardest part of the route lies ahead. On the northern side of the bridge the track begins a long climb up Pouākai on a partly forested ridge.

07 The 300m ascent to the junction with the **Pouākai Track** is a one- to 1½-hour effort, with the first 20 to 30 minutes being the steepest part. The track then levels briefly through a mossy forest, before continuing at a more gentle incline. If the day is nice, you can distract yourself from the knee-bending effort by pausing to enjoy the views back across the swamp and Mt Taranaki rising above it. If it's raining or if the sun is beating down, this can be a real slog, even with all the steps that have been installed.

08 Two hours from Holly Hut, you top out at a **saddle** that opens up to views of New Plymouth. Head right, as the track sidles around the north side of the Hump (1292m), then makes a short descent to a signposted junction with Mangorei Track. Those with sharp eyes will see a corner of Pouākai Hut well before you reach it.

09 Although the official Pouākai Crossing heads straight down Mangorei Track, you'd be remiss not to take the 15-minute walk down to the **Pouākai Tarns**. Here's where all of those classic shots of Taranaki are taken, showing the elegantly proportioned mountain perfectly reflected in what looks like a

Mt Taranaki

Art & Artefacts

New Plymouth is home to arguably Aotearoa/New Zealand's best regional art gallery in the **Govett-Brewster** *(govettbrewster.com),* which presents contemporary – and often experimental and provocative – local and international shows.

The shimmering building attached to it is dedicated to prominent NZ artist Len Lye (1901–80). It's an interlocking facade of tall, mirror-clad concrete flutes, with internal galleries linked by ramps housing Lye's works – kinetic, noisy and surprising.

Also worth a visit is **Puke Ariki** *(pukeariki.com),* an excellent museum with an extensive collection of Māori artefacts, plus colonial, mountain geology and wildlife exhibits.

Mangorei Track

large lake. If you ever wanted a demonstration of the difference between Instagram and real life, this is the place to come. Instead of a lake, you'll find a shallow pond not much bigger than a backyard swimming pool. Inevitably, there's a row of anxious 'influencers' lined up at one end, cameras on tripods, waiting for that magical moment when the cloud lifts and the wind stops rippling the surface of the tarn long enough for them to capture an image that's already been captured countless times before. Amusing as the social-media circus is, this is actually a very pretty spot – and an ecologically important and culturally significant one. Stick to the boardwalks, which protect the slow-growing spongy moss surrounding the two small tarns (only one of which can be accessed), and don't touch the water, which local Māori consider to be *tapu* (sacred). Māori know this place as Ruahumoko, after its guardian spirit, and the water was used for rituals.

10 The walk back up to the **Mangorei Track** junction takes around 25 minutes, and **Pouākai Hut** (16 bunks, long-drop toilets) is just five minutes down this track. Nestled on the west side of the ridge, it has grand views from its veranda over the curved coastline and New Plymouth. The sunsets can be spectacular from this perch, followed by the lights of the city gradually flickering on.

11 The **Mangorei Track** continues steadily downhill on a stepped boardwalk for about two hours to reach the road's end. Be sure to pause to appreciate the views of northern Taranaki and the coastline before you drop below the bushline.

From here, the track continues its constant descent through lush **rainforest** broken only by one of the last stands of mature rimu and miro to escape the last eruption of Mt Taranaki. Around 30 minutes later, you will emerge at a gravel road; follow it for five minutes to reach the Mangorei Rd car park.

18

Wilkies Pools

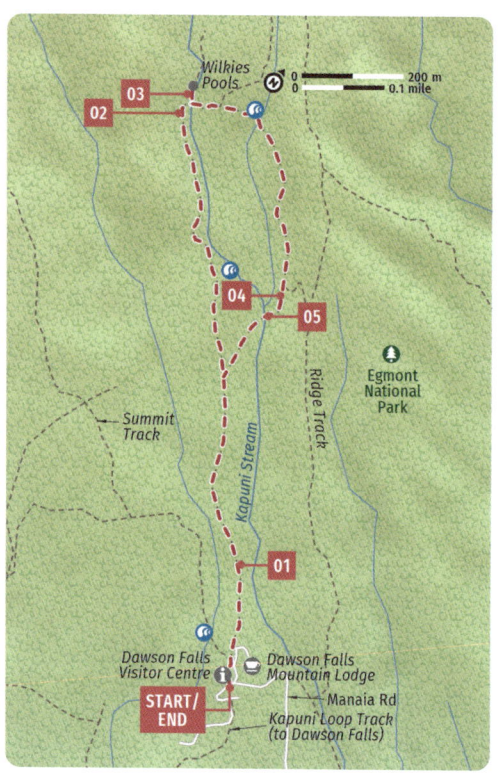

DURATION	DIFFICULTY	DISTANCE	START/END
1hr 20min	Easy	1.9km	Dawson Falls Visitor Centre
TERRAIN		Mountain, forest, excellent track	

This easy walk on the slopes of Taranaki is hugely fun for kids while being gloriously scenic for adults. Highlights include an enchanting 'goblin forest' and a set of lava-formed pools with a natural rock slide – we told you kids would love it! It's a short stroll but there are plentiful options for extending it into something more substantial by joining up with adjacent tracks.

Getting Here
The closest town is Stratford, 23km away, or you can drive here from the city of New Plymouth in less than an hour.

Starting Point
The Dawson Falls Visitor Centre has a large car park with a toilet and a replica of the former Syme Hut rebuilt inside.

01 From the visitor centre, cross the lawn and look for the well-labelled start to the track. The first 900m is touted as being wheelchair accessible, although you'll need arms like Popeye for the steep section a little further on. The track heads straight into one of Taranaki's famous **'goblin forests'**, a gorgeous mossy, fern-filled subalpine wonderland, where the trees all sport long, straggly lichen beards.

02 After a steeper incline, the path reaches the **Kapuni Stream** and offers magnificent views of Mt Taranaki, directly ahead. You can easily see why the picture-perfect volcano was

Wilkies Pools

Extend Your Trek

If 80 minutes isn't enough to get your blood pumping sufficiently, there are various options for continuing your walk. The simplest is to cross the **Dawson Falls** Visitor Centre car park and look for the start of the **Kapuni Loop Track**, a one-hour (1.4km) circuit through more 'goblin forest' alongside the Kapuni Stream to the base of the 18m-high Dawson Falls. The track then climbs steeply to the falls lookout, crosses the road and continues back through forest to the visitor centre.

Alternatively, you can link the Wilkies Pools and Kapuni Loop Tracks via the **Ridge Track** (one hour). This also avoids the short double-back at the end of the Wilkies Pools Track.

cast in the role of Mt Fuji in the 2003 Tom Cruise flick *The Last Samurai*. The path then follows the gurgling rock-strewn stream until it crosses it via a bouncy **suspension bridge**.

03 Just across the bridge, a short track leads to the **Wilkies Pools**, a set of small pools formed within 20,000-year-old lava, with waterfalls tinkling into them. A short, steep natural rock slide connects them, which hardy kids delight in swooshing down. Being hardy is a necessity: the water originated from snow melts further up the mountain and is bracing, to say the least. A wet suit is sensible attire.

04 Pick up the trail again, which is a little rougher and damper on the return loop (it's still fine, but definitely not wheelchair accessible, and muddy in places). It heads back through more **goblin forest** and steps down to some picturesque little waterfalls and a small stream.

Just after the junction of the Ridge Track, look out for the **intake weir** for the hydroelectric power station, which you can visit later, just off the road near the car park (built in 1899, it's the world's oldest continuously operating power generator).

05 Metal steps head down to the **Kapuni Stream**, which is easy enough to cross by hopping between the rocks (although it's impassable after heavy rain). The loop then rejoins the wheelchair-accessible part of the main track; turn left to head back to the visitor centre.

Take a Break

Stock up on picnic food in New Plymouth or Stratford and enjoy a snack by the pools. Set in a beautiful 1920s buildng, Stratford's award-winning **Baking Company** has a cabinet groaning with fresh-baked pastries, pies, sandwiches, cream doughnuts and salads, as well as meals.

19

Manawatū Gorge

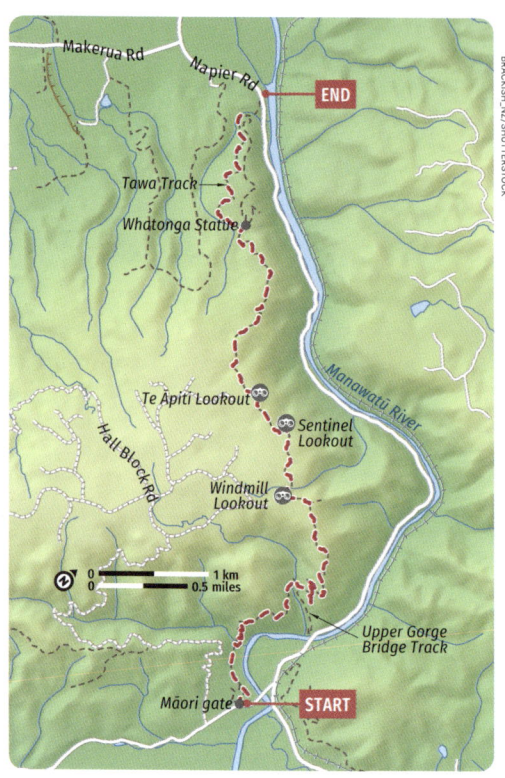

DURATION	DIFFICULTY	DISTANCE	START/END
3½hrs	Moderate	11km	Balance Gorge Rd/ Napier Rd

TERRAIN	Well-defined track, forest

Nīkau (tree palms) and giant maidenhair ferns give a Jurassic edge to this shady walk through native bush, high above the Manawatū River.

There's no transport serving this track, so, unless you have a car to leave at each end or can catch a lift from someone, you may have to reconsider this as a seven-hour hike. Park in the designated area just over the road bridge at the **Woodville** end and enter through the **carved Māori gate**.

The path climbs for the first 30 minutes before starting to flatten out and, 30 minutes later, loops down to a **gurgling creek** lined with nīkau palms.

After the junction with the Upper Gorge Bridge Track (at the 3.5km mark), it gently snakes its way up again. The first two short spur tracks to lookouts are barely worth bothering with, although the **Windmill Lookout** at the 5.5km point does have a toilet and a picnic table. The **Sentinel Lookout**, 800m further, is better, offering views down to the river and over the surrounding countryside. However, you don't even have to leave the main track for **Te Āpiti Lookout**, 600m further on.

A 6.2m-high stylised steel **statue of Māori chief Whatonga** stands sentinel over the junction of the Tawa Loop Walk. The riverside section of the Tawa Loop Track is closed due to a hazardous tree, so take the left-hand branch of the track until it pops out near the car park.

Carved Māori gate

20

Kāpiti Island Summit

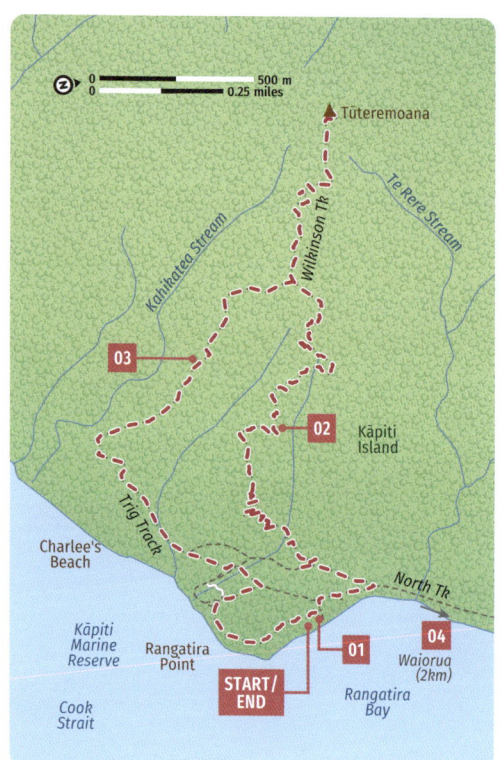

DURATION	DIFFICULTY	DISTANCE	START/END
4hrs	Moderate	6km	Kāpiti Island Rangatira Shelter

TERRAIN	Bush track, can be muddy and slippery

This large, protected, predator-free island off the western coast north of Wellington is a nature reserve flourishing with rare birdlife and regenerating forest. There are several rewarding day hikes available on Kāpiti in just two publicly accessible areas, one of which is described here. Check with tour operators to see which walk best suits your needs.

Getting Here
Paraparaumu Beach, about an hour's drive north of Wellington, is your gateway to Kāpiti. It is well signposted just a few minutes off SH1.

Starting Point
Kāpiti is only accessible via tour operator **Kapiti Island Nature Tours** (kapitiisland. com), which operates a ferry service for self-guided walkers. Boats leave from Kapiti Boating Club at Paraparaumu Beach.

01 Kāpiti Island Nature Tours' ferries mean you can enjoy a half-day or full-day walk on the island at your own pace. Self-guided tours ($129/79) include return ferry tickets, a DOC permit and an introductory *kōrero* (talk) with a guide. From the **Rangatira Shelter**, at Rangatira in the middle of the island, start your walk on the **Rangatira Loop**, an easy trail through wetland, coastal shrubland and regenerating forest. At 1.8km (one hour 30 minutes total), this loop is great for families. Completing the whole loop will take you past a historic *whare* (home) and whaling artefacts, before beginning to head up into the older forest on the Wilkinson Track.

Tīeke (saddleback)

Kāpiti Coast

The national walking trail, Te Araroa, traverses part of the wide, smooth beach running along the Kāpiti Coast, so you might see trampers laden with large packs straggling along the sands. You, however, will be entranced with the opportunity to stroll, dine and sunbathe on this beautiful stretch of coastline, one of the jewels in the Wellington region.

Across a short stretch of water, **Kāpiti Island** sits on the horizon like a low green dragon, and the beach is vast enough to give you a pleasant sense of being away from it all, despite it being lined with homes. **Paekākāriki** is a particularly nice little settlement, with a popular cafe.

02 The well-formed **Wilkinson Track** takes you past a hihi feeding station and a picnic area on the way to Kāpiti's 521m summit, **Tūteremoana**, a two-hour walk over 3.8km. Enjoy the bird's-eye views!

03 It's back down the hill now on the much steeper **Trig Track**, a more challenging 2km walk on a track that can be muddy and slippery with narrow or unstable sections. Keep your ears and eyes peeled for birdlife; on these upper tracks you can hope to see hopping little tīeke, with their orange saddles; the very rare hihi or fat blue takahē; and kākā, the raucous parrot. After about two hours, you'll encounter the Rangatira Loop again and can make your way back along the rest of the path to the **shelter**, where there are bathrooms and a water tap (it's recommended to treat it before use).

04 For those wanting more of a human connection and story, visit the more open and peopled **Waiorua** area at the northern end of the island. The summit walk here is a gentle, 2h loop to 198m, with good views.

Take a Break

You'll need to bring your lunch and snacks to Kāpiti for the day, but Paraparaumu has plenty of options if you're staying the night on the coast. Popular cafe **Two Fat Chefs** has large, delicious portions of Kiwi cafe favourites like beef cheeks, corn fritters and portobello mushroom burgers.

21

Paekākāriki Escarpment

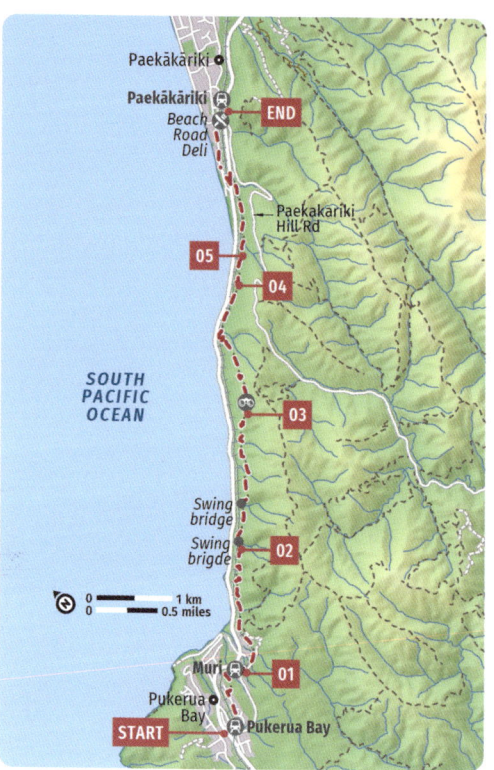

DURATION	DIFFICULTY	DISTANCE	START/END
3½hrs	Moderate	10km	Pukerua Bay/ Paekākāriki

TERRAIN	Good dirt track, exposed ridges

Spectacular ocean views are a constant along this popular, well-marked track. And there's a train station at each end, making it a breeze to access via public transport. You'll need a head for heights, though. The two swing bridges aren't a problem, but much of the track hugs the edge of the escarpment, which makes it unsuitable for small children or during high winds. Still, those views over Kāpiti Island are well worth it.

Getting Here

If you're driving, ditch your car at Paekākāriki and catch the train to Pukerua Bay ($4). Alternatively, train here directly from Wellington.

Starting Point

There's an information board with a map on the Pukerua Bay train platform. The nearest toilets and shops are 250m away.

 01 Follow the signs from the station up to suburban Sea Vista Dr. Eventually, it turns into a cul-de-sac where there's a sign reading 'foot access to Muri Reserve'. Cut across the reserve then walk alongside the train tracks to the tiny, disused **Muri Station** building. Stop to admire the mural by Bruce Freestone entitled *Accents of Angels* (2015).

02 After the 1km marker, you'll reach the track proper, which continues to follow the railway line before climbing to incredible

Paekākāriki Escarpment

views over Pukerua Bay and distant Kāpiti Island. Just before the 3km mark, you'll reach the first **swing bridge**. The second, which is 15 minutes further along the track, is the longer of the two. While both are quite high, the enclosed sides mitigate any potential nerves. And you'll be quite thankful that you don't need to walk down the gully and back up again!

03 From here, the track steps up steeply until you can see all the way to the South Island. At this point, the path is quite narrow, with some sheer drop-offs to your left. Here's where the nerves may kick in, particularly if there's any wind. Trudge up the stairs to the 5km marker; you're now halfway. Near the highest point of the walk there's a **viewpoint** with a large U-shaped seating area and a display pointing out the landmarks on the horizon.

04 By the 6km mark you'll be stepping down towards the train tracks. The route flattens out by the 7km mark and passes through a **karaka grove**, followed by a gentle climb to the site of a long-gone Māori village called **Pari Pari**.

☕ Take a Break

Stocked with home-baked goodies (chubby muffins, bagels, pastrami-stuffed baguettes), Paekākāriki's **Beach Road Deli** *(beachroaddeli.co.nz)* is heaven-sent for the hungry hiker. The coffee's as good as it gets, made by happy staff whistling along to a jazzy soundtrack. Pizzas happen from noon on Fridays.

05 A little further along, a **former quarry** has been turned into a haven for lizards. From here, you'll pass through some pleasant, shady patches of native bush, rich with birdlife. Eventually, the route ducks under the busy highway and comes out on the footpath. You can turn left here and head directly back to Paekākāriki train station, but we'd recommend turning right for a more pleasant meander through the village via Ames St.

22

Otari-Wilton's Bush Loop

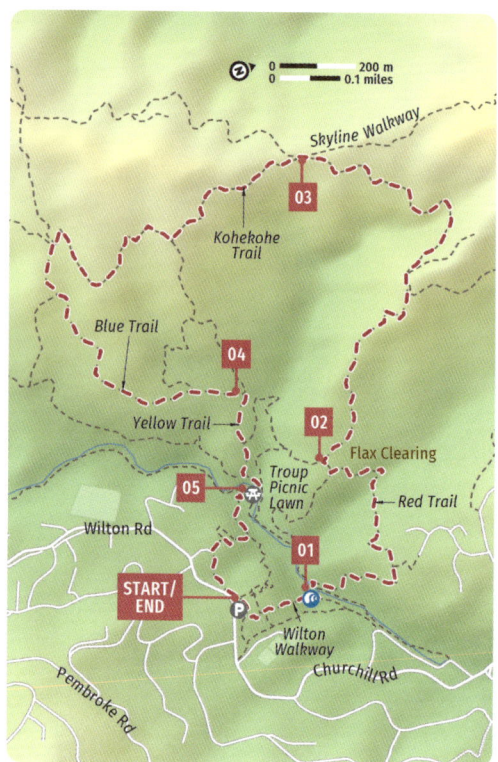

DURATION	DIFFICULTY	DISTANCE	START/END
3hrs	Moderate	7km	Main entrance, 160 Wilton Rd

TERRAIN	Dirt track through native bush

Meet some of Wellington's oldest trees on a lush, shady walk through the capital's largest remaining stand of native forest. The route then heads up to a section of the Skyline Walkway for views over the harbour. It's easily reached by public transport and mainly sheltered – making it doable even in the face of one of the city's legendary gales.

Getting Here

Otari-Wilton's Bush botanic garden and reserve is 5km from the centre of Wellington. Catch the no 14 (Wilton) bus from Lambton Quay.

Starting Point

The information centre has toilets and a useful map brochure. Start on the Wilton Walkway near the car park.

01 The reserve's designated tracks are short, so we've devised a route combining several of them while also heading outside of its boundaries. Start by meandering through the patch of bush near the main entrance, stopping to read the labels and information panels as you go. There's no single route to choose here, but look out for signs pointing down to the **waterfall**. It's not much of a waterfall, but it is a pretty spot nonetheless.

02 Turn left at the junction after the waterfall, continue downhill and cross the stream. Look for the beginning of the **Red Trail**

Nature's Larder

Otari-Wilton's Bush is the only botanic gardens in Aotearoa/New Zealand specialising in native flora, showcasing more than 1200 plant species. The virgin and regenerating podocarp-broadleaf forest at its heart is a type of evergreen forest unique to Aotearoa/New Zealand.

Before the arrival of the British, this diverse patch of forest was an important larder for the local tribes. Otari means 'place of snares', a reference to the birds such as kerurū (wood pigeon), weka (woodhen) and kiwi that were caught here. Seasonal berries were also harvested, and kumara (sweet potato) was planted on some of the north-facing slopes.

opposite and slightly to the left. The track leads through the lovely dappled light of a tawa forest. It's a bit up and down, but mainly up. In about 25 minutes, you'll reach the **Flax Clearing** – an expanse of lawn with a few park benches.

03 Cut across the clearing, looking for the sign to 'Skyline Walkway'. The gentle walk up through the bush opens out after around 15 minutes and joins up to a dirt road. After another 15 minutes, it intersects with the **Skyline Walkway** (p99), a 13.4km track following the ridges of the hills surrounding Wellington. If you feel inspired, you could walk in either direction to one of the nearby peaks. At 255m, this junction is the highest point of our walk and the views are extraordinary: Wellington Harbour and Somes Island/Matiu to the left, Tinakori Hill directly in front (hiding the central city), and the airport and heads to the right.

04 Hop over the stile and take the path known as the **Kohekohe Trail**, which starts by cutting through long grass and low scrub. Eventually, you'll reach another stile and head back into the forest, passing through a sheltered grove. At the track junction under the pines, turn left and take the steps down through the bush. After a short spell, you'll reach a junction with the **Blue Trail**; take the left-hand fork. You're now in the heart of the old forest. The big fella with his own seating area is an **800-year-old rimu**.

05 At the next junction, where the Blue and Yellow Trails meet, turn right and head down towards the **Troup Picnic Lawn**. Be sure to say hi to the eels in the stream. From here, zigzag up to the more formal botanic section of the gardens, where a canopy walkway leads back to the start.

☕ Take a Break

There are no cafes nearby so pack a picnic to enjoy on the Flax Clearing or the Troup Picnic Lawn. The latter has the advantage of free barbecues and toilets.

Skyline Walkway

Best for

ESCAPING THE CITY

SOUTHERN NORTH ISLAND 22 OTARI-WILTON'S BUSH LOOP

Also Try...

Mt Taranaki Summit

KLANARONG CHITMUNG/SHUTTERSTOCK

Mt Taranaki Summit

DURATION	DIFFICULTY	DISTANCE
8–10hrs	Hard	12.6km

Climb to the 2518m pinnacle of the slumbering Taranaki volcano on this challenging but rewarding track.

It's said to be the most climbed mountain in Aotearoa/New Zealand, and in ideal summer conditions most fit hikers can make it to the summit, but you need to prepare – many people have been killed on its slopes. It's an ascent of around 1570m – a very big day out – so don't take it lightly, whatever the conditions. Check the forecast, and be prepared to turn tail and retreat if the weather deteriorates (check in with the Taranaki/Egmont National Park Visitor Centre before you set out for up-to-date information). The best time of year to attempt the climb is from January to March, when the mountain is mostly clear of snow and ice, other than in the crater.

Sunrise Track

DURATION	DIFFICULTY	DISTANCE
4½–5½hrs	Moderate	12km

This gentle, well-graded track climbs through gorgeous forest to a hut with high views and an easily attained alpine saddle.

This is the perfect introduction to mountain walking in Aotearoa/New Zealand, rising slowly through changing forest to offer a glimpse of alpine country. If you're new to life above the bushline, it could be love at first sight. The gradient and changing scene make the Sunrise Track a good option for families, but it's also more than just a taster of the mountains. The bush that drapes the slopes of the Ruahine Range is spectacular, with the track setting out through red beech, rimu and kahikatea forest and rising through mountain beech and mountain cedar (kaikawaka) to top out among subalpine herb fields.

Mt Holdsworth

Mt Holdsworth–Jumbo Circuit

DURATION	DIFFICULTY	DISTANCE
3 days	Hard	24km

A long-time favourite of local hikers, this circuit includes nights at two scenic huts above the bushline, and a day following alpine ridges.

This classic Tararua tramp climbs through beech forest to quickly ascend to the alpine tops of the range. Mt Holdsworth (1470m) brings wraparound views, while the huts along the route also provide expansive panoramas, bringing a serene sense of removal as you look out to the lights of Masterton in the evening.

Skyline Walkway

DURATION	DIFFICULTY	DISTANCE
5hrs	Hard	13.4km

Admire Wellington from above on this track along the city's ridges.

As well as views over the city and harbour, on a clear day you can see all the way to the Marlborough Sounds and Kaikōura Ranges on the South Island. Choose your day carefully, though – the track is extremely exposed, with no shelter from either the sun or Wellington's notorious wind. The full route stretches from Karori to Johnsonville but there are multiple entry points.

Wharariki Beach (p104)

Top of the South

23 **Green Hills & Wharariki Beach**
Hike to one of Aotearoa/New Zealand's most striking beaches. **p104**

24 **Pupu Hydro Walkway**
Engineering and nature combine on this short bush walk. **p106**

25 **Abel Tasman Day Walk**
Take a bite out of Aotearoa/New Zealand's most popular Great Walk. **p108**

26 **Mt Robert/Pourangahau Circuit**
Climb a mountain and turn around, descending through mossy forest. **p112**

27 **Queen Charlotte Day Walk**
Traverse a remote fold of the Marlborough Sounds. **p114**

Explore

Top of the South

Consisting of the fertile Tasman and Marlborough Districts, with the chilled-out city of Nelson squeezed in between, the 'Top of the South' boasts renowned coastal holiday spots – particularly Golden Bay/Mohua, Tasman Bay and the curlicued emerald inlets of the Marlborough Sounds. There are also three national parks (Nelson Lakes, Abel Tasman and Kahurangi) and three of the country's most famous multiday hikes (the Abel Tasman Coast, Heaphy and Queen Charlotte Tracks). If you're arriving by ferry from often-blustery Wellington, it's an impressive introduction to what South Islanders refer to as 'the Mainland'.

Tākaka

Boasting Aotearoa/New Zealand's highest concentration of yoga pants, dreadlocks and bare feet in the high street, Tākaka is a lovable little town (population 1240) and the last 'big' centre before the road west ends at Farewell Spit. You'll find most things you need here, and a few things you don't, but we all have an unworn tie-dyed tank top in our wardrobe, don't we?

Motueka

Motueka (pronounced maw-tu-eh-ka; population 8300) is a bustling agricultural hub and the closest decent-sized town to the Abel Tasman and Kahurangi National Parks. It has a good selection of accommodation and cafes, a large supermarket and roadside fruit stalls.

Nelson

Dishing up a winning combination of beautiful surroundings, sophisticated art and culinary scenes, and lashings of sunshine, Nelson (population 55,200) is hailed as one of Aotearoa/New Zealand's most liveable cities. In summer, it fills with local and international visitors, all there to take advantage of its proximity to both the Marlborough Sounds and the diverse natural attractions of the Tasman District. It has everything you'd expect from a city of this size, including multiple supermarkets, bakeries and breweries, and an oversized range of outdoors and camping stores. The best restaurants congregate at the cathedral end of Trafalgar St, while other good options spread along Hardy St.

WHEN TO GO

The forecast is good: this area soaks up some of Aotearoa/New Zealand's sunniest weather, with January and February being the warmest months. From around Christmas until the end of January, the whole region teems with Kiwi holidaymakers, so plan ahead during this time and be prepared to jostle for position with bucket-and-spade-wielding families. June and July are the coldest months, averaging highs of 12°C. However, the Top of the South sees some wonderful winter weather, with frosty mornings often giving way to clear skies and T-shirt temperatures.

Picton

Half asleep in winter, but hyperactive in summer (with up to eight fully laden ferry arrivals per day), boaty Picton (population 4700) clusters around a deep and beautiful gulch at the head of Queen Charlotte Sound/Tōtaranui. Over the past few years, this little town has really bloomed, and offers visitors plenty of reasons to linger even after the obvious attractions are knocked off the list. Picton has plenty of cafes, a good supermarket and an excellent Dutch-style bakery.

TRANSPORT

Picton is the South Island's main interisland ferry port, with multiple daily sailings to and from Wellington. Nelson has the busiest domestic airport, followed by Blenheim and Picton. Buses link the region to Canterbury and the West Coast. From October to April, KiwiRail's Coastal Pacific train takes the scenic journey between Picton and Christchurch.

WHERE TO STAY

Picton has good motels and B&Bs and some brilliant hostels – the best of which is **Tombstone Motel, Lodge & Backpackers** (tombstonelodge.co.nz). Nelson isn't too shabby when it comes to hostels either – our favourite is **Tasman Bay Backpackers** (tasmanbaybackpackers.co.nz) – and it has some great motels, too. There are plenty of options around Motueka and its surrounds, particularly the quirky **Eden's Edge Lodge** (edensedge.co.nz) in Riwaka and the **Kaiteri Motels & Apartments** (kaiterimotelsandapartments.co.nz) in Kaiteriteri. If you're looking for beachside luxury in Golden Bay/Mohua, try **Adrift** (adrift.co.nz).

WHAT'S ON

Marlborough's biggest event is the **Marlborough Wine & Food Festival** (marlboroughwinefestival.com), held in February at Renwick Domain, out of Blenheim.

The city of Nelson has a lively events calendar, including the **Nelson Jazz Festival** (nelsonjazzclub.com) in January and the **Nelson Arts Festival** (nelsonartsfestival.nz) in October.

Resources

Picton i-SITE
(marlboroughnz.com)
Maps, track information and bookings.

**DOC Whakatū/
Nelson Visitor Centre**
(doc.govt.nz)
The main DOC centre for the Top of the South, including Kahurangi and Abel Tasman National Parks.

**DOC Nelson Lakes
Visitor Centre**
(doc.govt.nz)
Park-wide information.

Motueka i-SITE
(facebook.com/motuekaisitenz)
Local information and DOC passes.

Golden Bay Visitor Centre
(goldenbaynz.co.nz)
Free tourist map, bookings and DOC passes.

23

Green Hills & Wharariki Beach

DURATION	DIFFICULTY	DISTANCE	START/END
3hrs	Moderate	11km	Wharariki car park

TERRAIN	Farmland, bush, hill and beach

With crazy rock formations and pounding surf, beaches don't come much more dramatic than isolated Wharariki. This track heads through farmland for a loop among native bush to wild sea cliffs. At low tide, you can then return back along the seal-populated beach.

Getting Here
The nearest major townships are Collingwood (29km) and Tākaka (54km); the last 6km of the road is unsealed. There's no public transport to the trailhead.

Starting Point
There's a seasonal cafe and a toilet at the Wharariki car park, but that's about it.

01 From the car park, follow the signs to **Green Hills Track**, which starts by following a 4WD road through farmland. After about 15 minutes, it skirts a marshy lake. Continue through a couple of farm gates (leave them as you found them) and, eventually, you'll see the **Green Hills Stream** below, lined with manuka, nīkau palms and cabbage trees.

02 Take the little bridge over the stream and through another **farm gate**, then turn right when you get to the junction marked 'Green Hills Creek Loop'. You'll likely have this track to yourself, as it's immediately obvious that it's not well trodden. However, it's not especially

Best for

OFF THE BEATEN PATH

Wharariki Beach Track

Farewell Spit

Bleak, exposed and positively sci-fi, **Farewell Spit** is a wetland of international importance and a renowned bird sanctuary. At low tide a large sandy intertidal zone is exposed on the Golden Bay/Mohua side – the summer home of thousands of migratory waders, notably the godwit, Caspian tern and Australasian gannet. Unfortunately, the shallow waters are also notorious for mass strandings of pilot whales – in one incident in February 2017, over 400 beached themselves simultaneously.

Walkers can explore the first 4km of the spit via a network of tracks. Beyond that point, access is limited to trips with **Farewell Spit Tours** (farewellspit.com).

difficult and there are handy marker poles to follow. The track heads up through a thick patch of native bush to a scrubby clifftop viewpoint, where the waves crash over the rocky islets below. This is the very top of the South Island's famously wild West Coast and the views are invigorating.

03 Continue around the hill and take the marked one-minute detour along the fenceline to the **Boundary Lookout**, where there are further views of exposed cliffs, farmland and the forest-shrouded mountains of Kahurangi National Park in the distance. Complete the loop around the grassy side of the hill (look out for the poles as the track isn't always clear), and then drop down through the small section of bush to the loop junction. From here, backtrack along the road you came in on, looking out for the sign on your left pointing to Whariki Beach.

04 Hop over the stile and follow the marker poles along the fenceline so you don't bother the sheep. The track then cuts across the field, over another stile and then through a brief but particularly beautiful expanse of bush before...wow! Suddenly you're facing wonderful **Wharariki Beach**, with its rolling waves, layered limestone and Archway Islands in the distance.

Be warned: this beach is incredibly dangerous and only the foolhardy would attempt to swim here. And it can be unpleasant when the westerly wind blows a sandy dermabrasion your way. It is glorious, though. Chances are you'll see seals (keep your distance). At low tide, you can make your way around the rocks and along the sand to a short track connecting to the car park. Otherwise, return the way you came.

 Take a Break

The **Archway Cafe** by the car park is theoretically open from October to Easter, weather depending, and serves the likes of sandwiches, muffins and cake. For a more substantial meal, head to Collingwood where there are couple of good cafes.

24

Pupu Hydro Walkway

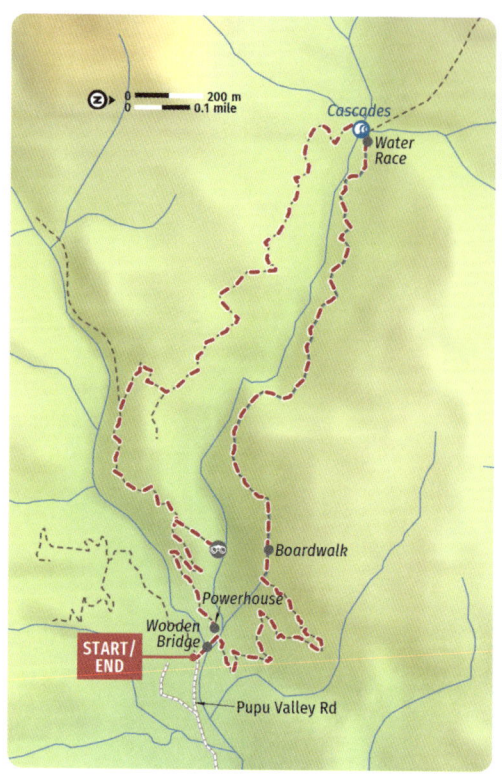

DURATION	DIFFICULTY	DISTANCE	START/END
2hrs	Moderate	5.5km	Pupu Valley Rd

TERRAIN	Gravel road, bush track, boardwalk

Combine a bush walk with historic engineering on this short track through the fringes of vast Kahurangi National Park. A lookout along the way provides views over Golden Bay/Mohua. Combine it with a visit to the breathtakingly beautiful Te Waikoropupū Springs just down the road.

Have a good look at the information panels by the entrance then cross over the **wooden bridge**, where there's a little **waterfall**. After about a minute, you'll reach the junction of the main loop. We'd recommend heading left, as the climb is more gradual in this direction.

Very shortly, you'll reach the hydroelectric **powerhouse**. It is now fully restored and, once again, generating sustainable electricity for the surrounding houses; peer through the window at the workings. The route then heads up a broad gravel road, known as **Jim's Track**. Along the way, take the 160m diversion through the bush to the **lookout**, where the views stretch all the way to the eastern end of Golden Bay/Mohua.

The road ends at a bridge over a stream where there are pretty **cascades** and the beginning of the water race. Originally built for gold mining, it was converted for use in power generation in 1929. The track then heads through bush following the fern-lined **water race** along a ridge. It may be an illusion, but the crystal-clear water in the channel seems to cool the air on a summer's day.

At the end of the water race, the track narrows into a slim **boardwalk** along a cliff. It's fenced, but not great for small children. The downward section of the track isn't in the best shape but it eventually flattens out into a very pretty bush walk.

Boardwalk, Pupu Hydro Walkway

25

Best for

COASTAL SCENERY

Abel Tasman Day Walk

DURATION	DIFFICULTY	DISTANCE	START/END
6hrs	Moderate	17km	Medlands/ Apple Tree Bay

TERRAIN	Well-formed bush track, beaches

Fur seals, Abel Tasman National Park

Aquamarine waters and golden-sand beaches backed by quintessential NZ coastal forest: there's a reason the five-day Abel Tasman Coast Track (p116) is the most popular of the country's official Great Walks. Boats stop at jetties all along the route, making it perfect for a day walk, too. This section covers a substantial chunk of the middle of the track, including great beaches, glorious views and a gorgeous swimming hole set in dense native bush.

Getting Here

Boats leave from both Kaiteriteri and Mārahau, offering water-taxi services, set tours and timetabled ferries. Some offer packed lunches and pick-ups from Motueka and Nelson. In summer, allow time before your departure to find parking. The operators include **Wilsons** *(abeltasman.co.nz)*, **Abel Tasman Sea Shuttle** *(abeltasmanseashuttles.co.nz)*, **Abel Tasman AquaTaxi** *(aquataxi.co.nz)* and **Marahau Water Taxis** *(marahauwatertaxis.co.nz)*. All the companies have set timetables for their drop-offs and pick-ups, allowing you to choose your own adventure between the various bays and beaches.

Starting Point

There's nothing at Medlands Beach except a long-drop toilet and water that needs to be boiled or filtered before drinking. Kaiteriteri and Mārahau both have toilets and cafes, and Kaiteriteri has a general store selling the likes of sunblock (essential), insect repellent (also essential) and seasickness tablets (probably not necessary).

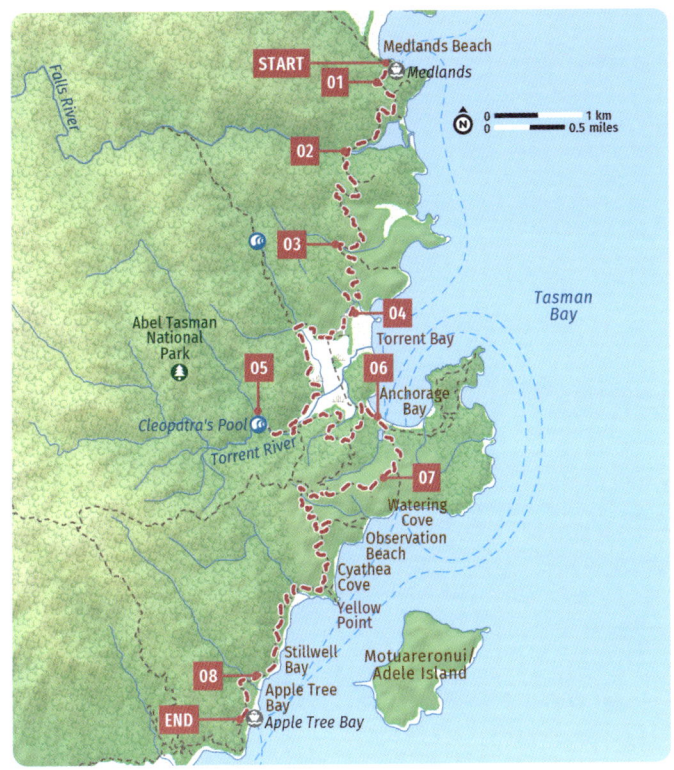

Abel Tasman National Park

Coastal **Abel Tasman National Park** blankets the northern end of a range of marble and limestone hills. At 22,530 hectares, it's NZ's smallest national park. It take its name from the great Dutch explorer who dropped anchored in Golden Bay/Mohua in 1642, becoming the first European to discover Aotearoa.

There are various tracks in the park, although the **Coast Track** is what everyone is here for. The main reason for the track's popularity is that it traverses some of NZ's (and arguably the world's) finest golden-sand beaches. Only a few can be reached by road, but non-walkers can access others by kayak or boat.

01 It takes under an hour to reach **Medlands Beach** by boat. Use the time to apply sunblock and insect repellent. Sandflies can be a nuisance on this track. They don't tend to bite while you're on the move but will swoop in when you stop, leaving highly itchy bites in their wake.

The magic starts as soon as the boat sets out, giving you a teaser of the beauty to come. If you're departing from Kaiteriteri, chances are your boat will take a quick detour into Ngaio Bay to gawk at the unusual rock formation known as **Split Apple Rock**. This dramatically fractured 135-million-year-old granite boulder looks pretty much as its name suggests; it will eventually wear down to form the golden sand typical of this coast. Your starting point, **Medlands Beach**, is a pretty little beach with a stream down one end, immediately south of the better-known Bark Bay. As you disembark, look for the **Māori carving** on the hill. Here's where the track starts.

02 The Abel Tasman is not a typical, rugged Aotearoa/New Zealand track. It's better serviced than any other track in the country: well cut, well graded and well marked. It's difficult to get lost and can be hiked in a pair of running shoes. An added advantage of this is that you'll probably get your feet wet – indeed, you'll probably want to get your feet wet. Head south along the track and, within 15 minutes, you'll glimpse ominous-sounding Sandfly Bay, far below. Within another 15 minutes, you'll reach a **suspension bridge** over the **Falls River**, one of the largest rivers in the national park; you'll get a great view of it a little further on.

03 The track carries on through dense native forest. After around 20 minutes, you'll reach the well-marked **Halfway Pool**, a tiny swimming hole at the side of the track.

04 Press on for 40 minutes more and you'll reach **Torrent Bay/Rākauroa**, the national park's main settlement. There are terrific views over the beach and estuary as you descend. Unlike some other countries, it's unusual to find residences within NZ's national parks. However, the private dwellings here already existed when the park was established in 1942. Try not to be too envious of the lucky families who have holiday homes in this tiny enclave of car-free paradise. Torrent Bay/Rākauroa is a great spot for a swim and a picnic, and there are long-drop toilets, should you need them. There are no shops of any kind, however.

05 From here, there are two options to proceed. If the tide is right and the water low enough, you can zip straight across the estuary for 1.4km to Anchorage Bay, usually you have to be within two hours of low tide to cross. Daylight tide times are published on the DOC website (doc.govt.nz). The recommended route, however, is to follow the coast path around the estuary, taking the bridges over the three little feeder streams that gave Torrent Bay/Rākauroa its name. Although this option is 3.4km longer, it's well worth coming this way, even at low tide, to take the 15-minute side track to beautiful **Cleopatra's Pool**. We're fairly sure that the Ancient Egyptian queen never actually visited here, but if she did she would surely have taken a dip in the natural swimming holes fed by the Torrent River. The cold, freshwater is invigorating after a day in the sun and sea. Kids and the young at heart love to hurtle down the natural stone slide separating the upper and lower sections. Keep an eye out for eels and inquisitive weka (woodhens), the latter of which will make a lunge for any food left unattended.

06 Return to the main track and at the next junction it's possible to save some time by bypassing **Anchorage Bay** completely and continuing south. We wouldn't recommend this unless you're really pressed for time. Instead, we suggest you take the left-hand fork, and follow the signs to this blissfully long stretch of sandy beach. It's only 2.8km from Cleopatra's Pool, but you do need to climb up and over a bushclad hill to get to it. There's a 34-bunk DOC hut and campsite down the far end, along with long-drop toilets. The bay becomes a makeshift marina at the height of summer, with kayaks, water taxis and yachts coming and going, or sitting anchored offshore.

07 Pick up the track halfway along the beach and puff your way back up and along the ridge. Be sure to take time to stop, turn around and admire the views, which are among the most breathtaking in the entire park. Far below, a little tannin-stained lake makes the sea alongside it seem even more brilliantly green and blue in contrast. From here the track follows a high ridge through lush **beech forest**, resounding with the pealing song of korimako (bellbirds) and the chattering of pīwakawaka (fantails).

☕ Take a Break

There's nowhere to buy food within the park, so you'll need to stock up before arriving. You can order packed lunches in advance from the main boat operators for $15 to $25. Kaiteriteri has a few eating options, but none of them are great. Mārahau fares better, with two decent cafes and the **Fat Tui** burger bar.

Anchorage Bay

Through the trees you'll catch views of **Adele Island/Motuareronui**. The latter name was given to it by French explorer Jules Dumont d'Urville, who charted this coast in the 1820s; Adele was his wife. Other d'Urville-related names on this stretch include Watering Cove, where his crew collected freshwater from a creek; Observation Beach, where he studied the stars for six days in 1827 in order to ensure the accuracy of his maps; and Cyathea Cove, which he named after the ponga/silver fern *(Cyathea dealbata)*. A short spur track leads to **Yellow Point**, named for the yellowish lichen found here. After 5.5km, you'll pass **Stillwell Bay**, which takes its name from a pioneering family who built holiday homes here in the 1920s.

08 Press on for another kilometre to **Apple Tree Bay**, named after an orchard planted here by early settlers. There's not much here now except for another DOC campsite and long-drop toilets. Hopefully, you'll have time for a swim at this pretty little beach before your boat arrives. After all, enjoying these remote bays is a large part of what this walk is all about.

Kayaking the Abel Tasman

Sea kayaking is a popular way to explore the Abel Tasman coastline, and the possibilities and permutations for guided or freedom trips are vast. You can kayak from half a day to up to three days, staying in DOC huts or campsites (book in advance online before entering the park) or in any of the other park accommodation. You can kayak one day, camp overnight and then walk back, or walk further into the park and catch a water taxi back.

Most operators offer similar trips at similar prices, focusing on the safer southern half of the park (as far as Onetahuti Beach). Mārahau is the main base, but trips also depart from Kaiteriteri. There are numerous day-trip options, including guided tours often departing from Mārahau and taking in bird-filled Adele Island/Motuareronui (around $200).

26

Mt Robert/ Pourangahau Circuit

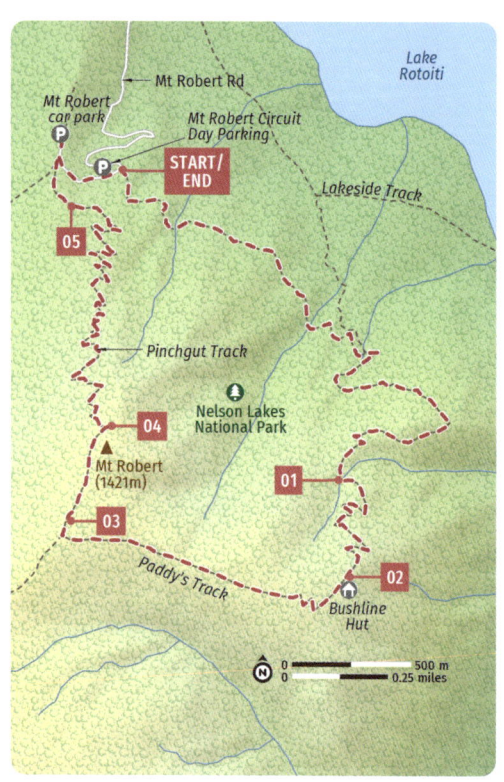

DURATION	DIFFICULTY	DISTANCE	START/END
4hrs	Hard	9.6km	Mt Robert Circuit Day Parking

TERRAIN	Mountainous, exposed ridge, forest

Climb to a high ridge for lofty views over Nelson Lakes National Park then descend through a mossy forest. Lake Rotoiti is laid out below, as are the valleys of the Travers River, running into the lake, and the Buller River, running out. You'll traverse a variety of landscapes, including beech forest and classic South Island tussock grasslands.

Getting Here
The trailhead is 4.5km along unsealed Mt Robert Rd, which starts 2km west of St Arnaud village. There's no public transport.

Starting Point
The Mt Robert Circuit Day Parking area is the lower of the two car parks. There's a toilet at the main Mt Robert car park, 600m further up the road.

 In winter, be sure to check in with the DOC **Nelson Lakes Visitor Centre** in St Arnaud before starting out. There's no point attempting the circuit in bad weather as you'll miss out on the views and it can be dangerous. In summer, bring insect repellent, plenty of water and sunscreen, as long sections are exposed to the elements.

This circuit can be walked in either direction, but we suggest heading clockwise for a gentler ascent. Start by taking **Paddy's Track**, just across the road from the parking area. After a brief climb through bush, there's a gentle downhill before it starts sloping consistently up along the northern slopes of Mt Robert/

Best for

MOUNTAIN VIEWS

Mt Robert/Pourangahau Circuit

Nelson Lakes National Park

Nelson Lakes National Park surrounds two lakes – Rotoiti ('small lake') and Rotoroa ('long lake') – fringed by sweet-smelling beech forest with a backdrop of greywacke mountains. Located at the northern end of the Southern Alps and with a dramatic glacier-carved landscape, it's an awe-inspiring place to get up on high.

Part of the park, east of Lake Rotoiti, is classed as a 'mainland island' where a conservation scheme aims to eradicate introduced pests (rats, possums and stoats) and regenerate native flora and fauna. The park is flush with birdlife and is famous for brown-trout fishing.

Pourangahau. After about an hour, the path flattens out onto a ridge, with views of the lake below and the summit ahead. Ten minutes further on, there's a shady cleft with a gurgling stream; a great place to catch your breath on a scorching day.

02 The track continues to climb through grass and then tussock for another 30 minutes until you reach the **Bushline Hut**. Content yourself with the knowledge that this is the halfway mark, and the hardest part lies behind you. The hut has sleeping swabs, a log fire, long-drop toilets and drinkable water.

03 Continue through the forest behind the hut and then zigzag up to the ridge, where the views embrace the Travers River valley. A slip zone to the right of the track demonstrates the risks during snow, high winds or heavy rains. After 1.5km, you'll reach a 'T' intersection where the Robert Ridge Route heads left. Instead, turn right onto the **Pinchgut Track**.

04 Shortly past the junction you'll reach a single-room shelter where there's water but nothing else. The track heads downhill and, after about 10 minutes, you'll find a park bench, perfectly positioned for romantic views over the lake.

05 The track then plunges back under the bushline and descends steeply through a moss-lined forest; in summer, it's deliciously cool. There's one more exposed section through the bracken and low mānuka (tea tree) bushes before you're enveloped by the lofty canopy of the beech forest. After around an hour, you'll reach the upper **Mt Robert Car Park**. Follow the road for 600m to complete the loop.

 Take a Break

There's very little in St Arnaud, but you can grab a snack from the small grocery store and basic cafe attached to the petrol station. A better option is the pub-like bistro at **Alpine Lodge** (*alpinelodge.co.nz*).

27

Queen Charlotte Day Walk

DURATION	DIFFICULTY	DISTANCE	START/END
5hrs	Moderate	17km	Ship Cove/Meretoto/Furneaux Lodge
TERRAIN		Bush tracks along coastal hills	

Explore a landscape of sea-drowned valleys and forested hills virtually unchanged since the *Endeavour* dropped anchor here in 1770. The Marlborough Sounds are displayed in all their wiggly wonder along the Queen Charlotte Track (p116), offering some of New Zealand's finest coastal scenery. It doesn't have the golden-sand beaches of the Abel Tasman Coast Track, but neither does it have the number of visitors. Mostly, it will be just you, the birds and the summertime chorus of cicadas.

Getting Here

Picton's Town Wharf buzzes with tour operators and water taxis all offering trips out on Queen Charlotte Sound/Tōtaranui. The journey to Ship Cove/Meretoto takes around an hour.

Starting Point

Remote Ship Cove/Meretoto has a shelter and a proper flush toilet, but you'll need to stock up on supplies before you leave Picton.

01 Ship Cove/Meretoto's English name relates to the journeys of James Cook, who first anchored the *Endeavour* here in January 1770 and then returned many times, spending 168 days in the bay over a seven-year period. On that first voyage, he established good relations with the local Māori and left pigs, chickens and goats as a permanent larder. You can read all about it on the fascinating display boards, and pause to admire the European-style monument and Māori *pou* (carved wooden pole).

Queen Charlotte Track

Marlborough Sounds

The **Marlborough Sounds** are a maze of peaks, bays, beaches and watery reaches, formed when the sea flooded deep river valleys after the last ice age. They are very convoluted: Pelorus Sound/Te Hoiere, for example, is 42km long but has 379km of shoreline. The main gateways are **Havelock**, at the base of Pelorus Sound/Te Hoiere, and Picton, at the apex of Queen Charlotte Sound/Tōtaranui.

The wiggly 35km route along **Queen Charlotte Drive** between the two is a great Sounds snapshot. There are loads of hiking, kayaking, boating and biking opportunities, and there's diving as well – notably the wreck of the *Mikhail Lermontov*, a Russian cruise ship that sank in 1986.

The well-labelled, well-formed track starts climbing through shady native bush. Within half an hour, there are good views through the bush towards the mouth of the sound. In another 20 minutes, you'll reach the **Ship Cove Saddle**, where there's a seat and views to Motuara Island on one side and Resolution Bay on the other.

02 From here, it's fairly flat for a while, then the track gently meanders down to the strikingly green waters of **Schoolhouse Bay** where there's a DOC campsite with a long-drop toilet. Before long, you'll pass side tracks to private land on Resolution Bay; where the route is unclear, take the tracks leading up and to the right. After about an hour, you'll reach the **Tawa Saddle**. Sit on a bench and enjoy the views of Mt Stokes/Parorangi, the highest point in the Marlborough Sounds.

03 The track continues downward on a gentle slope for about an hour until it reaches a pretty little pebbly beach at the beginning of the **Endeavour Inlet**. It then shadows the coastline for another 40 minutes, passing a handful of private houses and lodges set within the bush. Yes, some lucky people do indeed live in these isolated bays, with the only access being on foot or by boat. Eventually, the track will pass the rear of **Furneaux Lodge**, where you can wait for your return boat. The full Queen Charlotte Track continues on from here for another 69km, ending in Anakiwa.

Take a Break

The only place to eat or drink on this section of the track is **Furneaux Lodge** *(furneaux.co.nz)*, where you can reward your efforts with an ice-cold drink or a meal. Otherwise, stock up in Picton on picnic supplies. The **Picton Village Bakkerij** *(facebook.com/PictonVillageBakery)* is a good place to start.

Also Try...

Queen Charlotte Track

Abel Tasman Coast Track

DURATION	DIFFICULTY	DISTANCE
5 days	Moderate	60km

Think of this as a beach holiday on foot. Arguably the most beautiful of the Great Walks, the full Abel Tasman Coast Track expands on what's offered in our Abel Tasman Day Walk: a seductive combination of reliably pleasant weather, sparkling seas, golden sand and native coastal forest.

The Abel Tasman is better serviced than any other track in the country, it's difficult to get lost and can be hiked in a pair of running shoes. Such is the pulling power of this track that it now attracts more than 37,000 hikers and kayakers each year, who stay at least one night in the park. Don't expect to just turn up and hike; you'll need to plan and book your Great Walks huts and campsites online, well in advance, especially if you're planning to hike in January.

Queen Charlotte Track

DURATION	DIFFICULTY	DISTANCE
3-5 days	Moderate	71km

The complete Queen Charlotte Track (qctrack.co.nz) continues on from our Queen Charlotte Day Walk (p114), meandering past gorgeous coastal scenery all the way to Anakiwa. The coastal forest is lush, and from the ridges there are views into both Queen Charlotte Sound/Tōtaranui and Kenepuru Sound.

The well-defined track, suitable for people of most fitness levels, can be walked in either direction, though Ship Cove/Meretoto is the usual (and recommended) starting point. This is mainly because it's easier to arrange a boat from Picton to Ship Cove/Meretoto than the reverse. There are six DOC camping grounds along the route, while other accommodation ranges from homestays to luxury lodges. This is one of the draws of the track – the chance to spend the day hiking, then to enjoy a hot shower and a cold beer at the end of it.

Heaphy Track

Heaphy Track

DURATION	DIFFICULTY	DISTANCE
5 days	Hard	78.5km

The popular Heaphy Track is a Great Walk in every sense. It traverses diverse terrain – dense native forest, the mysterious Gouland Downs, secluded river valleys and beaches fringed by nīkau palms.

Although quite long, the Heaphy Track is well cut and benched, making it easier than any other extended tramp found in Kahurangi National Park. That said, you may still find it arduous, particularly in unfavourable weather. As with all of the Great Walks, you'll need to book huts and campsites in advance.

St Arnaud Range Track

DURATION	DIFFICULTY	DISTANCE
5hrs (return)	Hard	11km

This popular up-and-down day walk provides one of the best viewpoints of Nelson Lakes National Park and beyond.

It's around a 1000m ascent (and subsequent descent) from lake to ridge, but achy legs will be soothed by the splendour of beech forest – red, silver and mountain – that gradually changes with altitude. Equally diverting is the chatter of native birds, the population of which is bolstered by the work of the Rotoiti Nature Recovery Project, through which this track passes.

Hooker Valley Track (p138)

Canterbury

28 **Godley Head/Awaroa**
Join the Christchurch locals on a beautiful circuit through wartime history. **p122**

29 **Sign of the Packhorse**
A trek along summits to a historic roadhouse strewn with harbour views. **p124**

30 **Kaikōura Peninsula Walkway**
Wander with wildlife around low cliffs and rocky coast. **p126**

31 **Avalanche Peak**
A steep climb to the heart of the Southern Alps, rewarded with wraparound views. **p128**

32 **Bealey Spur**
Ascend a relatively gentle spur to a historic hut. **p130**

33 **Woolshed Creek Hut**
A feature-filled walk stitching together water caves, an old coal mine and swims aplenty. **p132**

34 **Mt John (Ōtehīwai)**
Rise from the shores of Lake Tekapo to the observatory-topped summit of this low mountain. **p136**

35 **Hooker Valley**
Grab an audience with Aotearoa/New Zealand's highest mountain on this flat and spectacular track. **p138**

36 **Mueller Hut**
A tough climb amply rewarded with one of the country's most dramatically located huts. **p140**

Explore

Canterbury

Aotearoa/New Zealand's largest region is a place of stark natural contrasts, with a vast agricultural plain ramping up into mountains that include the tallest in the country, 3724m Aoraki/Mt Cook. It's among the mountains – the Southern Alps – that Canterbury's signature walking trails wriggle through valleys and ascend to alpine heights: the magnificent Hooker Valley, so blessed with features it could have been custom-made by a walker; the heady heights of Mueller Hut; and the equally dramatic Avalanche Peak in the ever-steep terrain of Arthur's Pass. The coast also brings its share of walking treats, be it trails past lounging seals or windswept headlands still bearing the ghosts of wartime worry.

Christchurch

Welcome to a vibrant city in transition, coping creatively with the aftermath of Aotearoa/New Zealand's second-worst natural disaster. Traditionally, the most English of the country's cities, Christchurch's heritage heart was all but hollowed out following the 2010 and 2011 earthquakes that left 186 people dead.

Today, Christchurch is in the midst of an epic rebuild that has completely reconstructed the city centre, where over 80% of buildings needed to be demolished after the quakes. Scaffolding and road cones will be part of the city's landscape for a while yet, but don't be deterred; exciting new buildings are opening at an astonishing pace, and sights are open for business.

Kaikōura

Kaikōura is a pretty peninsula town backed by the snowcapped Seaward Kaikōura Range, 180km north from Christchurch. Few places in the world are home to such a variety of easily spottable wildlife: whales, dolphins, Aotearoa/New Zealand fur seals, penguins, shearwaters, petrels and several species of albatross live in or pass by the area.

In 2016, the Kaikōura region was struck by a severe magnitude 7.8 earthquake but, following the re-establishment of badly damaged transport links, the town can once again be reached easily.

WHEN TO GO

For the most part, you're likely to be walking in the mountains, where the optimum time to be walking is December to April. Note that the Southern Alps have a volatile climate regardless of time of year – when these mountains aren't attracting bad weather, they're creating it – and you can expect to encounter cold, wind and rain any time. Down on the Canterbury Plains and coast, you're suddenly in one of the country's driest areas, making walking possible throughout the year.

Lake Tekapo

Born of a hydropower scheme completed in 1953, Lake Tekapo, which is slowly assuming its correct Māori moniker Takapō, is booming off the back of a tourism explosion, though it has long been a popular tour-bus stop on the route between Christchurch and Queenstown. Its popularity is well deserved: the town faces out across the turquoise lake to a backdrop of snowcapped mountains.

Such splendid Mackenzie Country and Southern Alps views are reason enough to linger, but there's infinitely more to see if you wait till dark. In 2012, the Aoraki Mackenzie area was declared an International Dark Sky Reserve, one of only 22 in the world.

WHERE TO STAY

On the coast and the Canterbury Plains, accommodation types and choices are many and various, but it's worth preparing ahead when you head into the mountains. Arthur's Pass and Aoraki/Mt Cook Village are tiny settlements with just a smattering of hotels and motels. They both have a campground and a YHA hostel, as well as a **New Zealand Alpine Club** *(alpineclub.org.nz)* lodge, where bunks can be booked by non-members (though they are cheaper for members).

The region's headline hotel is the **Hermitage** *(hermitage.co.nz)*, which completely dominates Aoraki/Mt Cook Village – a mountain of a hotel with suitably fine mountain views.

TRANSPORT

Christchurch is the transport hub of the South Island, making for easy access into Canterbury. Simplifying things further is the fact that in Kaikōura, Arthur's Pass and Aoraki/Mt Cook, where the bulk of the region's walks are found, you can pretty much step straight off a bus and onto the trails. Private transport is still the easiest and quickest way to get about – Christchurch is the place in which to organise car hire.

WHAT'S ON

Coast to Coast
(coasttocoast.co.nz)
This famed 243km multi-sport race traverses the South Island each February, squeezing through Arthur's Pass and ending in Christchurch.

Great Kiwi Beer Festival
(greatkiwibeerfestival.co.nz)
A one-day January celebration of all things beery and cheery in Christchurch's Hagley Park.

WORD Christchurch
(wordchristchurch.co.nz)
A five-day spring festival of books, writers and reading, featuring more than 70 events with more than 100 Kiwi and international writers, readers and thinkers.

Resources

Department of Conservation
(doc.govt.nz/parks-and-recreation/places-to-go/canterbury)
Parks and walks throughout Canterbury.

ChristchurchNZ
(christchurchnz.com)
For all things Christchurch.

Kaikōura
(kaikoura.co.nz)
Kaikōura i-SITE for exploring this region.

Lake Tekapo New Zealand
(laketekaponz.co.nz)
Official Tekapo tourism website.

28

Godley Head / Awaroa

DURATION	DIFFICULTY	DISTANCE	START/END
2½–3hrs	Moderate	9.1km	Taylors Mistake

TERRAIN	Wide, well-formed track with several climbs

Poking into the sea at the eastern end of Christchurch's Port Hills, Godley Head/Awaroa combines a dramatic coastline with an unexpected tale of WWII history, making for a fascinating loop walk with vast ocean views just a half-hour drive from the city centre. The walk described here takes the longest and most spectacular possible course, running along the very edges of the head.

Getting Here

Taylors Mistake is 17km southeast of Christchurch's city centre, just beyond Sumner. There's no public transport.

Starting Point

The walk begins at the end of Taylors Mistake Rd, where there's a large car park with a toilet block, picnic tables and a surf beach.

01 From behind the toilet block, cross the stream and follow the track below the line of holiday shacks and past the beach's southern edge. From here, climb a set of stone steps and set out through the head's grass-covered slopes. After zigzagging down to cross above a **rocky cove**, the track soon passes a mesh metal fence – this is a predator-proof fence to protect a colony of white-flippered penguins below the cliffs.

02 The track continues through the grasslands above the sea. At suitably named **Boulder Bay**, a side track ducks down through

Best for

ESCAPING THE CITY

Godley Head/Awaroa

Godley Gunners

It was just six days into WWII when gunners were sent to Godley Head/Awaroa to protect Lyttelton Harbour/Whakaraupō to guard against an enemy landing.

At the height of the war, more than 500 defence personnel were based on the head, with large guns and searchlights strung along its ocean-facing coast.

The guns were never fired in anger, but the idea that Christchurch – so far from the battle lines of war – might ever be attacked wasn't mere fantasy. Ten German mines were found laid across the approaches to the mouth of Lyttelton Harbour/Whakaraupō, though none exploded.

macrocarpas to an incongruous set of baches (holiday homes). If you turn right at the shore and walk along the front of the baches, you'll come to a path signposted rather grandiosely as 'Roberts Rd', which climbs back to the main track.

03 Here, begin a sustained climb, and on a fine day you might be treated to views as far north as the Kaikōura Range. Near the head's tip, the track passes between the concrete remains of **Taylor Battery**, where a pair of large guns were situated during WWII.

04 The track climbs around the point of the head, passing more buildings and gun emplacements of the **Godley Head Battery**. Stay on the gravel path to skirt the campsite, and soon you'll coil steeply down to **Battery Observation Post II** – one of three on the head – right at the entrance to Lyttelton Harbour/Whakaraupō, Christchurch's port. The track climbs back up the slopes, rising past the green **engine room**, where power was generated for the battery. A few steps ahead, cross through a fence to reach the Godley Head/Awaroa car park.

05 Crossing another fence, carry on along a track signed to Breeze Col. The track crosses the slopes, about 200m above the harbour, crossing above Breeze Bay to reach **Breeze Col** – the name is a clue to conditions here some days.

06 Turning inland, you cross a stile and then Summit Rd as the track cuts across the grassy neck that attaches this head to the body of the South Island. As you descend to Taylors Mistake, head out onto the **beach** and walk back to the car park along the sands.

Take a Break

Grab one of the famed cinnamon rolls or other delicious yeasty treats at **Bohemian Bakery** (bohemianbakery.co.nz) for a trail-side picnic out on the head.

29

Sign of the Packhorse

DURATION	DIFFICULTY	DISTANCE	START/END
4hrs return	Moderate	12km	Gebbies Pass Rd car park

TERRAIN	Paddocks and pine forest

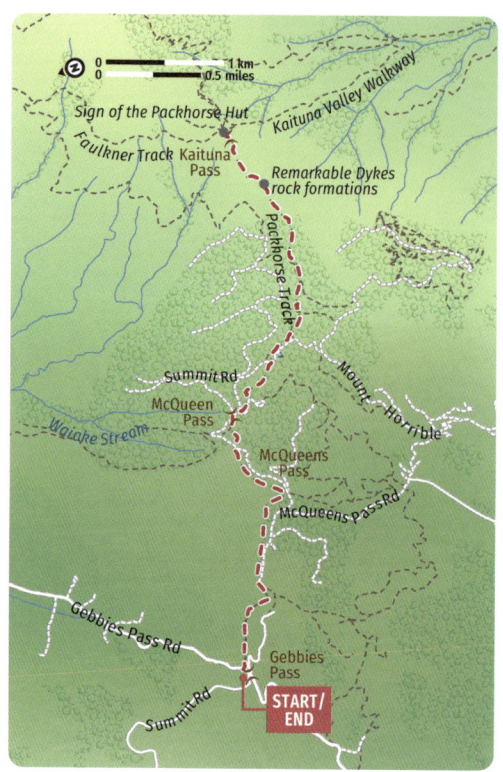

Take in an intriguing slice of Canterbury history with your walk during a visit to Sign of the Packhorse, one of a chain of several attractive stone buildings in the Christchurch hills, built as rest stops in an early-20th-century vision for a grand Summit Rd to Awaroa. The roadhouse is now a DOC hut that can be booked for overnight stays, but the walk there and back makes for an enjoyable half-day before or after exploring the nearby city.

It's a 30-minute drive out of Christchurch to the trailhead, a small car park on Gebbies Pass Rd on the Lyttleton side of the Port Hills. The route, part of the Mt Herbert Walkway and Summit Walkway/ Te Ara Pātaka, has steep sections and can be rough in places, although it's the easiest of the three tracks to the nine-bunk **Packhorse Hut**. It's a total ascent of 450m.

A track below a logging road eventually sets you walking across paddocks, your way guided by orange-topped poles. They'll give you plenty of airspace to enjoy views across Lyttleton Harbour/ Whakaraupō to blue ranges beyond, although some of the recently logged forest tracks can be muddy after rain.

After a climb through pine forest, the track takes you back out onto open land until you encounter the imposing **Remarkable Dykes** volcanic rock formations, which mark the boundaries of a crack in the side of an extinct volcano. The trachyte rock is steep and perfect for scrambling; indeed, it has been a popular local climbing spot since the 1930s.

It can be cold and windy up here, with low cloud – make sure you've got good clothing, even for this short walk. Lambing season may send you along a diverted track between 8 August and 15 October.

Best for

OFF THE BEATEN PATH

CANTERBURY 29 SIGN OF THE PACKHORSE

Packhorse Hut

30

Kaikōura Peninsula Walkway

DURATION	DIFFICULTY	DISTANCE	START/END
3–4hrs	Easy	11.7km	Kaikōura i-SITE

TERRAIN	Wide smooth paths with mostly gentle gradients

Take a walk with wildlife on this wonderful circuit of the history-rich Kaikōura Peninsula. The walk takes in a seal colony and wraparound coastal views from the peninsula's clifftops. The seals are the stars of the show, but the walk is highly scenic in its own right.

Getting Here

InterCity *(intercity.co.nz)* buses from Christchurch, Blenheim and Picton stop outside the i-SITE, which is also the walkway's starting point.

Starting Point

The walk begins at the i-SITE (there's a large display on the walkway inside) in Kaikōura's town centre. There's metered all-day parking on the i-SITE's northern side.

 01 Kaikōura's most famous feature is its abundance of marine wildlife, and it extends to this walk as you set out from town along the Esplanade towards a seal colony. Pass through the whalebone arches in Anzac Park and along the edge of the town's **stony beach**. At times, you're on a footpath; other times just the road verge (but well removed from traffic). Information boards detail local history. Just beyond the beach, you'll come to the 1885-built **Pier Hotel**, where you veer right into Avoca St.

 02 Avoca St wriggles around the coast, becoming Fyffe Quay beside the former whaling station of **Fyffe House**. A final section of

Best for

SPOTTING WILDLIFE

New Zealand fur seal, Point Kean

Wildlife Tours

Kaikōura's stock-in-trade for tourism is wildlife tours. Few places in the world are home to such a variety of easily spottable marine life, with an upwelling of nutrients from the ocean floor created as the southerly ocean current hits the continental shelf just offshore.

On offer are whale-watching tours, dolphin-watching tours and albatross-viewing tours. You can kayak or snorkel with seals and spot whales from the air. Get a full rundown on the town's official website (kaikoura.co.nz).

roadside boardwalk ends at the large Point Kean car park. This is the site of a **colony of New Zealand fur seals**. Take some time to wander out onto the rock platforms, among the colony, but keep 10m between yourself and any seals.

03 Cross through the car park and make the short steep climb to the **Point Kean Viewpoint**, overlooking the seal colony. The clifftop section of the walkway begins here, providing continual ocean views as you walk. Past the predator-proof fence of the Hutton's/Rae O Atou Titi shearwater colony, you'll come to **Whalers Bay Lookout**. If you want to revisit the shores, there's a short track down from here.

04 The walkway now crosses a stile and skirts around a high headland. Across the next stile, the track turns right but, if you turn left, you can follow a side track up to the top of a bluff and an old *pā* (fortified village) site with views over South Bay and Whalers Bay. Continue down to the **South Bay Viewpoint** platform, which, as the name on the tin suggests, has views across South Bay to the Kaikōura Range.

05 Keep descending towards South Bay, following the roads closest to the shore, passing the boat ramp and **marina**. Continue on Moa Rd (despite the 'no exit' sign) to cut across a boat and trailer parking area to South Bay Pde, turning right at the blue walker sign to join the **South Bay Track**.

06 The final section of the walkway climbs through **pine forest** to cross the peninsula's ridge. Atop the ridge, swing right onto **Tom's Track** and descend into town. Head straight down Brighton St to the Esplanade, turning left to return to the i-SITE.

Take a Break

Situated in a primo seaside spot, 2.5km along the walk, the **Pier Hotel** *(thepierhotel.co.nz)* has a menu ruled by crayfish and paua (abalone).

31

Avalanche Peak

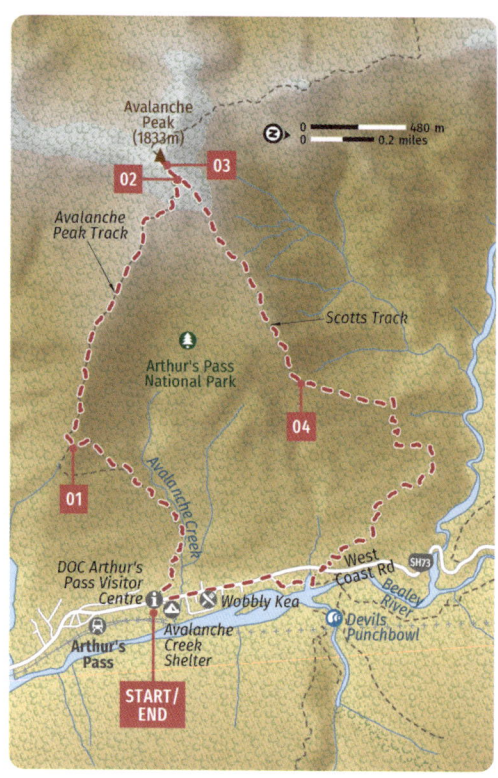

DURATION	DIFFICULTY	DISTANCE	START/END
6-8hrs	Hard	7km	Arthur's Pass

TERRAIN	Steep and rugged climb and descent, with narrow and exposed sections

Airy Avalanche Peak (1833m) is unquestionably the most popular mountain climb in Arthur's Pass National Park. On a clear day, the alpine world experienced on the steep haul is stunning (on a not-so-clear day, it just shouldn't be attempted). The total climb and descent is around 1100m, so it's one for the fit walker.

Getting Here

The start is located five minutes' walk from the Arthur's Pass train station, where **TranzAlpine** (great journeysofnz.co.nz/tranzalpine) trains stop daily on their mountain crossing between Christchurch and Greymouth. **Atomic Shuttles** (atomictravel.co.nz) and **East West Coaches** (eastwestcoaches.co.nz) run buses to Arthur's Pass from Christchurch and Greymouth.

Starting Point

The walk starts beside the DOC Arthur's Pass Visitor Centre. There's a large car park with toilets directly across the road; the town store is 300m up the road.

01 There are two routes – Avalanche Peak Track and Scotts Track – that ascend Avalanche Peak. It's best to use the steeper and trickier Avalanche Peak Track for the ascent, and the more gradual Scotts Track for the return, when your legs will be tired. From beside the visitor centre, **Avalanche Peak Track** sets out parallel to SH73 and straight into forest, where it turns up a set of stone steps and the big climb begins, rising beside a string of waterfalls. There's a succession of short scrambles up rock faces, but all have good hand and footholds. After about 1½ hours, the tracks pops through the bush line to **vast mountain views**. Welcome to the alpine world.

Avalanche Peak

Detour: Devils Punchbowl Falls

If you still have any juice in your legs by the time you return to the valley, **Devils Punchbowl Falls** make for a good side trip.

From the falls' car park, it's about a 30-minute walk (with a lot of steps, if you're already on tired legs) up to the base of the 131m-high waterfall, which seems to pour down the cliffs in waves.

02 There's no let-up in the gradient as the track turns up a steep ridge, following yellow markers along the edge of a steep slip. Past the slip, the ridge broadens and Avalanche Peak comes into view ahead. The final part of the ridge walk ascends through a scree field before meeting the Scotts Track just below the summit, amid a jumble of **boulders**.

03 Turn left, heading up the ridge and scrambling through the boulders. The final approach is narrow, exposed and spectacular, with steep drops to either side. The view from the **summit** is 360-degree mountains, dominated by nearby Mt Rolleston (2271m), with Crow Glacier bending and buckling down its slopes.

04 Return to the top of the Avalanche Peak Track, but continue straight ahead (following the orange poles) to begin descending on the **Scotts Track**. At first, it's rocky and narrow but then broadens out into a virtual **meadow**. Here the going gets a bit easier, and there are good views across the valley to Devils Punchbowl Falls. Back below the bushline, the gradient eases as the track turns back on itself, heading up the valley towards Arthur's Pass. It drops down beside SH73 just out of town. Cross the highway and turn right onto a walking trail that dips through the Devils Punchbowl car park, finishing along a roadside footpath into the village.

Take a Break

Arthur's Pass is light on for food and drink options – **The Alpine Parrot** offers breakfast until midday, and then an unexpected Mexican offering in remote, alpine Aotearoa/New Zealand: nachos, burritos or a quesadilla for lunch and dinner.

32

Bealey Spur

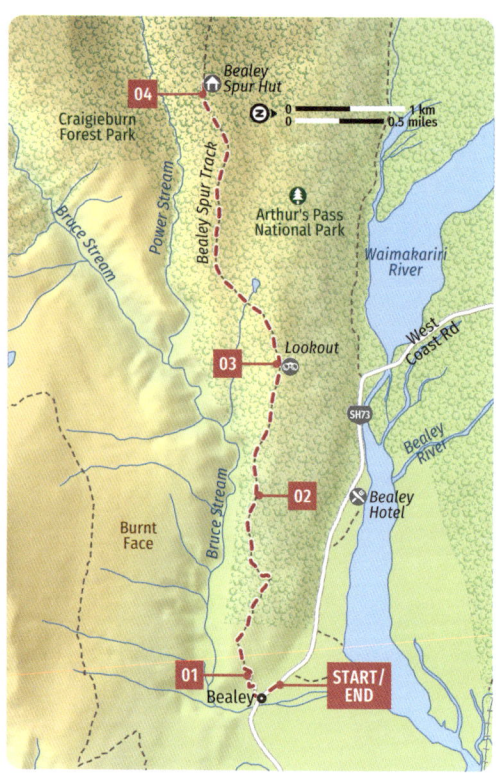

DURATION	DIFFICULTY	DISTANCE	START/END
4–6hrs	Moderate	13.5km	Cloudesley Rd

TERRAIN	Sustained but moderate incline over uneven ground

Bealey Spur is a rare exception to the rule that climbing almost anything in Arthur's Pass National Park is steep work. On this walk, reward far exceeds effort, with a steady but not steep 600m ascent to a historic hut, with grand views over the Waimakariri Valley and the surrounding peaks. Bealey Spur sits east of the Main Divide, meaning it can be dry here even when northwesterly winds are bringing rain to Arthur's Pass.

Getting Here

Cloudesley Rd is 14km southeast of Arthur's Pass. You can be dropped off and collected by various passing bus services with prior arrangement – try **Atomic Shuttles** *(atomictravel.co.nz)*.

Starting Point

Makeshift parking is along a gravel track accessed from Cloudesley Rd but immediately beside SH73. You can drop walkers off at the top of Cloudesley Rd, cutting out the 500m of uphill road walking, but you can't park here, so the driver at least still has to make the climb.

 In an area of steep slopes and often brutal terrain, Bealey Spur is a gentle finger of land that begins its rise from directly beside the main highway (SH73). The first part of the walk is along sealed Cloudesley Rd, climbing for about 500m through a cluster of holiday homes to the **trailhead**.

 The track rises through sparse beech forest before swinging west, ascending parallel to the Waimakariri Valley. It's a gentle climb, at times even flat, along the top of the broad spur. As the forest cover thins, the walk heads along the

Bealey Spur

Meet the Kea

While you're around the Arthur's Pass area, it's quite likely that you'll encounter Aotearoa/New Zealand's most gregarious character, the mischievous kea.

Whether the world's only alpine parrot, which is a green ball of personality with orange underwings, is destructive or playful by nature is open to interpretation – they are notorious for pulling things to pieces (including car wiper blades, tents and backpacks). Sadly, kea numbers are in decline, and the DOC wants visitors to report all sightings; head to *keadatabase.nz* for more information.

lip of the deep gouge carved by Bruce Stream. As this waterway turns away into the mountains, a small side track to the left reveals a good **view through the gorge** and across to Mt Bruce. The peak to the far right is the top of the spur, just beyond Bealey Spur Hut.

03 The walk continues straight ahead, leaving the stream and becoming slightly steeper. It heads through a low cover of bush and finally out into tussocks, rising to a **knoll with superb views** straight down onto the confluence of the Bealey and Waimakariri Rivers.

04 From here, the track dips in and out of beech forest and across a marshy shelf of small tarns on a **boardwalk**. The final climb rises out of forest and cuts across tussocky slopes to attain the crest of the spur as it re-enters a section of beech forest. It's a bit of an enchanted forest up this high, with the beech trees strung with lichen like Christmas tinsel.

The track crosses one more patch of tussocks and, as it emerges into another clearing about 100m on, you arrive at **Bealey Spur Hut**. This green, corrugated-iron hut, which sleeps six people, was built by a pair of local station owners in 1925 and originally used as a shelter for annual sheep musters. If you plan to spend a night here (bookings not required), note that even one of its early owners considered the bunks uncomfortable. Return back down the spur on the same track.

☕ Take a Break

The **Bealey Hotel** (*thebealeyhotel.com*) has a full bar and delicious meals.

33

Woolshed Creek Hut

Woolshed Creek Hut

DURATION	DIFFICULTY	DISTANCE	START/END
5–7hrs	Moderate	14km	Jig Rd, Mt Somers

TERRAIN	Narrow track on uneven ground, with a few steep climbs

The Mt Somers Track is a popular two-day circuit walk at the edge of the Southern Alps, but you needn't hike the whole thing to get a sense of its compelling attractions. At Mt Somers' western edge, a pair of trails connect to form a loop walk to Woolshed Creek Hut (one of the two huts along the Mt Somers Track) that's full of fascinating features. You'll step through mining history, find a classic trampers' hut, scurry through a large rock overhang and discover a couple of sublime swimming holes. Our tip...set out early to allow time to make the most of the swimming opportunities.

Getting Here

The walk begins at the Woolshed Creek car park at the end of Jig Rd. From the town of Mt Somers on the SH72 Inland Scenic Route, follow Ashburton Gorge Rd for 10km. Then turn onto unsealed Jig Rd and drive 4km to the car park. There's no public transport.

Starting Point

The sizeable car park on the banks of Woolshed Creek reflects the popularity of walks on Mt Somers and around the creek area. It has toilets and signboards with maps and time and distance details for all walking tracks on Mt Somers.

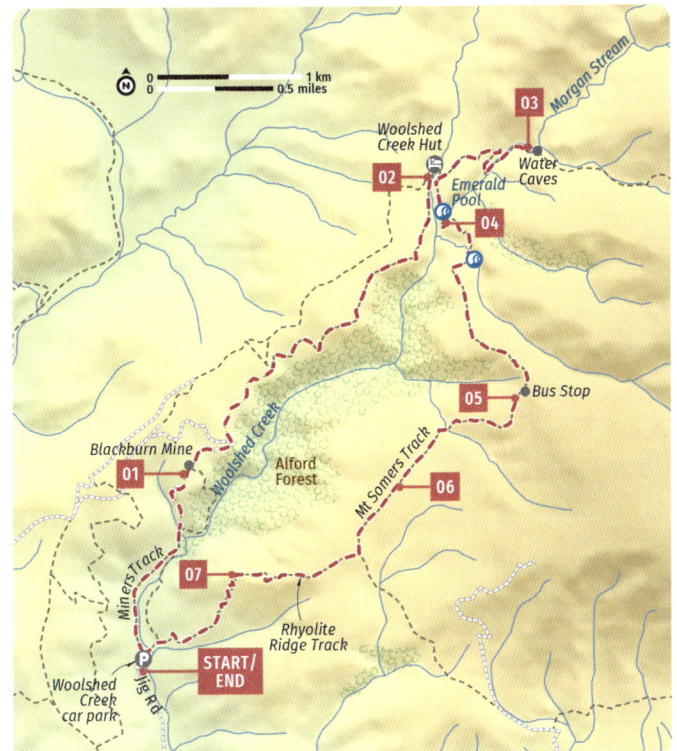

Mt Somers Track

The full **Mt Somers Track** is a 26km loop around its namesake 1688m peak, taking most walkers two days.

From the traditional starting point at Sharplin Falls car park, it's a three-hour walk to **Pinnacles Hut** and then another three hours over 1170m Somers Saddle and past the water caves to **Woolshed Hut**.

The second day climbs to the **Bus Stop**, as described on p134, and turns onto the **South Face Track**, where there's also the possibility of taking a side track up to Mt Somers' summit.

The Mt Somers Track is popular, and between October and April huts must be booked ahead through DOC.

01 The easiest route to Woolshed Creek Hut is the **Miners Track**, which begins to the left as you enter the **Woolshed Creek** car park. It sets out through a thin cover of forest with Woolshed Creek flowing below the track. The track rises gently but consistently, staying beside the creek and, after about 1km, passes the crumpled remains of one of the hopper wagons that used to bring coal down from the Blackburn coal mine. The wagon is off to the right, almost dangling above the creek. Ignore the trail that turns back beside the hopper wagon and continue straight ahead, crossing a side stream. This marks the beginning of a steeper climb to the **Blackburn mine site**, rising 170m above Woolshed Creek. The entrance to the mine is still here, along with some mining debris and tailings. You can step inside the mine entrance, where signs explain some of the history of the abandoned operation.

02 The gorse-lined track now flattens out, and is, at first, as wide as a vehicle track before soon narrowing to a skinny path that skirts along the edges of the tree cover. After crossing through a fence, you'll begin another steeper climb, rising into more rugged and rocky terrain before angling more steeply still up a narrow ridge. It's a climb that brings with it the blessing of good views, back over Woolshed Creek and the coal mine and west through the wide Stour Valley towards Mt Arrowsmith and Couloir Peak in the Southern Alps. When the climb tops out, a gentle traverse along the ridge brings you to a view over a beautiful gorge, with **Woolshed Creek Hut** to its left. Descend to the hut, which is cradled in a grassy valley horseshoed by peaks. It's thought that a hut originated here for mustering in the 19th century, with a hut for walkers first built in 1987 – it was replaced by this farm-like building in 2006. It sleeps 26 people, but is a popular destination – if you decide to stay a night between October and April, you must book ahead; at other times it's first-come, first-served.

03 You can simply head back to Jig Rd from Woolshed Creek Hut, but it's well worth continuing a little further along the Mt Somers Track to the so-called **'water caves'**, about 20 minutes' walk from the hut. Cross Woolshed Creek directly in front of the hut and head to the track junction 50m to the right. Turn left, climbing up and over the low ridge before winding down to a second creek. Crossing this creek, the track turns upstream, rising to a junction with a side track that's signed to the water caves, five minutes away. The 'caves' are fancifully named, and are, in fact, an unruly mess of boulders, with **Morgan Stream** pouring through them – the dark spaces between the boulders form the caves. Some of them interconnect, making for a maze of tunnels, while most also have deep, inviting pools. Walk through them, wade through them, swim through them. Just be sure to explore.

04 Turn back here, returning to the track junction opposite Woolshed Creek Hut. The easiest way back to Jig Rd from here is to retrace your steps along the **Miners Track**, but the more interesting return is on the Mt Somers Track, though it's rougher and has a lot more climbing. We describe the latter here, but if you're feeling tired already, think about heading back on the Miners Track because most of the hard work is still ahead.

To continue along the **Mt Somers Track**, swing left at the track junction and, in a few minutes, you'll come to a suspension bridge. Immediately before the bridge, look for a side track to the left that leads down to the gorgeous swimming hole of **Emerald Pool**, looking like something out of the Australian outback. At the rock outcrop above the pool, a makeshift trail heads right to drop down onto the pool's little beach while, if you go left, you'll discover a fine view through the gorge. Even if you've had a swim at the water caves, it's well worth grabbing another here, especially as the toughest of the day's climbs is about to begin.

05 Cross the suspension bridge and climb steeply above the gorge. You'll probably have a sweat up again by the time the track briefly flattens out, cutting beneath layered cliffs, before it dives quickly down again to cross a high gully that splits the cliff. A few steps ahead, there's a detour up beside the stream to a waterfall, five minutes' walk away. The walk's toughest and most sustained climb begins here, with the compensation that Woolshed Creek Hut comes back into view behind you. Ahead, you'll see the Bus Stop rock overhang notched into the cliffs like a wound.

Take a moment for one final look back at Woolshed Creek Hut, as it's about to disappear from view. The track draws level with the **Bus Stop**, and then sidles across to the rock overhang, which is the highest point on the walk. There is indeed a bus stop sign here, clipped to the cliffs, but it'd be a very long wait.

Woolshed Creek Hut, Mt Somers

☕ Take a Break

Call into the cute **Staveley Store & Cafe** (staveleystore.co.nz) for the best coffee for miles around, as well as a cabinet of goodies – the chicken and cranberry sandwiches and their locally famous sausage rolls – that you can take on the trail.

06 The track now flattens out through scrub and, to the west, you'll be able to see the Blackburn coal mine far below you. Past a short section of boardwalk through tussocks, the first descent begins, plunging down onto a very **wide ridge**. The track heads along the ridge for a while, finally coming to a junction with the **Rhyolite Ridge Track**.

07 Turn right onto this track (the path straight ahead is the continuation of the Mt Somers Track loop), which crosses the ridge before swooping steeply down, **zigzagging between cliffs**. At the base of the ridge, cross the bridge over Woolshed Creek and you're back at the Jig Rd car park.

Blackburn Coal Mine

In 1929 the **Blackburn coal mine** opened high above Woolshed Creek and, even though it went bankrupt within a year, coal was ultimately mined here for 40 years.

One of the most striking features of the mine was its incline railway, used to transport the coal down to the creek, where a tramway then carted it off to the railway at Mt Somers village.

The incline railway plunged 170m and it would take just two-and-a-half minutes for a coal-laden four-tonne hopper wagon to go from top to bottom, pulling an empty hopper back to the top as it did so.

34

Mt John (Ōtehīwai)

DURATION	DIFFICULTY	DISTANCE	START/END
3hrs	Moderate	9km	Tekapo Springs car park

TERRAIN	Smooth paths and vehicle tracks; flat beside the lake, with some short steep climbs on the mountain

At the western edge of Lake Tekapo (Takapō), Mt John (Ōtehīwail; 1031m) is a small mountain that also happens to be one of the world's great stargazing destinations, giving it an extra sense of sparkle. The mountain is lower and simpler to climb than almost any other peak around the Southern Alps areas, and this walk combines two routes to its summit to create a loop with wonderful views over Lake Tekapo (Takapō), and far beyond.

Getting Here

Tekapo Springs, a commercial hot-springs complex, is at the end of Lakeside Dr, 2km from the centre of Lake Tekapo town. **InterCity** *(intercity.co.nz)* has daily buses to Lake Tekapo from Christchurch, Aoraki/Mt Cook Village and Queenstown. From town, it's about a 30-minute walk to the trailhead.

Starting Point

The walk begins from a large car park beside Tekapo Springs. There's a cafe at the springs if you want a shot of caffeine to propel you up the hill.

 01 From the car park's far end, set out on the shores of fabulously turquoise Lake Tekapo on a dirt road set a few metres in from the water. The town of Lake Tekapo is directly across the water – if you look closely you can see the **Church of the Good Shepherd**, probably one of the most photographed spots in Aotearoa/New Zealand. Beyond a small pier, take the upper road, climbing slightly and cutting through the lower reaches of the **conifer forest**. Just before a locked gate, turn left onto a dirt walking track.

Mt John Observatory

Mt John Observatory

Mt John (Ōtehīwai) sits at the heart of an international dark sky reserve. The University of Canterbury's **observatory** (part of which was once also a US spy station) on its summit has four main telescopes, including the largest in Aotearoa/New Zealand.

Nightly visits to the observatory, which include a guided tour of the sky from qualified astronomers, are run by **Dark Sky Project** (darkskyproject.co.nz).

For indoor, virtual astronomy experiences, including Māori astronomy, visit the Project's beautiful new restaurant and dark-sky centre on the lakeshore, which also has a range of star-themed gifts and books for sale.

02 In a couple of minutes, you'll leave the cover of the forest and enter open grasslands, with good views across the lake to Mt Edward and the Two Thumbs Range. The track sidles across the slopes until, just past another farm gate, it begins to climb, veering away from the lake. Atop a small rise, the track U-turns and arrives at a pair of wooden benches with an absorbing **view** of the surrounding mountains. Take a break ahead of the climb still to come.

03 Here, the track swings up the ridge, running pinched between the summit road and a farm fence. Near the top of the next rise, cross the fence on a stile and, within a few steps, the observatory on Mt John (Ōtehīwai)'s summit comes into view. After a short final climb, turn left onto the observatory circuit track, following the **'South Summit'** sign, to cut below the summit to a rocky knoll – the South Summit – with a good view down onto Lake Tekapo town.

04 Continue along the observatory circuit track, turning right at a T-junction and heading uphill. Follow the 'cafe' signs to rise onto the **summit**, which is capped by the observatory and the **Astro Café**, with wraparound views across the Mackenzie Basin and Lake Tekapo, looking like spilled blue paint below. Retrace your steps to the T-junction before the South Summit but continue straight ahead, descending into the forest and zigzagging down to the Tekapo Springs car park.

 Take a Break

The views are so good at the glass-walled **Astro Café** (Mt John University Observatory) atop Mt John (Ōtehīwai) that they've had to put up a 'no standing on tables' sign to stop folks seeking that even-better photo. Tuck into a salmon bagel or a stonking slice of cake before your descent back to Lake Tekapo.

35

Hooker Valley

DURATION	DIFFICULTY	DISTANCE	START/END
3hrs	Easy	10km	White Horse Hill Campsite

TERRAIN	Wide, smooth path through a flat valley

Few walks reward so readily as this short track into the orbit of Aotearoa/New Zealand's highest mountain. It's a visual extravaganza of glaciers, lakes, icebergs, swinging suspension bridges and a personal audience with 3274m Aoraki/Mt Cook. The walk follows a remarkably flat track, given its proximity to such a tall mountain, so it's no surprise that it's very popular – set out in the early morning if you want to beat the crowds.

Getting Here

White Horse Hill Campsite is a 3km drive from Aoraki/Mt Cook Village. You can also begin walking from the village, following the Kea Point Track from the Hermitage hotel and veering away to the campsite. This adds around 30 to 45 minutes of walking either end.

Starting Point

There's a large car park at White Horse Hill Campsite, but it still often becomes full to overflowing. An enclosed public shelter has tables, treated drinking water and attached toilets.

01 A valley so near to a country's highest mountain has no right being so flat, but it makes for a walk that's kind from the outset. From the campsite, cross a wooden bridge, turning immediately left and burrowing through a section of bush to pass **Freda's Rock**, about 20m off the track. Australian Freda du Faur was the first woman to climb Aoraki/Mt Cook in 1910, and a famous photo of her was taken by this rock on her return from the summit. A sign beside the rock shows the old photo.

Alpine Memorial

The Shrinking Mountain

All mountains grow or shrink incrementally, but on Aoraki/Mt Cook, change happened all of a sudden. On 14 December 1991, the summit of the mountain collapsed, with 12 million cubic metres of rock falling away into the Tasman Valley.

In 2014, measurements showed that the collapse had sheared 30m off the height of the peak. Once 3754m in height, Aotearoa/New Zealand's tallest mountain now measures 3724m.

02 The track begins to round the base of **White Horse Hill**, coming quickly to a short side trail up to the pyramidal **Alpine Memorial**, which is studded with memorial plaques to climbers killed in the national park.

03 The main track continues to cut across the valley before rising gently to **Mueller Lake Lookout**, perched atop an old moraine wall and peering over the mud-brown glacial lake to the imposing Mt Sefton.

04 The track descends to cross the Hooker River on a long suspension bridge before turning up the valley. After about 15 minutes, a short set of wooden steps leads up to another **lookout** over Mueller Lake and back to Aoraki/Mt Cook Village.

05 Past a second suspension bridge, the track flows along beside the Hooker River, and Aoraki/Mt Cook rises into view. A small wooden bridge crosses **Stocking Stream**, from where an elevated boardwalk cuts across tussocky ground to the final **suspension bridge**.

06 The track's only real climb begins just beyond here, but detour away first to the signposted alpine tarn just off the track. In still conditions, it provides good reflections of Aoraki/Mt Cook. From here, the track winds up through a moraine to the **Hooker Lake viewpoint**. The lake is typically afloat in icebergs calved from Hooker Glacier, with Aoraki/Mt Cook rising behind.

When you're ready, retrace your steps back to the campsite.

Take a Break

Sit and admire the view of where you just walked in the **Old Mountaineers' Cafe (mtcook.com/restaurant)**. The best eatery in Aoraki/Mt Cook Village has an all-day menu offering burgers and fries, fish and chips and pizzas.

36

Mueller Hut

DURATION	DIFFICULTY	DISTANCE	START/END
6–8hrs	Hard	10km	Aoraki/Mt Cook Village

TERRAIN	Steep alpine slopes with scree, boulder hopping and some scrambling

This classic alpine walk elevates you into a mountaineers' landscape without the need to be a mountaineer. The track ascends more than 1000m to the barren tops of the mountains, and, at the top of the climb, is the little red shed of Mueller Hut, one of the most magnificently positioned of all NZ's tramping huts. You can stay the night to enjoy a mountain sunset and sunrise, but bookings are required as it's a popular roost.

Getting Here

InterCity *(intercity.co.nz)* buses run to Aoraki/Mt Cook Village from Christchurch, Lake Tekapo and Queenstown, stopping at the Hermitage (the starting point of the walk).

Starting Point

The walk starts outside the front doors of the Hermitage, the hotel complex that dominates Aoraki/Mt Cook Village. Look for the 'Kea Point' sign on the paved path across the lawns.

 01 Since Mueller Hut was first constructed in 1914, there have been five incarnations of the building, which is testament to the fierce and brutal nature of the landscape in which it sits – you should set out from the lawns of the Hermitage only in fine weather. After descending steps to cross Terrace Rd, the **Kea Point Track** runs flat through the valley, with good views (on a fine day) to Aoraki/Mt Cook. For the moment, ignore the Mueller Hut turn-off and continue straight ahead, rising gently through a moraine wall to **Kea Point**, 10 to 15 minutes' walk ahead. This lookout is perched directly above Mueller Lake, near the terminus of **Mueller Glacier**.

Best for

MOUNTAIN VIEWS

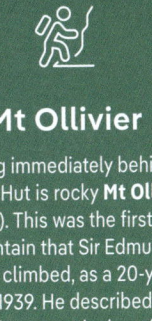

Mt Ollivier

Rising immediately behind Mueller Hut is rocky **Mt Ollivier** (1933m). This was the first real mountain that Sir Edmund Hillary climbed, as a 20-year-old in 1939. He described the experience as 'the happiest day I had ever spent'. Fourteen years later, with Tenzing Norgay, he would become the first person to summit Mt Everest.

If you want to emulate Sir Edmund, it's about a 30-minute rock scramble along the obvious ridge behind Mueller Hut to the summit, which has views down onto Aoraki/Mt Cook Village and out to the edge of Lake Pukaki.

Mueller Hut Route

02 Return to the Mueller Hut track junction and turn right. Suck in some deep breaths; the big climb starts here. At first, the ascent isn't particularly steep, but from the moment you pass a wooden seat, it gets into its precipitous stride. The difficulty of the climb (though not the gradient) is alleviated by the presence of steps that lead all the way to **Sealy Tarns**, a trio of lakes pooled along a narrow shelf in the mountain 500m above the valley.

03 The now rocky path continues steeply up, with a few straightforward scrambles through some rocky bluffs. The final part of the main ascent grinds up a scree slope, rising to the crest of a ridge that looks directly across to the finger-like glaciers on Mt Sefton. The **rocky knoll** to the right provides a good outlook over Mt Sefton and down into the Hooker Valley.

04 Here, the track turns left, skirting beneath the ridge before regaining it again a short way ahead, where **Mueller Hut** pops into view for the first time. In a few minutes, across a lunar landscape, you'll reach the red hut (which has 28 bunks) and its ultimate loo with a view. Expect to see a kea or two flying about here – leave your gear outside and unattended at your own peril. Return to Aoraki/Mt Cook Village along the same path.

☕ Take a Break

The gargantuan **Hermitage** (hermitage.co.nz) has several food and drink options, including a cafeteria-style cafe attached to the Sir Edmund Hillary Alpine Centre. The Alpine Restaurant and the Snowline Bar get the best mountain views in the village – sunset is prime time.

Also Try...

Castle Hill Peak

TOBIN AKEHURST/SHUTTERSTOCK

Castle Hill Peak

DURATION	DIFFICULTY	DISTANCE
5-7hrs	Hard	12km

This popular but unmarked climb has views that stretch as far as Aoraki/Mt Cook, and provides a serious alpine outing at the edge of the Southern Alps.

The Castle Hill Peak trail sets out from a highway pullout behind a guard rail at Porters Pass on SH73 and climbs abruptly (rising 800m in 2.7km) to the summit of Foggy Peak - if the morning fogs of the Canterbury Plains are pressing against the edge of the mountain, it will feel well named. Foggy Peak is connected to Castle Hill Peak by a long ridge that is at first broad and then quite narrow. The final ascent is on loose, exposed and slippery scree, but it flattens out as you rise onto the summit. The view is vast, and The Gap - one of the most striking features seen along the Christchurch–Arthur's Pass drive - is right below the summit.

Bridle Path

DURATION	DIFFICULTY	DISTANCE
1½hrs	Moderate	2.4km

Following the course of the original packhorse route used by settlers to cross the Port Hills, this short, steep walk creates a fun link between Christchurch and Lyttelton.

The ascent begins beside the base station of the Christchurch Gondola (suitably at the end of Bridle Path Rd), rising up the grassed slopes of the Port Hills. Along the way, you'll pass boulders dislodged from Castle Rock by the Christchurch earthquakes of 2010 and 2011. The path crosses Summit Rd beside the Pioneer Women's Memorial, commemorating the courage and hard work of the region's pioneering women, and then makes an equally steep descent into the port town of Lyttelton. You can return to Christchurch on bus 28 through the Lyttelton road tunnel.

Rakaia Gorge Walkway

Arthur's Pass Walking Track

DURATION	DIFFICULTY	DISTANCE
2½–3hrs	Easy	6.8km

Almost every trail in Arthur's Pass goes steeply skyward, but this walk ambles along the valley floor, picking off highlights through the valley.

From the village, the track heads west, passing the trail to Devils Punchbowl Falls (see p129) and reaching the Bridal Veil Falls lookout. Past a restored road worker's cottage, it then reaches the summit of Arthur's Pass proper, where there's a memorial to Arthur Dobson, the surveyor who gave his name to the pass. Return back through the valley.

Rakaia Gorge Walkway

DURATION	DIFFICULTY	DISTANCE
3–4hrs	Easy	10.4km

As the Rakaia River, one of Aotearoa/New Zealand's largest waterways, pours out of the Southern Alps, it carves a deep and impressive gorge, along the top of which runs a scenic walkway.

Making a lollipop loop out from SH72 (the Scenic Inland Route), the walk snakes along the top of the gorge's cliffs, passing old coal mines and offering great views into the gorge and to the Southern Alps beyond. Near the walk's northern end, a side trail descends 120m to the river's edge.

Franz Josef Glacier/Kā Roimata o Hine Hukatere

West Coast

37 **Charming Creek North Walkway**
Follow an old railway track up to a waterfall and rusting relics. **p148**

38 **Punakaiki-Pororari Loop**
Enjoy Pancake Rocks on this fun bush and river walk. **p150**

39 **Ōkārito Pack Track & Coastal Walk**
Both bush and beach are involved on the Three Mile Lagoon walk. **p152**

40 **Alex Knob**
Climb high for brilliant alpine views of Franz Josef Glacier/Kā Roimata o Hine Hukatere. **p154**

41 **Lake Matheson**
Short walk legendary for its reflections of Aoraki/Mt Cook. **p156**

42 **Monro Beach**
Hike to an isolated beach, known for its Fiordland crested penguins. **p158**

Explore

West Coast

Take a walk on the wild side, literally. The West Coast echoes with memories of lawless gold rushes and its weather often appears equally lawless – locals say that if you can't see the mountains here then it's raining – and, if you can see them…it's about to rain. And, yet, the West Coast is one of the most dynamic hiking regions in Aotearoa/New Zealand, with an emerging network of tracks. The undoubted natural stars of the West Coast are a twinset of glaciers– Franz Josef Glacier/Kā Roimata o Hine Hukatere and Fox Glacier/Te Moeka o Tuawe – that leak from the Southern Alps towards the Tasman Sea. You can walk on the ice itself with a guided helihike.

Westport

The 'capital' of the northern West Coast is Westport. The town's fortunes have waxed and waned on coal mining but, in the current climate, it sits quietly stoked up on various industries, including dairy and, increasingly, tourism. It boasts respectable hospitality and visitor services and makes a good base for exploring the fascinating coast to the north.

Greymouth

Greymouth is the largest town on the West Coast and the region's 'Big Smoke'. For locals, it's a refuelling and shopping pit stop, while for travellers it's a noteworthy portal to tramping trails. Arriving on a dreary day, it's no mystery why Greymouth, crouched at the mouth of the Grey River, is sometimes the butt of jokes. But with gold-mining history, a scattering of jade shops and worthy walks in its surrounds, it pays to look beyond the grey.

Franz Josef Glacier/Kā Roimata o Hine Hukatere

Franz Josef Glacier/Kā Roimata o Hine Hukatere (population 530) is more action-packed than Fox Glacier/Te Moeka o Tuawe, but heavy tourist traffic often swamps both towns from December to February. Geologist Julius von Haast led the first European expedition here in 1865, and named the glacier after the Austrian emperor. The dismal forecast of a rainier, warmer future spells more shrinkage for Franz Josef Glacier/Kā Roimata o Hine Hukatere, whose trimlines (strips of vegetation on the valley walls) mark out decades of dramatic glacial retreat.

WHEN TO GO

December to February is peak season, so book accommodation at least a couple of months ahead. The shoulder months of October/November and March/April are increasingly busy. The West Coast has plenty of sunshine but serious rainfall (in places, up to 5m annually). May to September has fewer crowds and cheaper accommodation; though mild (for NZ), it's reliably rainy. All year round, walkers should check conditions with local DOC office staff. Rivers can be treacherous and snow hangs around longer than you may think.

Fox Glacier / Te Moeka o Tuawe

Fox Glacier/Te Moeka o Tuawe (population 300), 23km south of Franz Josef Glacier/Kā Roimata o Hine Hukatere, is the quieter of the two glacier towns. The 13km glacier (named for former New Zealand prime minister Sir William Fox) has been steadily retreating over the past century. Compared with the glacier, the township isn't nearly so dramatic. Surrounded by farmland, its cafes and tour operators are strung along the main road, along with hotels and motels catering to visiting crowds that descend over the summer.

Haast

A small township at the yawning mouth of the Haast River, Haast acts as a springboard to forests, sand dunes, craggy coast and tree-knotted lakes. Only in 1965 was Haast linked to the rest of the West Coast Hwy and the untouched feel endures. It's a handy stop for filling the tank and tummy if you're travelling between Otago and the West Coast glaciers. If you're heading north, check your fuel gauge as Haast petrol station is the last one before Fox Glacier/Te Moeka o Tuawe.

TRANSPORT

Air New Zealand (airnewzealand.co.nz) flies between Hokitika and Christchurch.

Originair (soundsair.com) connects Westport and Wellington.

One of the world's great train journeys, the **TranzAlpine** (greatjourneysofnz.co.nz) traverses the Southern Alps daily between Christchurch and Greymouth, through Arthur's Pass National Park.

Buses run the length of the coast, over the Southern Alps to Christchurch, south to Wānaka and Queenstown, and north to Nelson.

Rental wheels will give you the opportunity to really explore.

WHAT'S ON

Westland A&P Show (westlandapshow.co.nz)
Held on the last Saturday in January at the Hokitika Racecourse.

Coast to Coast (coasttocoast.co.nz)
Legendary February multi-sport race from the West Coast's Kumara Beach to Christchurch.

Hokitika Wildfoods Festival (wildfoods.co.nz)
One-day festival of daredevil eating in early March. Fish eyes, pigs' ears and huhu beetle grubs usually grace the menu.

Resources

Tourism West Coast
(westcoast.co.nz)

Destination Westport
(destinationwestport.com)

Punakaiki
(punakaiki.co.nz)

Greymouth i-SITE West Coast Travel Centre
(westcoasttravel.co.nz)

Hokitika
(hokitika.org)

Franz Josef & Fox Glaciers
(glaciercountry.co.nz)

DOC Paparoa National Park Visitor Centre
(doc.govt.nz)

DOC Westland Tai Poutini National Park Visitor Centre
(doc.govt.nz)

DOC Haast Visitor Centre
(doc.govt.nz)

 WHERE TO STAY

There are good places to stay the length of the West Coast thanks to the booming tourism industry. Book ahead for the summer; there are also plenty of camping options.

37

Charming Creek North Walkway

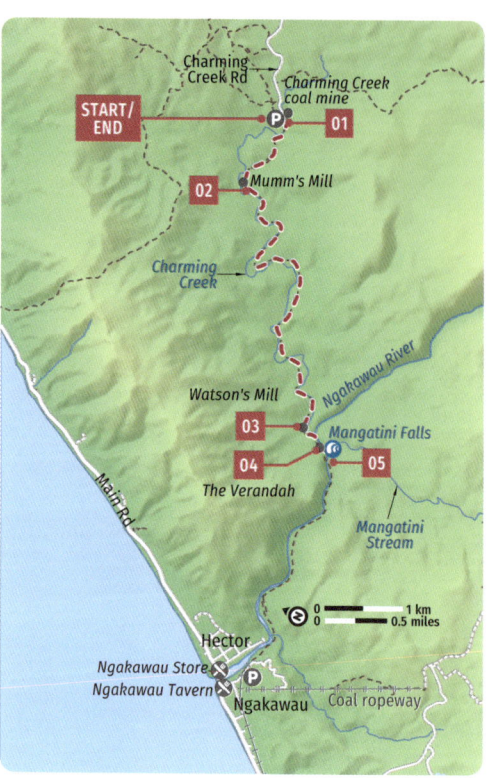

DURATION	DIFFICULTY	DISTANCE	START/END
4hrs return	Easy	11km return	Charming Creek Rd end

TERRAIN	Low gradient following old railway

Once a single track, a large slip has split it into two: North and South, the latter of which is closed. But the North is a beautiful day walk from Seddonville; you'll follow an old train line into the Ngakawau Gorge to Mangatini Falls and return. The walk features rusty relics, tunnels, waterfalls, and interesting plants and geological formations.

Getting Here

Seddonville, the now-sleepy site of New Zealand's first state-owned coal mine, is 50km north of Westport on the banks of the Mokihinui River, which is worth a swim in its deep green waters. There is no public transport in the area so you'll need your own wheels.

Starting Point

The trailhead is 10km south of Seddonville, at the end of the gravel Charming Creek Rd. A bridge brings you over the river to begin the track.

The walk, along a historic bush tramway, starts at the abandoned **Charming Creek coal mine** site, which has plenty of old equipment slowly decaying into the bush. The Charming Creek rail track was built in the early 1900s by brothers Bob and George Watson to access and bring out timber from the Ngakawau Valley, then later for coal. The coal was sent by rail to Westport and shipped to Wellington, but the enterprise ended in 1958.

Best for

OFF THE BEATEN PATH

Mining remnants, Charming Creek North Walkway

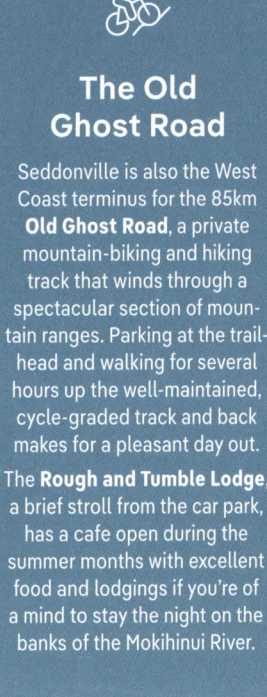

The Old Ghost Road

Seddonville is also the West Coast terminus for the 85km **Old Ghost Road**, a private mountain-biking and hiking track that winds through a spectacular section of mountain ranges. Parking at the trailhead and walking for several hours up the well-maintained, cycle-graded track and back makes for a pleasant day out.

The **Rough and Tumble Lodge**, a brief stroll from the car park, has a cafe open during the summer months with excellent food and lodgings if you're of a mind to stay the night on the banks of the Mokihinui River.

02 A short downhill section followed by some uphill steps will bring you to a flatter part of the track, and then the former **Mumm's Mill**, where there are sawmill relics to check out. Infographics abound; take the time to learn about Aotearoa/New Zealand's nascent coal mining history.

03 After Mumm's Mill, the next hour sees you cross Charming Creek a number of times on wooden bridges, traversing country more open than you'll soon experience in the gorge. At historic **Watson's Mill**, there's a restored boiler and more rusty relics in the regenerating bush.

04 Follow old railway tracks and past impressive rock overhangs called **'The Verandah'**, with views of the confluence of the Ngakawau River and Charming Creek, and the upper Ngakawau Gorge - the only known habitat for the rare and protected Ngakawau Gorge white daisies.

05 Walkers pass through a 50m tunnel and reach the impressive **Mangatini Falls**, a 25m-high multi-step waterfall at the point where the Mangatini Stream joins the Ngakawau River. Retrace your steps to Charming Creek car park.

☕ Take a Break

Ngakawau Tavern, on SH67, is a bar and cafe, and offers simple accommodation. Just across the river is **Ngakawau Store**. Heading south towards Westport, Waimangaroa's **Coffee on the Go** trailer makes renowned homemade pies, definitely worth stopping for. Drinks and ice creams are also available.

38

Punakaiki-Pororari Loop

DURATION	DIFFICULTY	DISTANCE	START/END
3–4hrs	Easy	11.5km	Waikori Rd car park

TERRAIN	Undulating well-maintained track

This popular walk in Paparoa National Park heads up the bouldery Punakaiki River, pops over a hill and comes down the Pororari River with its spectacular limestone gorge to rejoin the highway near the sea. From there, it's an amble along the road to Pancake Rocks and Paparoa National Park Visitor Centre, then back to wherever you left your car. A feature of the area is the numerous nikau palm trees.

Getting Here

Punakaiki is 45km north of Greymouth and 56km south of Westport. The DOC Paparoa National Park Visitor Centre is directly opposite the entrance to Pancake Rocks.

Starting Point

There are three starting point options – at the DOC Paparoa National Park Visitor Centre car park, 1km north at the mouth of the Pororari River, and 2.5km southeast at the car park on Waikori Rd. Wherever you start, you can walk the loop in either direction. (The described walk is anticlockwise from the Waikori Rd car park.)

 From the Waikori Rd car park, follow the **Inland Pack Track**, crossing the Punakaiki River on the **footbridge**. This historic track, carved by gold miners in 1867 to bypass the rugged coast, is these days, a popular two-day, 25km hike – the day walk described here takes in the first part of the Inland Pack Track.

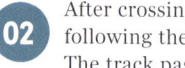 After crossing the bridge, head northeast, following the large orange track markers. The track passes through logged swamps to the base of the hill that separates the Punakaiki River from the Pororari Valley to the north. A well-

Pancake Rocks

Pancake Rocks

Whatever you do, before, after or during your walk, don't forget to head out to **Pancake Rocks**. Punakaiki's claim to fame is Dolomite Point, where a layering-weathering process called stylobedding has carved the limestone into what looks like piles of thick pancakes.

Aim for high tide (tide timetables are posted at the visitor centre; hope that it coincides with sunset) when the sea surges into caverns and booms menacingly through blowholes. See it on a wild day and be reminded that Mother Nature really is the boss. Allow 20 to 30 minutes for the straightforward walk, which loops from the highway out to the rocks and blowholes (longer if you want to take photos). Parts of the trail are suitable for wheelchairs.

benched track climbs through **mature rainforest** to a low saddle and then drops gently into the Pororari Valley.

03 When you hit a signposted junction, head upstream along the Inland Pack Track for a short distance to the **swing bridge** for a lovely spot to take a break.

04 Head back downstream and carry on out towards the coast from the track junction. The trail follows the river closely along its south bank, through a spectacular landscape of towering **limestone bluffs** graced by nīkau palms and tree ferns. Keep an eye on the river's deep-green pools for trout or eels, or perhaps you might feel inclined to take a dip at one of the spots where there is easy access to the river.

Take a Break

Almost inevitably, pancakes are the pride of the menu at **Pancake Rocks Cafe** (pancakerockscafe.com) opposite Pancake Rocks trail, heaped with bacon, berries, cream and other tasty toppings. Even better are the pizzas, from whitebait to four cheese (with a few good veggie options too). Time a visit for summer open-mic nights from 6pm on Fridays. The conservatory area – all wooden benches and fairy lights – is a pleasant spot for a drink around sundown.

05 When you hit SH6 and the Pororari River Track car park, turn left and a 10- to 15-minute walk will take you to **Paparoa National Park Visitor Centre**. From there, it is a 2.5km walk back along the road to the car park at the described starting point. Walkers can use the SH6 bridge over the Punakaiki River on the upstream side.

39

Ōkārito Pack Track & Coastal Walk

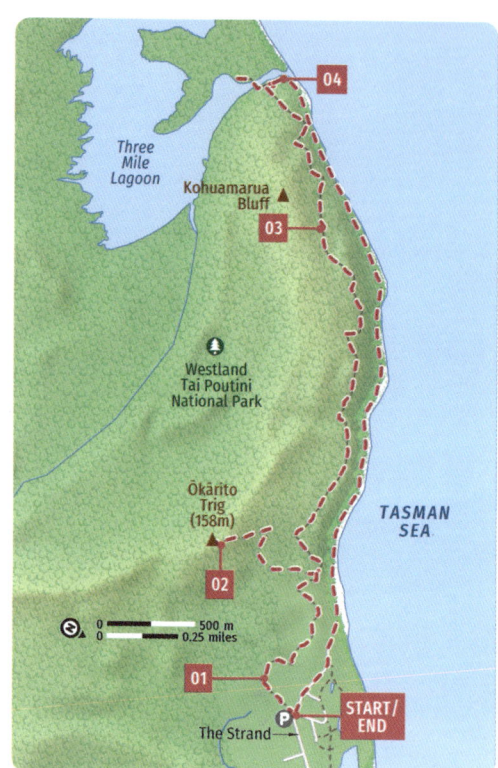

DURATION	DIFFICULTY	DISTANCE	START/END
3½hrs	Easy	10km	The Strand car park

TERRAIN	Well-maintained track; coastal walk

Ōkārito boasts one of the few navigable river bars on the West Coast, which made it a booming port of 1500 souls during the gold rushes of the 1860s. The pack track was constructed to give miners an alternative inland route to the 'dangerous' coastal route to get to the gold-bearing sands of Three Mile and Five Mile Lagoons to the south. These days, the walk to Three Mile Lagoon makes a top half-day hike when combined with the coastal route back along the beach.

Getting Here

Turn off SH6 at the Forks-Ōkārito Rd turn-off, 18km north of Franz Josef Glacier/Kā Roimata o Hine Hukatere and 13km west of Whataroa. Follow the sealed road 13km to Ōkārito township.

Starting Point

The car park is next to the old Ōkārito School House on The Strand. If you're walking the coastal route first, there's an alternative car park at the end of The Strand. Both have tide times posted. DOC says that walking along the beach between Ōkārito township and the Three Mile Lagoon should only be undertaken within one hour each side of low tide. Walkers should allow 1½ hours to walk along the beach and should check tide times as posted at the car parks, or look up Ōkārito on *tide-forecast.com*. Choose whether to do the inland route or coastal route first based on the tide times. The treacherous section of the coastal walk is below the bluffs towards Three Mile Lagoon.

Best for

COASTAL SCENERY

Ōkārito

The seaside hamlet of Ōkārito is surrounded by a pounding surf beach with the snowcapped Southern Alps as a backdrop, forest-clad hills and an expansive lagoon. With a present population of around 30, it's hard to believe that during the height of the gold rush 1500 people lived here.

Ōkārito Lagoon is the largest unmodified wetland in NZ. More than 76 bird species glide among its waterways, including kōtuku (white heron). Hiding out in the forest are rowi kiwi, the rarest species of NZ's iconic land bird. Consider joining a tour run by **Okarito Kiwi Tours** (okaritokiwi tours.co.nz), a paddle on the lagoon with **Okarito Kayaks** (okarito.co.nz), or a bird-spotting trip with **Okarito Boat Eco Tours** (okaritoboat tours.co.nz).

Kōtuku (white heron), Ōkārito

01 If doing the inland route first, from the car park follow the **Ōkārito Wetland Walk** on a boardwalk before entering the forest and climbing to a viewpoint over the estuary.

02 Ten minutes further on, an optional side track climbs up to the **Ōkārito Trig viewpoint** (158m), which offers impressive views of the coast, inland mountains and the possibility of spotting Aoraki/Mt Cook, almost directly south. Add 40 minutes to your hike time if you walk this side track.

03 Continue through coastal forest and climb over the **Kohuamarua Bluff**. The track winds its way through wind-battered rimu, rata and silver pine forest before dropping down to the sheltered estuary of **Three Mile Lagoon**. Up to 2500 miners lived here and at Five Mile Lagoon in the 1860s; children made the return walk to Ōkārito School from here on a daily basis.

04 There's a **footbridge** across the lagoon that's worth exploring. To head back to Ōkārito, carry on out to the coast and follow it back to where the beach widens, then inland to the township and your car. Keep your eyes open for fur seals (kekeno), little blue penguins and sea birds, such as black backed gulls, oyster catchers and shags along the way.

☕ Take a Break

Ōkārito has no shops so stock up before you go. **Okarito Kayaks** may have its locally famous homemade ice cream and espresso for sale; it's open 8am to 5pm. Ōkārito is 26km west of Whataroa and 31km north of Franz Josef Glacier/Kā Roimata o Hine Hukatere. Franz offers vibrant eating and drinking options for after your hike, while you'll find a more limited range of options in sleepy Whataroa.

153

40

Alex Knob

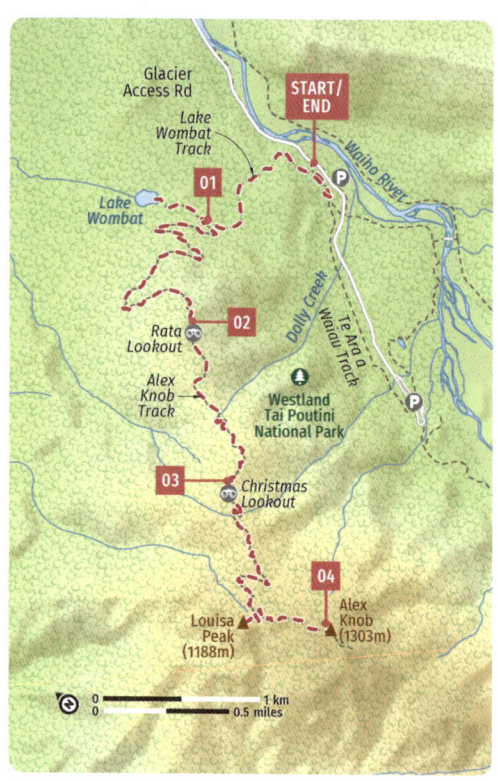

DURATION	DIFFICULTY	DISTANCE	START/END
8hrs	Hard	17km	Glacier Access Rd car park

TERRAIN	Bush and alpine trail climbing to altitude

Walkers need to be experienced and well-prepared for the full 1125-vertical-metre climb to Alex Knob (1303m) and its impressive views, but there are other spots, such as Lake Wombat, Rata Lookout and Christmas Lookout, where you can turn around and shorten the walk. The first views of Franz Josef Glacier/Kā Roimata o Hine Hukatere are from Rata Lookout (allow 3½ to four hours return). Check conditions with the Westland Tai Poutini National Park Visitor Centre before heading out. Afternoon cloud is common, so get an early start to reach the summit as early as possible, before cloud builds to obscure views.

Getting Here
Drive or walk south from the Franz Josef township across the Waiho River Bridge and onto Franz Josef Glacier Access Rd.

Starting Point
The Alex Knob Track starts 2km down Glacier Access Rd, signposted on the right side of the road. There is car parking here.

01 From the access road, the track is initially easy as it passes through rainforest for 30 minutes to the **Lake Wombat Track** junction. Named after a miner whose nickname was Wombat Jack, the small lake is a depression ground out by the glacier that subsequently filled with water, and is reached on a 30-minute (return) side track. Lake Wombat makes a good destination for those looking for a short walk and takes 1½ hours return from the access road.

Franz Josef Glacier/Kā Roimata o Hine Hukatere

Glacier Helihiking

If skies are blue and choppers are flying, seize the chance to helihike on a glacier. Franz Josef Glacier/Kā Roimata o Hine Hukatere is the more popular of the two glaciers, with its steepness intensifying the drama of crevasses and ice formations, while Fox Glacier/Te Moeka o Tuawe is longer and faster moving.

The two major operators offering helihikes have primo standards on safety and technical expertise. **Franz Josef Glacier Guides** *(franzjosefglacier.com)* is a well-oiled machine, while family-run **Fox Glacier Guiding** *(foxguides.co.nz)* prides itself on a friendly, personalised experience. They're comparable on price (around $480 with three hours on the ice) and both offer photo-ops in the famous blue ice caves.

02 From the turn-off to Lake Wombat, the Alex Knob track steepens, turns into a rough mountain track and zigzags steeply up to 700m above sea level to **Rata Lookout** for your first view of the glacier and the main divide. Along the way, you'll catch views out to the coast and valley below. This is the toughest part of the climb, with scrambling over large boulders, fallen trees and exposed tree roots.

If Rata Lookout is your target for the day, head back down from here, allowing 3½ to four hours for the return hike.

03 It is then a more gentle gradient to **Christmas Lookout**, at 900m and the 6km mark, where there is a good rest spot and spectacular views of the glacier. If this is your target for the day, allow 4½ to five hours for the return hike.

04 For the final hour of the climb, the trail switches back and forth through subalpine forest before reaching the bushline. From here, the track continues through snow tussock to the **Alex Knob summit**, where a plane table has information on the spectacular surrounding features. Alex Knob is the first peak of the Fritz range, the main ridge to the west of Franz Josef Glacier/Kā Roimata o Hine Hukatere. It's named after West Coaster Alex Graham (1881–1957), a local mountain guide. Head back down to the access road when ready.

 ## Take a Break

In Franz Josef township, head to **Landing Restaurant & Bar** *(thelandingbar.co.nz)*. Portions are huge at this popular spot on the main street, from whopping whitebait patties to unfinishable nachos and bulky burgers. The patio, complete with sunshine and gas heaters, is a good place to warm up after a day in the wilds.

41

Lake Matheson

DURATION	DIFFICULTY	DISTANCE	START/END
1½hrs	Easy	4.4km	Lake Matheson Rd car park

TERRAIN	Undulating track; it is wheelchair accessible to Jetty Viewpoint

Surrounded by ancient forest, Lake Matheson (Te Ara Kairaumati), 6km west of Fox Glacier township, is famous for its mirror views of Aotearoa/New Zealand's two highest peaks, Aoraki/Mt Cook and Mt Tasman.

Lake Matheson sits in a small glacier-carved depression west of the Southern Alps. It was formed when Fox Glacier/Te Moeka o Tuawe retreated from its last significant advance about 14,000 years ago. During the last major ice age, the glacier spread across the coastal plains towards the sea, grinding out a depression that later filled with water, forming the lake. Its reflecting properties are thanks to the dark brown colour of the water, the result of organic matter leached from the forest floor.

The popular track around the lake, a good option for families, features three viewpoints. The first, **Jetty Viewpoint**, is around 20 minutes from the car park when heading clockwise around the lake; this bit of track is suitable for assisted wheelchairs.

Twenty-five minutes further walking will bring you to the **View of Views** at the northern end of the lake. After another 10 minutes, you'll reach **Reflection Island**. A number of viewing platforms here make it a great spot for that photograph. It will take 30 minutes back to the car park from here.

The best time to visit is early morning, or when the sun is low in the late afternoon, although the **Lake Matheson Cafe** (lakematheson.com) here surely has one of the best cafe outlooks in the world. Next to the car park, this cafe does everything right: sharp architecture that maximises inspiring mountain views, strong coffee, craft beers and upmarket fare.

Lake Matheson

42

Monro Beach

DURATION	DIFFICULTY	DISTANCE	START/END
1½hrs	Easy	5km	Monro Beach Walk car park

TERRAIN	Undulating track through dense rainforest

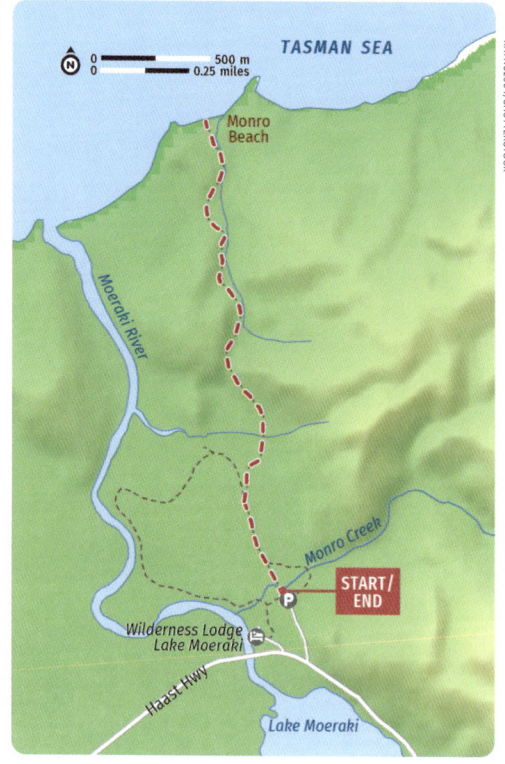

This lovely short walk from the car park near the Lake Moeraki outlet, 30km north of Haast, takes about 45 minutes in each direction and gives walkers the opportunity to see a Fiordland crested penguin (tawaki) at rugged and isolated Monro Beach.

The trailhead for this walk is off SH6, on the northern side of the bridge that crosses the Moeraki River, and down a short road next to **Wilderness Lodge Lake Moeraki** (wildernesslodge.co.nz). Park in the small car park and, on starting the walk, you're immediately within luxuriant **coastal rainforest**. The track is popular and well maintained. Cross a **suspension bridge** and patches of boardwalk before the track winds its way downhill to the beach through magnificent rainforest with lots of tree ferns. When you reach the **pebbly beach**, head left or right towards rocky outcrops at either end of the beach. Find a good spot to sit and observe.

With its distinctive broad, yellow eyebrow stripe, the tawaki nests among tree roots and rocks in dense coastal forest. The best time of year to see **tawaki** is during the breeding season from July to November, though they can also sometimes be seen during the moulting season from mid-January to early March. The best time of day to see one is early morning or late afternoon. The tawaki population is between 2500 and 3000 breeding pairs and is in decline. Tawaki are very timid, so do not disturb or approach birds, nests or areas of beach where there are penguin tracks. Learn more at the **Tawaki Project** (tawaki-project.org).

Tawaki (Fiordland crested penguin)

Also Try…

Moria Gate Arch, Ōpārara Basin

PETER UNGER/GETTY IMAGES

Harihari Coastal Walkway

DURATION	DIFFICULTY	DISTANCE
2½–3hrs	Easy	7.6km

This trail near Harihari offers spectacular views while walking through estuaries, bogs, a swamp forest and along the beach.

From Harihari, 72km southeast of Hokitika on SH6, take Wanganui Flat Rd, then La Fontaine Rd 20km out to the car park and trailhead beside the Wanganui River. The walk forms a loop from the car park, heading out along the Wanganui River to the Tasman Sea, turning south along the beach to the Poerua River mouth before returning via a historic pack track and parts of a bush tramway to the car park. At the southern end, a boardwalk continues over wetlands to the mudflats and lagoon at the river mouth. The beach and Wanganui River estuary section of track are only suitable within two hours of low tide. Check the tide times posted at the start of the walk.

Ōpārara Basin

DURATION	DIFFICULTY	DISTANCE
2½hrs (both walks)	Easy	6km (both walks)

Two excellent short walks to impressive rock formations start at the Arches car park, about a 45-minute drive northeast of Karamea.

Lying within Kahurangi National Park, the Ōpārara Basin is a hidden valley concealing limestone arches and caves within a thick forest of massive, moss-laden trees. The valley's signature sight is the 200m-long, 37m-high Ōpārara Arch, spanning the picturesque Ōpārara River, tannin-stained brown, which winds alongside the easy walkway (50 minutes return) north from the car park. From the same car park, a lovely forest loop walk taking about 1½ hours takes in the smaller but no less stunning Moria Gate Arch (43m long, 19m high); and Mirror Tarn. The arches were formed by collapsed limestone cave systems, while Mirror Tarn is known for its forest reflections. The tracks are easy to walk and perfect for families.

Cape Foulwind Walkway

Cape Foulwind Walkway

DURATION	DIFFICULTY	DISTANCE
1¼hrs one-way	Easy	3.4km one-way

Screaming gulls are the soundtrack to Cape Foulwind, as wind-battered a walk as its name promises.

Located 11km directly west of Westport, Cape Foulwind was named by Captain Cook when he was blown off course in 1770. The trail traverses farmland and coastal hills between Omau and Tauranga Bay. Towards the southern end is a seal colony where up to 200 fur seals loll on the rocks. Further north, the walkway passes a replica astrolabe (a navigational aid) and lighthouse.

Point Elizabeth Walkway

DURATION	DIFFICULTY	DISTANCE
1¾hrs one-way	Easy	5.5km one-way

North of Greymouth, this walkway rounds Point Elizabeth and continues on to the small town of Rapahoe.

The walkway car park is at the end of North Beach Rd, directly north of Cobden, about 6km from Greymouth. An enjoyable walk (3½ hours return), the track skirts around a richly forested headland in the shadow of the Rapahoe Range to an impressive ocean lookout, before continuing on to Rapahoe (11km from Greymouth) – small town, big beach, friendly local pub.

Roys Peak (p170)

Otago

43 **Rob Roy Track**
Walk a narrow gorge to spectacular glacier views west of Wānaka. **p166**

44 **Diamond Lake & Rocky Mountain**
A 360-degree panorama of lakes and mountains. **p168**

45 **Roys Peak**
A big climb, but a chance to take that image you've seen on Instagram. **p170**

46 **Ben Lomond**
Climb high above Queenstown and Lake Wakatipu. **p172**

47 **Bob's Cove**
A gentle, fun family walk near Queenstown. **p176**

48 **Lake Hayes**
Circumnavigate this photogenic lake near Arrowtown. **p178**

49 **Routeburn Track Day Walk**
Valley walking at the eastern end of this legendary hike. **p180**

50 **Sandymount & Sandfly Bay**
Spectacular scenery on the Otago Peninsula near Dunedin. **p184**

51 **Long Beach**
The kids will love this beach near Dunedin, with a massive sea cave at the end. **p186**

Explore

Otago

Few places ignite a sense of adventure quite like Otago's Queenstown, Wānaka and Mt Aspiring/Tititea National Park – even the sedentary get drawn into hitherto unconsidered activities here. Some of Aotearoa/New Zealand's finest mountain country awaits, including the Routeburn Track. Just as enticing is the Matukituki Valley further north, providing a jaw-dropping gateway to hanging glaciers and airy passes. For all that, you barely need leave Queenstown or Wānaka to get an eyeful of mountains as you walk. Set out from Queenstown and you can rise to lofty Ben Lomond, while Roys Peak, with its photo-perfect perch over Lake Wānaka, is Wānaka's hike of the day every day. On the east coast, Otago Peninsula offers great coastal walks near the city of Dunedin.

Queenstown

Queenstown is as much a verb as a noun, a place of doing that likes to label itself the 'adventure capital of the world'. This mountain resort is famously the birthplace of bungy jumping, and the list of adventures you can throw yourself into here is encyclopedic, from alpine heliskiing to ziplining. But to pigeonhole Queenstown as just a playground is to overlook its cosmopolitan dining and arts scene, its fine vineyards, and the diverse range of bars that can make evenings as fun-filled as the days. Expect big crowds, especially in summer and winter, but also big experiences.

Wānaka

Like Queenstown, Wānaka is a lake and mountain resort town bristling with outdoor and adventure opportunities. Despite constant growth, Wānaka retains a fairly laid-back, lakeside, small-town atmosphere, though things get busy at the height of the winter ski season and in midsummer. A growing number of good cafes, restaurants and bars entice visitors to base themselves here and stick around.

WHEN TO GO

Queenstown and Wānaka are year-round resorts. Snow activities dominate in the winter, from June until September, while all sorts turn up the rest of the year.

The weather is generally settled from late December to March, with February often considered the best for walking. However, in alpine regions you must be prepared for sudden changes in weather and unexpected storms at any time of year. Snow can fall above 1000m in almost any month, with late winter and spring being high-risk times for avalanches.

Glenorchy

Perhaps best known as the gateway to the Routeburn Track, Glenorchy (population 410) sits on a shelf of flat land at the head of Lake Wakatipu. The small town is a great option if you want to be beside the lake and the mountains but prefer to stay away from the bustle and bluster of Queenstown. The hiking is sensational, and the town is also a base for horse treks, jetboat rides, helicopter flights and skydives.

Dunedin

Two words immediately spring to mind when Kiwis think of Dunedin: 'Scotland' and 'students'. The 'Edinburgh of the South' is immensely proud of its Scottish heritage, never missing an opportunity to break out the haggis and bagpipes on civic occasions. The very name Dunedin is derived from the Scottish Gaelic name for Edinburgh – Dùn Èideann. Dunedin locals love a drink, and none more so than the University of Otago students who dominate the city in term time. Dunedin is a great base for exploring the wildlife-rich Otago Peninsula, which officially lies within the city limits.

WHERE TO STAY

As resort towns, Queenstown and Wānaka offer a huge range of accommodation to suit all budgets in all seasons. Bookings are essential in high seasons and New Zealand school-holiday periods. Central Otago also makes a good living out of the tourism industry and you'll find all sorts of options everywhere. Consider staying in Glenorchy or Kinloch at the head of Lake Wakatipu if you're exploring southern parts of Mt Aspiring/Tititea National Park. Dunedin also has a good range of places to sleep.

TRANSPORT

The hub for Central Otago and Wānaka is Queenstown International Airport with domestic flights and direct flights from Australia. Dunedin Airport, 27km southwest of the city, is the hub for Dunedin and the east coast of Otago. Buses crisscross the region, linking Queenstown and Wānaka with Christchurch, Aoraki/Mt Cook and Te Anau, as well as Dunedin. Many visitors make use of the huge fleets of rental cars at Queenstown Airport to explore the region.

WHAT'S ON

Winter Pride
(winterpride.co.nz)
Held every August, the festival has been celebrating love and diversity in Queenstown since 2003.

Arrowtown Autumn Festival
(arrowtownautumnfestival.co.nz)
Five days of fun in mid to late April.

Rhythm & Alps Festival
(rhythmandalps.co.nz)
Three-day music festival in the Cardrona Valley that finishes off the year.

Dunedin Fringe Festival
(dunedinfringe.nz)
The world's southernmost Fringe Festival takes over for 10 days in mid-March.

Resources

Discover Queenstown
(queenstownnz.co.nz)

Wānaka
(lakewanaka.co.nz)

Glenorchy
(glenorchyinfocentre.co.nz)

Dunedin
(dunedinnz.com)

DOC Mt Aspiring NP Visitor Centre
(doc.govt.nz)

DOC Queenstown Visitor Centre
(doc.govt.nz)

Dunedin i-SITE Visitor Information Centre
(dunedin.govt.nz)

43

Rob Roy Track

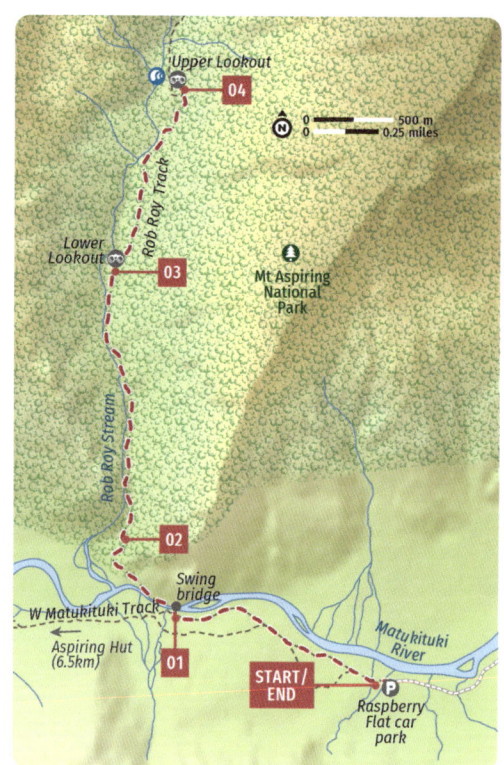

DURATION	DIFFICULTY	DISTANCE	START/END
4hrs	Easy-Moderate	10km	Raspberry Flat car park

TERRAIN	Maintained mountain track, steep in places

It's not uncommon to hear this walk – northwest of Wānaka – described as the finest day walk in the South Island. Few tracks provide such large-scale mountain scenery in such a short time frame, with the walk beginning along the Matukituki Valley before climbing 400m through beech forest into a high and dramatic enclosure of mountains and glaciers.

Getting Here

The tramp begins at the Raspberry Flat car park, an hour's drive from Wānaka. If you're coming in a rental car, check that you're covered for the drive – most of it is gravel road, with a series of creek fords along the way. Shuttles run from Wānaka to Raspberry Flat – check for the latest at the Mt Aspiring/Tititea National Park Visitor Centre in Wānaka.

Starting Point

There is plenty of parking, a shelter, toilets and information boards at the car park.

01 From the car park, follow the track straight up the valley with the sharp line of Cascade Saddle visible straight ahead. The trail is wide and well formed as it passes through open farmland. In 15 minutes, you'll come to a **swing bridge**, where you leave the West Matukituki Track, crossing the river.

02 Continue upstream through a beech forest on the opposite bank. The track emerges from the forest where there's a **seat with a perfect view** up the Matukituki Valley. Here, the track turns up and away from the valley, heading up into beech forest beside **Rob Roy Stream**. The stream quickly turns into a gorge, and there are

Rob Roy Track

Aspiring Hut

If you fancy a night in the Matukituki Valley, turn up the valley on your return and hike to the NZ Alpine Club's **Aspiring Hut** (alpineclub.org.nz). From the swing bridge over the Matukituki River, it's about a two-hour hike. Built by the NZAC in 1949, this stone-and-wood hut is a classic climbers' lodge, with an atmosphere of high adventure. The views are impressive, especially of the mountains at the head of the valley, including Mt Aspiring/Tititea (3033m) – try to nab a bunk under the big windows. The hut has gas cookers (only between late October and mid-April; bring your own stove at other times), wood stove, flush toilets and a water tank.

early glimpses through the crack of the gorge to a stunning glaciated mountainscape – a preview of things to come.

03 The track follows the line of the boulder-choked gorge, staying high on its bank. The beech forest gets mossier and more primeval as you ascend, with the stream below occasionally slowing into deeper, bluer pools.

One hour from the swing bridge, the track comes to a break in the forest that forms the **lower lookout**. If avalanche danger is present, access is restricted to here. A pair of waterfalls pour down from high above, and glaciers are scraped across the mountains like icing. On the opposite bank, the beech forest is strung with lichen.

04 Continue climbing through beech forest. At a large bend in the stream, the track turns up a tributary (beside a toilet), soon popping out from the bushline and into a maze of boulders. Among the boulders is the **upper lookout** (30 minutes from the lower lookout), with a series of interpretive signs sitting immediately below Rob Roy Peak and, most noticeably, **Rob Roy Glacier**, hanging precariously from its slopes. The waterfalls now sit almost directly across the stream, tumbling nearly 300m over the cliffs. Mountains wrap right around the lookout, and it's well worth taking some time to simply hang about here for a while before heading back down the track. You may be visited by a kea and it's quite likely that you'll get to witness bits of the glacier breaking away and avalanching down the mountain.

Retrace your steps to return to the car park.

Take a Break

When you have left Wānaka, there's nowhere to buy food or refreshments. Make sure to stock up before you head out, either at the supermarket or at **Doughbin Bakery** on the waterfront.

44

Diamond Lake & Rocky Mountain

DURATION	DIFFICULTY	DISTANCE	START/END
3hrs	Easy-Moderate	7km	Diamond Lake car park

TERRAIN	Good trail with a 450m climb and descent

This low-level hill climb past a beautiful lake to the summit of Rocky Mountain offers lovely views over Lake Wānaka, the mouth of the Matukituki River and a distant Mt Aspiring/Tititea. The walk effectively takes in three conjoined loops; walking the central loop anticlockwise to the Lake Wānaka viewpoint, as described here, provides the most gentle ascent.

Getting Here

The large car park at the start of the walk is on the Wānaka-Mt Aspiring Rd, 18km west of Wānaka. The road is sealed all the way. Shuttle buses from Wānaka stop by on their way to Raspberry Flat for the Rob Roy Track – check for the latest at the Mt Aspiring/Tititea National Park Visitor Centre in Wānaka.

Starting Point

Cross the stile at the end of the car park and enter the Diamond Lake Conservation Area.

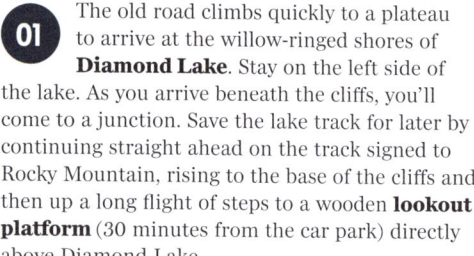

01 The old road climbs quickly to a plateau to arrive at the willow-ringed shores of **Diamond Lake**. Stay on the left side of the lake. As you arrive beneath the cliffs, you'll come to a junction. Save the lake track for later by continuing straight ahead on the track signed to Rocky Mountain, rising to the base of the cliffs and then up a long flight of steps to a wooden **lookout platform** (30 minutes from the car park) directly above Diamond Lake.

02 The track continues to climb. At the next junction, a couple of minutes past the lookout, keep right, following the path signed to the viewpoint. In another 10 to 15 minutes, detour

View of Lake Wānaka

right to the **Lake Wānaka Viewpoint**, where a seat at the mountain's edge stares out over the lake and across Glendhu Bay to Roys Peak.

03 Return to the main track and turn right. The track swings left, zigzagging steeply up the slopes, crossing a gully and then climbing steeply on a rugged section of track. The going quickly flattens out as you reach another **high plateau**.

04 Turn right onto the **Eastern Track**, climbing through the final rack of bluffs towards the summit. There are fine views as the trail creeps along the mountain's edge, but the grandstand view comes at the **summit** (775m; 1½ hours from the car park), as the scene peels open to reveal a cavalcade of features: Lake Wānaka, Treble Cone, Twin Falls and ahead, through the Matukituki Valley, the serrated summit of Mt Aspiring/Tititea.

05 Instead of returning on the same track, continue ahead onto the **Western Track**, which descends gently, rounds a couple of notches in the cliffs and then curls down to the high plateau. At the junction here, turn right (signed 'western track'), heading to the western edge of the mountain. The track descends through a damp gully, with a noticeable change in vegetation, cutting at times beneath overhanging cliffs. A steep set of tight switchbacks delivers you back to the track junction just above the Diamond Lake lookout platform that you passed earlier.

06 Turn right, passing the lookout, and descend to the lakeshore. Turn left here, completing the **lake loop** before returning to the car park.

☕ Take a Break

This is a great hike for bringing along a picnic. Get your supplies in Wānaka, then tuck into your goodies at either the Lake Wānaka Viewpoint on the way up or at the summit itself.

A Bit of History

Though Waitaha and Kai Tahu people occupied the area around Wānaka, there was no Māori presence when the first Europeans arrived here in 1853. Wānaka Station was established in 1859, and later divided into smaller runs, including Glendhu Station, which incorporated Rocky Mountain and Diamond Lake, in 1897. Recreational use began with the Wānaka Winter Sports Club, which used frozen Diamond Lake for ice skating from the 1950s.

In the 1990s, Stuart Landsborough came up with the idea of a walking track to the summit of Rocky Mountain, which he constructed with the support of the Glendhu Station landowners. The 106-hectare **Diamond Lake Conservation Area** was created in 2005.

45

Roys Peak

DURATION	DIFFICULTY	DISTANCE	START/END
6hrs	Moderate – Hard	16km	Wānaka–Mt Aspiring Rd car park

TERRAIN	Well-maintained mountain track; steep in parts

A long climb to a long view, this hike ascends to the summit of a 1578m peak along the rim of Lake Wānaka, passing one of the country's most popular mountain photo stops along the way. The climb to Roys Peak can be a grind, ascending 1220m from near the lakeshore to the antenna-tipped summit, but it's truly a spectacular walk. Many hikers aspire only to reach the ridge, about three-quarters of the way up, from where the famous selfie-with-Lake-Wānaka moment bombards Instagram.

Getting Here

The trailhead is around 6km from Wānaka, on the road to Mt Aspiring/Tititea National Park along the western shore of Roys Bay on Lake Wānaka. There's a sizeable car park if you drive here. Alternatively, walk or cycle 6.5km from town along the lakeside Glendhu Bay (Millennium) Track.

Starting Point

There's an information board with a map on the Pukerua Bay train platform. The nearest toilets and shops are 250m away.

 From the car park, the **Roys Peak Track** begins as it continues – climbing. Get used to that sting in your legs because it'll be steeply up most of the way, at first through **wide switchbacks**. About 30 minutes from the trailhead, the track crosses a fence on a stile as the switchbacks continue. The cars in the car park will already look like toys below.

 Some 10 to 15 minutes on, as the switchbacks uncoil, you'll come to three **graves** beside a pine tree, including that of Willis Scaife (1887–1965), the one-time owner of Glendhu

Best for

MOUNTAIN VIEWS

Roys Peak

#ThatWanakaTree

That coveted image taken from high above Lake Wānaka on the Roys Peak Track (#royspeak) may not even be Wānaka's biggest hit on social media. Top draw is a beloved crooked willow that grows on the shore of Lake Wānaka in Roys Bay.

Depending on lake levels, it is either surrounded by water or can be walked out to and visitors photograph it in droves. A favourite of Instagram fans worldwide, it has its own #That-WanakaTree hashtag and a Facebook and Wikipedia page.

It's a pleasant 15-minute stroll west of the Wānaka town centre along the waterfront. If you're having trouble finding it, look for the crowds!

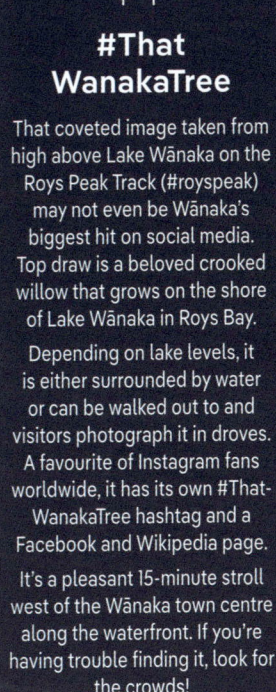

Station. There are also a couple of picnic tables here, so take a break and lap up the view of Lake Wānaka.

03 The gradient eases now as the track contours across the slopes for the next 20 minutes before the climb ramps up again, switchbacking through **tussocky farmland**, with Roys Peak now in view above you (if you've picked the right day). One to 1½ hours from the graves, you'll cross a stile and enter the **Stack Conservation Area**.

04 After another lengthy traverse, the track rises to the crest of the ridge (45 minutes from the stile). Just below the track to the right is the **knoll lookout** where all those Roys Peak photos are snapped.

05 The track turns up to the left from here, zigzagging up once again before crossing to the back of the ridge. After one final switchback, the track follows the summit ridge to the antenna-topped tip of **Roys Peak** (1578m), around 30 to 45 minutes from the knoll lookout. If you've come on a good day, the view is stunning – down onto Lake Wānaka and across to Mt Aspiring/Tititea.

Follow your ascent route for a knee-knocking descent to the car park.

Take a Break

Head to **Kai Whakapai Cafe & Bar** down on the Wānaka waterfront. This local institution is where the town seems to congregate on a sunny evening for a liquid sundowner over excellent pizza or salad. Locally brewed craft beers are on tap and there are Central Otago wines as well.

46

Ben Lomond

Best for

MOUNTAIN VIEWS

DURATION	DIFFICULTY	DISTANCE	START/END
6–8hrs	Moderate – Hard	15km	Bottom of Skyline Gondola

TERRAIN	Well-maintained track that is steep in parts

Ben Lomond Track

Climb high above Queenstown on a popular ridge-top hike with ever-widening views over Lake Wakatipu, Queenstown and finally Mt Aspiring/Tititea. If you stand in Queenstown, it might be the Remarkables that dominate the scene, but if you're on the opposite shore, looking across the lake towards Queenstown, it is the pyramidal figure of Ben Lomond, standing tall directly behind the town, that crowns the view. For walkers, it's the peak that also dominates thoughts of Queenstown.

Getting Here

One of the great joys of this tramp is its accessibility, with the Tiki Trail beginning directly beside the base station for the **Skyline Gondola** *(skyline.co.nz)*, a short walk from Queenstown's centre. The gondola offers the temptation of shortening the walk, either taking out the steep bits on the Tiki Trail on the way up or floating you back down into town after a tiring day out...or both.

Starting Point

For such an imposing mountain, Ben Lomond provides a surprisingly straightforward climb, complicated only by weather and the endurance of your legs – from Queenstown, the climb is 1438m to the summit. If time, energy or enthusiasm is short, you can ride the gondola to the top station, cutting out 2.5km of the approach walk and 500 vertical metres of climbing (and potentially descent at the end).

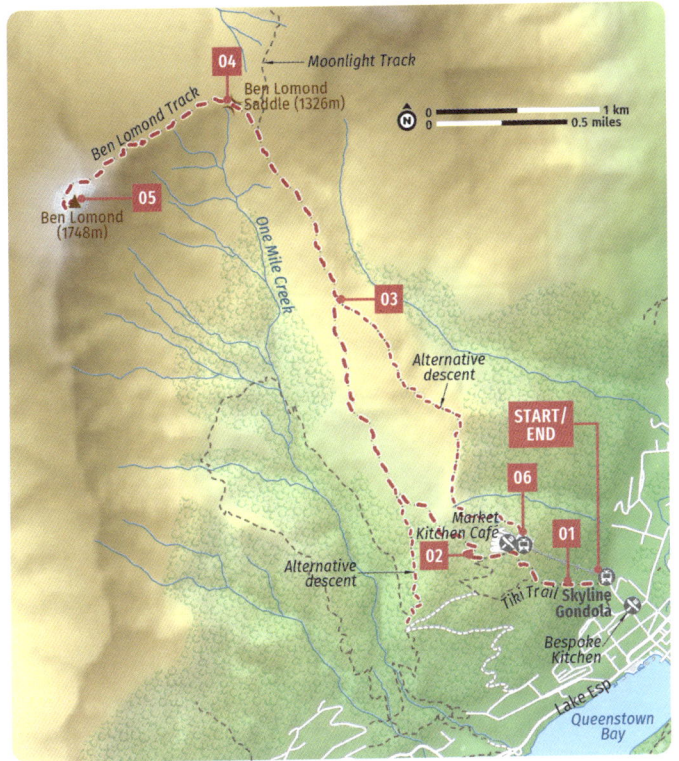

Lake Wakatipu

Beautiful **Lake Wakatipu**, sitting at 310m above sea level, is NZ's third-largest lake and reaches a depth of 399m – meaning the deepest spot actually sits well below sea level. Scientists have rated the lake's water as 99.9% pure. It's also very cold, hovering around 10°C throughout the year.

Māori tradition sees the lake's shape as the burnt outline of the evil giant Matau sleeping with his knees drawn up. Local lad Matakauri set fire to the bed of bracken on which the giant slept in order to rescue his beloved Manata, a chief's daughter who was kidnapped by the giant. The fat from Matau's body created a fire so intense that it burnt a hole deep into the ground.

01 The ascent of Ben Lomond begins on the **Tiki Trail**, which sets out from beside the base station for the Skyline Gondola, heading up beside a mountain-bike trail. Cross the bike trail after about 100m, from where the Tiki Trail coils steeply and tightly up the slopes through **Douglas fir forest**, passing platforms for the Ziptrek zipline tours through the forest. The trail crosses the Skyline vehicle road and mixes it with mountain-bike trails, and at times you'll hear Ziptrekers whizzing through the forest – it's a window into Queenstown's massive adventure industry. Past the Ziptrek office, you'll emerge into a clearing, one hour from the base station, and arrive at the gondola's top station. Pass through the station complex (take a break to enjoy the magnificent scenery from the viewing deck) to the **Market Kitchen Café**, where the Ben Lomond Track sets out not far from the luge chairlift.

02 The blue **Ben Lomond Track** signs will guide you out of the hubbub of people and the luge, and back into dark Douglas fir forest. Within 10 minutes, the track emerges from the forest to a view of the **peak of Ben Lomond** straight ahead. Soon you'll run into a track junction – some walkers make the climb up from lake level down at Fernhill Roundabout corner, about a kilometre along the waterfront from central Queenstown. Keep this track in mind for the descent if you're looking for a different way back into town.

03 Traverse beneath the ridge line, passing through a strip of beech forest before skirting the next, larger stand of beech, filling a deep gully, to rise to a **saddle** (1049m) in the ridge through tussocks and low subalpine scrub. Here, you'll notice a track heading off at a right angle, straight up the hill that sits between you and Queenstown. This is a great option for the descent, providing an alternative route back to the top of the Skyline Gondola, taking in amazing views and passing a **paraglider launching site** that makes an interesting stop on days that the tandem paragliders are operating. If you've decided at this junction that reaching the top of Ben Lomond is too formidable a task, following this alternative track back to the gondola makes a great loop trail for the day.

04 From the junction, the track simply follows the ridge line up, keeping left at the Moonlight Track junction and rising to **Ben Lomond Saddle** at 1326m, about an hour and a half from the top gondola station. Here you're greeted by an array of distant peaks, with a seat on which to sit and ponder the rest of the climb. The 1748m peak still looms high above and there's an hour of climbing to go.

05 The track now steepens as it rises up the neck of the mountain, following the line of the ridge just to its northern side. It continues to steepen as it rises, winding through bouldery schist and onto the **summit**, reached around one hour from the saddle.

The summit has an unbroken view over one of the most spectacular mountain regions in the country including Lake Wakatipu, the Remarkables and a distant Mr Aspiring/Tititea. If you're lucky, inquisitive and extremely intelligent kea (mountain parrots) may have decided to investigate you, as the latest intruders into their mountain paradise. Don't feed them, but enjoy their antics as they try to figure out how to steal your lunch.

06 Return back towards Queenstown, following the same track down to the saddle. From the junction another 20 to 30 minutes further down, as previously mentioned, there are a couple of options for getting back to the top of the gondola and the Tiki Trail. When there, if fatigue has set in, there's always the gondola for the descent – especially if you've decided to have a beer at Skyline's Market Kitchen Café.

☕ Take a Break

A great spot for refreshments is **Market Kitchen Café** (skyline.co.nz) at the top of the Skyline gondola. Many a walker has stopped in here for a cold drink before carrying on down the Tiki Trail back to Queenstown, only to succumb to the temptations of cold beer and taking the gondola down. Between the bottom of the gondola and central Queenstown is **Bespoke Kitchen** (bespokekitchen.co.nz), delivering everything you'd expect of a smart Kiwi cafe. There's a good selection of counter food, beautifully presented cooked options, a range of outside seating in sight of the mountains and, of course, great coffee. Within six months of opening, it was named NZ's cafe of the year.

Ben Lomond Saddle

Invasive Species

One of the greatest problems the environment around Queenstown faces is the growth of non-native species, such as the invasive Douglas fir (known locally as 'pines') and Scotch broom.

Turn up in November or early December, and the bright yellow flowers of the Scotch broom cover vast tracts – often to the delight of tourists – but much to the chagrin of conservationists. Douglas fir was originally sown on the lower slopes of Ben Lomond in the 19th century as a beautification project. The firs grow at a faster rate than in their original homeland of North America. The while DOC has tried to control them and local groups, such as the Wakatipu Wilding Conifer Control Group *(wakatipuwilding.co.nz)*, are trying hard too.

47

Bob's Cove

DURATION	DIFFICULTY	DISTANCE	START/END
1–3hrs options	Easy	4km	Bob's Cove car park
TERRAIN	Undulating, well-maintained track		

There are some magic hiking options for families at Bob's Cove, only a 15-minute drive from Queenstown. Take the kids on a one-hour jaunt to the beach and Bob's Knob, or add an hour for the Bob's Cove Bridle Track. Consider walking a couple of hours down to Twelve Mile Delta and back.

Getting Here
Drive southwest out of Queenstown on the road to Glenorchy at the head of Lake Wakatipu. Pass Wilson's Bay, Twelve Mile Delta and, about 15 minutes from Queenstown, Bob's Cove car park is on your left.

Starting Point
The start of the track is at the far end of Bob's Cove car park.

01 To do the easy walk with kids, turn left and down through the beech forest almost immediately on leaving the car park. Ten minutes will bring you down to the gorgeous, pristine, **pebbly beach** – a great spot for kids to learn to skip stones or take a swim. Bob's Knob is the little 385m 'mountain' not far to the south; lake level is around 310m above sea level. From the beach, head back onto the track for five minutes to reach an historic 1870s **lime kiln**. Gum trees were planted here to use as fuel for the kiln and some have grown to massive proportions in the ensuing years.

Bob's Cove

Bob Fortune

Bob's Cove is named after Bob Fortune, a boatman for Queenstown founder William Rees in the 1860s, and is one of the best-preserved examples of Lake Wakatipu's coastal past.

It's believed that between 20 and 40 million years ago the ocean penetrated from the southwest as far as the Wakatipu, and terraces around Bob's Cove contain fossils and shells, as well as bands of mottled limestone. Māori used the cove (Te Punatapu) as a campsite while on *pounamu* (greenstone) expeditions, and later the Wakatipu Lime Company built seven lime kilns here in the 1870s. Lime mortar was used in building the old Queenstown courthouse and the Kawarau River suspension bridge.

02 A few minutes further on, you'll pass a jetty down on your right. There are marvellous examples of the lancewood tree along this shore, with the long spiky leaves of the juveniles changing to the shorter, rounder leaves of the adult as the tree grows in height. Don't turn left at the track junction, but carry on around the shoreline of the peninsula. The track will gradually turn back on itself at **Picnic Point**, before making a scramble up to the top of **Bob's Knob** (385m). There are stunning views from here and it makes a great picnic spot.

03 Make the short scramble down the other side, and if you've had enough, take the track back to Bob's Cove beach from near the jetty you already passed; make your way back to the beach and car park. If you're up for more, after scrambling down off Bob's Knob, follow the coastal track along the edge of Lake Wakatipu for an hour to **Twelve Mile Delta**, a popular *Lord of the Rings* filming location. Along the way, you'll find a couple of beaches, beautiful native forest and possibly fossils of oyster shells and other molluscs at **Farry's Beach**. Allow two hours to walk down to Twelve Mile Delta and back.

Take a Break

A natural place for liquid refreshments after a walk at Bob's Cove is **1876** *(1876.co.nz)*, the bar that now occupies Queenstown's old courthouse, built in, you guessed it, 1876. Lime mortar from Bob's Cove was used between the stone blocks. Inside, you'll find the old judge's bench, while if you sit outside on the terrace, you can admire the 'Trees of Justice', two massive wellingtonia (sequoia) trees planted in the 1870s to provide shade for those awaiting justice.

04 A possible addition to the walk, either at the start or end of your adventure, is to wander along the **Bob's Cove Bridle Track**, part of the original track linking Queenstown with Glenorchy. The trail from the car park is well marked along the northern side of Bob's Cove and includes stands of massive red beech trees. Keep your eyes open for kererū (native pigeon).

48

Lake Hayes

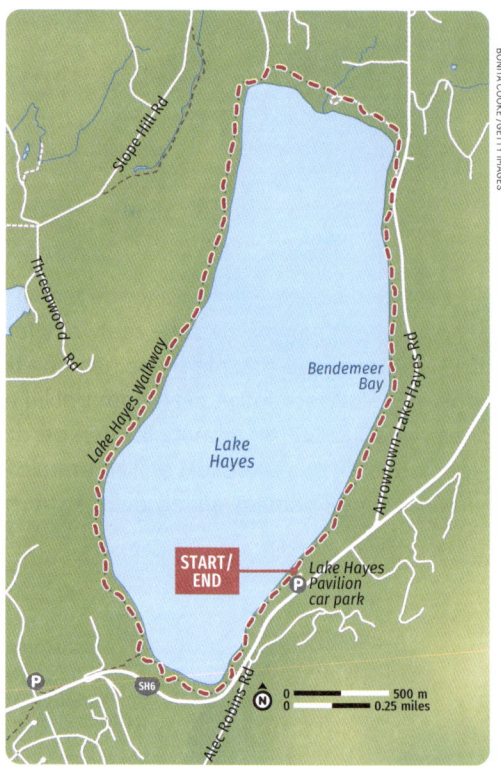

DURATION	DIFFICULTY	DISTANCE	START/END
3hrs	Easy	8km	Lake Hayes Pavilion

TERRAIN	A well-formed and maintained trail

Sitting placidly between Queenstown and Arrowtown, Lake Hayes often offers mirror-perfect reflections of the surrounding hills and mountains, leading some to claim it as the most photographed lake in New Zealand. Autumn colours are spectacular.

Around 14,000 years ago, little Lake Hayes was joined to the Frankton Arm of Lake Wakatipu. Now it sits in quiet isolation, 4km south of Arrowtown, on the road to Queenstown. Park at Lake Hayes Pavilion on SH6 and take the path down to the lake. You can walk the track in either direction. We suggest turning left and heading clockwise around the lake.

The southern end features boardwalks over **wetland** where you'll have a good chance of spotting local **birdlife** such as the Australasian crested grebe. When you are around the end of the lake, the track turns north and, on the western side, you'll be walking through pastoral farmland for about 3km to **Lake Hayes Reserve** at the lake's northern end. Lots of people camp here; there are public toilets and an attractive **swimming beach**.

Carry on around to walk south on the eastern edge of the lake, past holiday houses, some of the area's most notable homes, **Bendemeer Bay**, the Wakatipu Rowing Club and back to Lake Hayes Pavilion. Keep in mind that you're likely to be sharing the trail with runners and mountain bikers. Lake Hayes is particularly attractive in autumn when the willows, poplars and oaks that surround it turn to gold – worth as much to locals these days as that which was panned out of local rivers during the gold-rush days.

Lake Hayes

49

Routeburn Track Day Walk

DURATION	DIFFICULTY	DISTANCE	START/END
6–8hrs	Moderate	22km	Routeburn Shelter

TERRAIN	Well-maintained track that is steepish in parts

Routeburn Flats

Outdoor enthusiasts will have heard of the legendary Routeburn Track, the 32km, three-day hike that crosses the Southern Alps' Main Divide and is one of the country's Great Walks. This day walk involves walking at the eastern end of the Routeburn Track, approached from Queenstown and Glenorchy. We also have the Key Summit day walk on p198, which is at the western end of the Routeburn Track. The walk described here follows the Route Burn river up through dense beech forest to the tree line at Routeburn Falls Hut on an easy-to-follow track. It can be shortened to the one-hour Nature Walk or the four- to five-hour return walk up as far as Routeburn Flats Hut.

Getting Here

Routeburn Shelter, where the track starts, is 25km from Glenorchy, at the northern end of Lake Wakatipu. The last 9km of the road is gravel and very dusty in summer. Glenorchy, in turn, is a 44km drive from Queenstown. It's easiest to get to the track and explore the surrounding area if you have your own wheels. If not, there are plenty of transport options from Queenstown, including a number of companies offering guided day walks.

Starting Point

Routeburn Shelter has a sizeable car park, toilets, information boards, seating and a roof under which to shelter. There's nothing else in the way of facilities. Bring what you're going to need with you, including rain gear. The track starts on the far side of the road from the shelter.

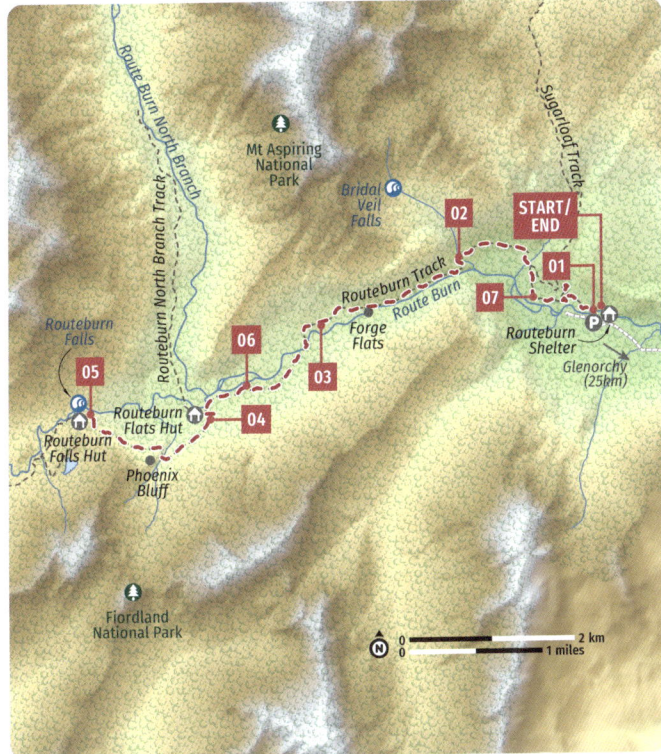

Mt Aspiring/ Tititea National Park

Alpine meadows, craggy mountains, braided glacial rivers, verdant valleys and more than 100 glaciers make **Mt Aspiring/ Tititea National Park** an outdoor enthusiast's paradise.

A national park since 1964, and later included in the Te Wāhipounamu (Southwest New Zealand) World Heritage Area, the park now covers 3555 sq km along the Southern Alps. Lording over it is colossal Mt Aspiring/Tititea (3033m), the highest peak outside the Aoraki/Mt Cook area. While the southern end of the national park near Glenorchy includes famed tramps, such as the Routeburn, there are also excellent walks such as the Rob Roy Track (p166) off the Matukituki Valley, close to Wānaka.

01 The track begins with a crossing of the Route Burn river on a **swing bridge** before winding through a forest of red, silver and mountain beech to a swing bridge over Sugar Loaf Stream. The lovely **Routeburn Nature Walk** is a loop trail in this first section of the track that takes about an hour to return to the car park and makes a more-than-worthy stroll should you only be looking for a short walk. The **forest** here is magnificent, with red beech trees towering overhead.

02 When you're across the stream, the track climbs gently for 20 to 25 minutes until it reaches a **bridge** over the small gorge carved by **Bridal Veil Falls**. You may have noticed the falls on the drive into the valley. Canyoning tours start at this bridge, with descents to the Route Burn.

03 More impressive rock scenery follows as the track sidles through **Routeburn Gorge**, providing ample opportunities to peer into the deep pools at the bottom. The dramatic views end at **Forge Flats**, a gravel bar along a sharp bend in the Route Burn and a popular place to linger in the sun. DOC has released a number of whio (blue ducks) in the Routeburn Valley, so keep your eyes out for this endangered species that features on the NZ$10 note and is one of few waterfowl worldwide that live year-round on fast-flowing rivers.

04 Just beyond Forge Flats, the track uses a long swing bridge to cross to the true right (south) side of the Route Burn and heads back into bush, where it skirts the grassy flats. It's an easy 30-minute stroll along a level track through the bush to a signposted junction, where the right fork leads to **Routeburn Flats Hut** (with 20 bunks), five minutes away. The hut overlooks the river, the grassy flats, a wide valley known as the Route Burn North Branch on the far side of river, and the snow-capped mountains to the north. If you're feeling enthused, wade across the river where there is a marker on the far side and follow the obvious trail into the **North Branch**, where you're unlikely to run into another walker. Many make the Routeburn Flats Hut their target for the day; if you return back to Routeburn Shelter from here, the return hike totals 16km and takes four to five hours.

05 Back at the track junction, if you're carrying on, the main track begins a steady ascent towards Routeburn Falls Hut. The track climbs 270m over 3km to reach the hut above the bushline. The Emily Creek footbridge is the halfway point of the climb and, just beyond it the track, sidles a steep rock face called **Phoenix Bluff**. The track soon crosses a huge slip, where a massive 1994 landslide sent trees crashing down to the flats below. The resultant forest clearing affords magnificent views of the valley and surrounding peaks. From the slip, you resume the steady but rocky climb to **Routeburn Falls Hut** (48 bunks),

the scene of many comings and goings. The hut is right at the bushline (1005m) and its long veranda offers views of the flats and the surrounding Humboldt Mountains. It's a short climb up to the impressive **Routeburn Falls**, which tumble down a series of rock ledges.

06 Follow the track back down to Routeburn Flats when you are ready to head back out. At the first grassy spot you meet past the junction (back on the main track on the flats), take the well-worn unmarked track that heads away at 90 degrees down to the river. Turn downstream and follow this track (it was the main Routeburn track before the 1994 floods) for a delightful wander through **open grassland**, then through riverside beech forest, that eventually links back up with the main track after about 20 minutes. Don't take this side track if it's been raining or you'll have wet feet.

07 When you're back on the main track, follow it back down through the gorge to Routeburn Shelter.

☕ Take a Break

There's nowhere to get food or refreshments after Glenorchy. Either stock up there or before leaving Queenstown.

For a stunning place to stay overnight, consider the **Kinloch Wilderness Retreat** (kinlochlodge.co.nz) at Kinloch on the western side of the northern tip of Lake Wakatipu, just 3km across the lake from Glenorchy by boat, but 26km by road. This wonderfully remote 1868 lodge offers heritage rooms, backpacker-style 'wilderness rooms' and a top restaurant and bar. The open-air hot tub has cracking mountain and lake views. The lodge is 20km south from the Routeburn Track trailhead, a similar distance north from the start of the Greenstone and Caples Tracks, runs track transport daily and makes a great base for exploring the area.

Routeburn Track

The Road to Paradise

Road signs in Glenorchy promote the town as the 'Gateway to Paradise' and it is...literally. Paradise lies around 15km to the north. The road from Glenorchy to Paradise, which is gravel from the Kinloch/Routeburn turn-off, heads up the broad valley, edging along the foot of the Richardson Range.

Approaching Paradise it cuts through a beautiful section of beech forest on the shores of Diamond Lake before fording the River Jordan – how's that for a biblical entrance to paradise! – passing Arcadia Station (think sheep not trains) and arriving at Paradise. There's not much here, but it sure is pretty. So pretty that *Lord of the Rings* legend Sir Ian McKellen described it as his 'favourite place on Earth'.

50

Sandymount & Sandfly Bay

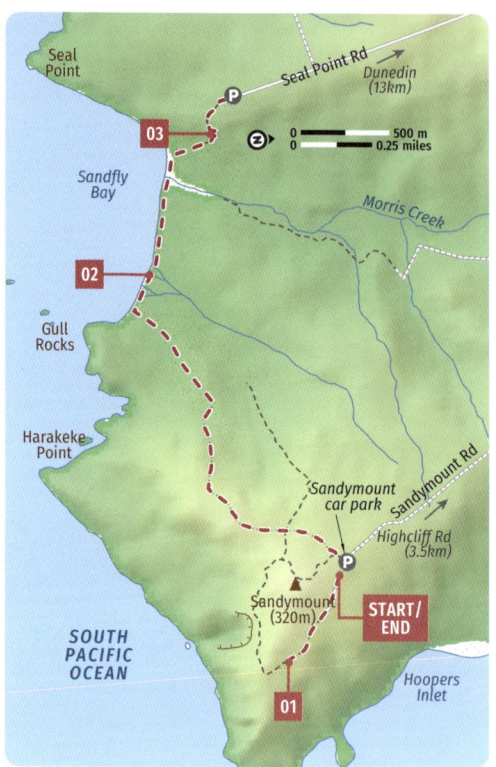

DURATION	DIFFICULTY	DISTANCE	START/END
1½ hrs	Easy – Moderate	4.4km return	Sandymount car park

TERRAIN	Sandy, well-defined trails

Otago Peninsula, within close proximity of Dunedin, offers some excellent walking options. Two particularly spectacular walks are a 30-minute 1.7km return track to a viewpoint at Sandymount and a walk to Sandfly Bay, a breathtakingly wild and beautiful southern beach. It's 1½ hours return from Sandymount car park down to Sandfly Bay, but an easier option is to drive to the car park at the end of Seal Point Rd and walk down to Sandfly Bay and back.

Getting Here

Both Sandymount Rd and Seal Point Rd are turns southeast off Highcliff Rd, the road that runs along the top of the spine of Otago Peninsula from Dunedin to Portobello. Both car parks are a 20- to 30-minute drive from central Dunedin.

Starting Point

The track starts at the Sandymount Recreation Reserve car park at the end of Sandymount Road. Park here and walk straight up through the stand of tall macrocarpa (Monterey cypress) trees.

01 As this track runs through private farmland, it is closed from 1 September to 15 October through the lambing season. The walk is 1.7km return to a viewpoint around **Sandymount** (320m) which, as its name suggests, is a mountain of sand, covered with native scrub and flora, including flax, which lines the track to the top. You'll have tremendous **views** over Hoopers Inlet, Allans Beach and out to Cape Saunders as you walk through working farmland, out to the DOC viewpoint. Return to walk to Sandfly Bay.

Best for

SPOTTING WILDLIFE

Sandfly Bay

Local Wildlife

Sandfly Bay has a small colony of yellow-eyed penguins (hoiho), though numbers are alarmingly on the decline. If you encounter a penguin on the beach keep well away and crouch down. The penguins will not come ashore if they feel threatened. New Zealand fur seals (kekeno) and sea lions (rāpoka) haul out on the rocks and beach and love to wallow in the sand. Also keep well away from sleeping sea lions and if you are in a group don't surround them. Seals and sea lions may look placid but they are powerful, wild predators and can be very dangerous if they feel you've come too close. Seabirds such as spotted shags, sooty shearwaters and variable oystercatchers are also common around here.

02 To get to **Sandfly Bay**, descend back to just short of the car park and follow the sandy track as it winds its way down to the beach, taking around an hour. The windswept landscape is spectacular – apparently Sandfly Bay got its name from the regular strong winds 'making the sand fly' rather than from the pesky little insect hated by walkers. Walk as far along the beach as you like, then make the long climb back up the same track to Sandymount car park.

03 If you're doing two separate hikes, after visiting the viewpoint at Sandymount, carry on down to the Sandymount car park. Drive back up to Hillcliff Rd, turn left and, in less that a kilometre, turn left down Seal Point Rd and drive to the car park at the end. Initially, the track crosses farmland to a **viewpoint** out over the bay, then drops down through sand dunes to the beach. Walk along on the sand and return when you feel like it. Allow one to 1½ hours.

☕ Take a Break

If you're up for refreshments after your walk, carry on along Highcliff Rd (away from Dunedin) until it descends into the small, inland harbour village of Portobello. Here, you'll find places such as **Portobello Treats & Sweets** for ice cream and milkshakes, **Penguin Cafe** and **1908 Cafe Restaurant** for meals, and the **Portobello Hotel & Bistro** should you be after fish and chips and a cold beer.

51

Long Beach

DURATION	DIFFICULTY	DISTANCE	START/END
2hrs	Easy	6km return	Long Beach car park
TERRAIN		Grass and sand	

This walk on the coast, about 20km northeast of central Dunedin, is one for families. Kids will love running down the windswept beach and exploring a spectacular large cave surrounded by cliffs.

The track starts at the car park, which has a simple playground, at the end of Mihiwaka Rd, off Purakanui Rd on the way to the small coastal settlement of Pūrākanui. A loop track to the right takes in a 600m grassy track at **Long Beach Recreation Reserve**.

After circling the loop track, head down the walking track off the car park to the very end of the beach to explore the sand dunes, rock formations and caves along this stretch of dramatic southern coastline. It's a popular swimming location but it will blow out the cobwebs; the wind can often be bracing here, but that's all part of the fun. You may see local climbers attempting some of the rock faces, too.

Allow kids (and adults) plenty of play time in the stunning **sea caves**, dunes and on the beach. Sea lions breed at Long Beach during the summer period, and kororā blue penguins have been known to use the caves to shelter and for nesting. Give them, and indeed all wildlife, a wide berth.

Best for

ESCAPING THE CITY

OTAGO 51 LONG BEACH

Long Beach

Also Try...

Makarora River, Blue Pools

Lake Rere

DURATION	DIFFICULTY	DISTANCE
4–5hrs	Easy-Moderate	14km

This walk starts at the Greenstone Track car park, 20km south of Kinloch at the northern end of Lake Wakatipu.

It initially involves following the Greenstone Track, a route used by Māori in centuries past to head out to the West Coast in search of greenstone, before it crosses the Greenstone River on a footbridge and climbs 200 vertical metres up to secluded Lake Rere. The track rounds the northern side of the lake before heading through a 'rock garden' of massive boulders that have tumbled down the slopes of Tooth Peak, high above, after which it descends out to Lake Wakatipu's Elfin Bay. This was a popular walk in the late 1800s for locals who enjoyed strolls and picnics beside the alpine lake, reaching Elfin Bay by steamer from Queenstown Bay. From Elfin Bay, walk 2km through farmland back to the car park.

Sawpit Gully

DURATION	DIFFICULTY	DISTANCE
3hrs	Moderate	7km

This walk is especially beautiful in autumn when leaves in the Arrowtown area turn a gorgeous gold.

This loop track can be walked in either direction from the car park at the Historic Arrowtown Chinese Settlement, 20km northeast of Queenstown. If walking anticlockwise, follow the Arrow River Trail as it climbs above the Arrow River until you reach signage for Sawpit Gully. The track climbs steeply northwest into a gully and, if it's been raining, you'll be getting your feet wet crossing the stream a number of times. Climb to the grassy saddle between German Hill and Brow Peak for spectacular views out over Lake Hayes and the Remarkables. Drop into Sawpit Gully, with its gold-mining tailings, then continue down through forest until the track runs into the Bush Creek Trail. Turn left and follow the wide track back to Arrowtown.

Queenstown Hill

Blue Pools

DURATION	DIFFICULTY	DISTANCE
45mins return	Easy	3km return

A great short walk for those travelling on SH6 over the Haast Pass, between Wānaka and Haast.

About 9km north of Makarora, from the Blue Pools car park, take the track through beech forest, across a bridge over the Makarora River, then on a boardwalk to a second bridge over a tributary creek. Below are the spectacular Blue Pools, natural wonders of pure glacial water gathered from the surrounding mountains. Drop down for some fun on the rocky beach and keep your eye out for mōhua (yellowhead).

Queenstown Hill

DURATION	DIFFICULTY	DISTANCE
3hrs	Easy–Moderate	7km

A favourite with Queenstown locals, this walk offers spectacular views of Lake Wakatipu and the surrounding mountains.

Walk from town or park in the small Belfast Tce car park before climbing 500m through pine forest to the summit of Te Tapu-nui ('mountain of intense sacredness'). Along the way you'll pass the *Basket of Dreams* sculpture as well as information plates explaining aspects of Lake Wakatipu and Queenstown. The view from the top takes in the Remarkables, Cecil Peak, Walter Peak, Ben Lomond, Frankton Arm and Queenstown Bay.

Gertrude Saddle Track (p198)

The South

52 **Milford Track Day Walk**
Take a boat ride and wander up the spectacular Clinton Valley. **p194**

53 **Gertrude Saddle**
Incomparable views of Milford Sound/Piopiotahi and the Fiordland National Park. **p198**

54 **Lake Marian**
This gorgeous alpine lake sits in its own hanging valley. **p200**

55 **Key Summit**
A 360-degree panorama of mountains and glacial-carved valleys. **p202**

56 **Mavora Walkway**
Amble through lakeside beech forest in this seldom-visited valley. **p204**

57 **Brod Bay to Te Anau**
Walk part of the Kepler Track and visit Te Anau's Bird Sanctuary. **p206**

58 **Rainbow Reach to Shallow Bay**
Easy walk through beautiful bush to Lake Manapōuri. **p208**

59 **Ulva Island - Te Wharawhara Marine Reserve**
Rakiura's predator-free island with a plethora of native birds. **p210**

60 **Port William/Potirepo to Halfmoon Bay/Oban**
Take a boat and walk back along the Rakiura Track to Halfmoon Bay/Oban. **p212**

Explore

The South

Fiordland National Park is almost a byword for Aotearoa/New Zealand hiking. Here, you'll find the track that was once billed as the 'finest walk in the world' along with the greatest representation of Great Walks in the country, with four of them – the Milford, Routeburn, Kepler and Rakiura Tracks – found in Fiordland and Stewart Island. They may all be multiday hikes, but parts of them can be accessed for some of Aotearoa/New Zealand's top day walks, and we have a portion of each described in this chapter. This is the deep-green deep south, a still-untamed outdoor treasure that's anchored by Aotearoa/New Zealand's largest national park.

Te Anau

Picturesque Te Anau is the main gateway to Milford Sound/Piopiotahi, Fiordland National Park and three Great Walks: the Milford, Kepler and Routeburn Tracks. The township borders Lake Te Anau, Aotearoa/New Zealand's second-largest lake, whose glacier-gouged fiords wind into secluded forest on its western shore. Visitors are spoiled for day-walk options if based here. Te Anau is a summer town, making its living between November and April by catering to sightseers and hikers, with plenty of accommodation options, cafes, restaurants and outdoor equipment shops.

The Fiordland National Park Visitor Centre is here, as is the opportunity to visit the town's bird sanctuary.

Invercargill

Any trip to Stewart Island/Rakiura inevitably includes a stopover in Invercargill, the southernmost city in NZ. Stock up on supplies here before heading to Stewart Island/Rakiura by ferry from Bluff, 28km to the south. You can also fly to Stewart Island/Rakiura from Invercargill's airport. As you'd expect of a city of 50,000, Invercargill offers plenty of places to sleep, eat and play.

WHEN TO GO

In a word, Fiordland is damp: waterfalls, lakes, fiords – and rain. Prevailing winds from the Tasman Sea dump up to 8000mm annually at Milford Sound/Piopiotahi on the western side of the Southern Alps, although Te Anau, to the east and sheltered by the mountains, averages just 1200mm. Overall, Fiordland NP averages 200 rainy days annually. Similarly Stewart Island/Rakiura's rainfall has been known to wreak hiking havoc. The annual measure at Halfmoon Bay may be a relatively low 1600mm, but it occurs over 275 days of the year. In general, you're likely to strike more rain in October/November than in February/March.

Halfmoon Bay/Oban

Tiny Halfmoon Bay/Oban, Stewart Island/Rakiura's only settlement, population 340 (give or take a few!) is a joy if you like far-flung isolated islands. With the ferry arriving here from Bluff, this is your entry point to Rakiura's tracks, wilderness and amazing birdlife. Rakiura has one of the largest and most diverse bird populations of anywhere in Aotearoa/New Zealand. Even in the streets of Halfmoon Bay/Oban the air resonates with birds such as tui, bellbirds and kākā, which share their island home with weka, kākāriki, fernbirds, robins and Rakiura tokoeka (brown kiwi). There are limited places to sleep and eat, so you may want to get organised before you go.

WHERE TO STAY
Te Anau is the gateway to Fiordland NP, especially for those who want to explore the Te Anau to Milford Sound road. There are plenty of places to stay here. Manapōuri, 20km south of Te Anau, is the access point to Doubtful Sound and a quieter option. If you're heading to Stewart Island/Rakiura, chances are you'll spend a night in Invercargill. There are various options in Halfmoon Bay/Oban.

TRANSPORT
Invercargill is the main transport hub within the region, with flights to and from Auckland, Christchurch and Stewart Island/Rakiura, and buses from as far afield as Queenstown and Dunedin. Te Anau has direct bus connections with Queenstown and Dunedin. Many of those intending to visit Milford Sound/Piopiotahi and Fiordland NP fly into Queenstown International Airport before making their way to Te Anau.

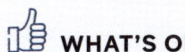
WHAT'S ON

Kepler Challenge & Luxmore Grunt
(keplerchallenge.co.nz)
Held annually since 1988 in Te Anau in early December, the Kepler Challenge involves running the full 60km of the Kepler Track. The Luxmore Grunt is a 27km race from Te Anau up Mt Luxmore and back, held on the same day.

Curio Bay Big Dig
(catlins.org.nz/events)
Sand modelling at Curio Bay in the Catlins in late December.

The Routeburn Classic
(goodtimesevents.net)
A race over the length of the Routeburn Track held in late April.

Resources

Destination Fiordland
(fiordland.org.nz)

Discover Southland
(southlandnz.com)

Stewart Island/Rakiura
(stewartisland.co.nz)

The Catlins
(catlins.org.nz)

DOC Fiordland National Park Visitor Centre
(doc.govt.nz)

DOC Rakiura National Park Visitor Centre
(doc.govt.nz)

Real Journeys
(realjourneys.co.nz)
Boat travel in Fiordland NP and to Stewart Island/Rakiura

Stewart Island Flights
(stewartislandflightsco.nz)
Air travel to the island

52

Milford Track Day Walk

Clinton Hut (p196)

DURATION	DIFFICULTY	DISTANCE	START/END
5hrs	Easy	11km return	Glade Wharf

TERRAIN	Well-maintained, easy-to-follow track

This day walk on the legendary Milford Track includes a boat trip from Te Anau Downs to Glade Wharf at the head of Lake Te Anau, hiking the track up to Clinton Hut, the first DOC overnight hut on the track for independent hikers, then retracing your steps to Glade Wharf and taking the boat back to Te Anau Downs. It's a teaser for walking the whole track, but an excellent option for those with limited time. Various companies in Te Anau operate fully guided package trips that include bus and boat transfers, guide and lunch, but you can also book the boat and do this day hike independently.

Getting Here

The Fiordland Outdoors boat leaves from Te Anau Downs, 27km from Te Anau on the road to Milford Sound/Piopiotahi, where there is a car-parking area. If you don't have a car, book a return bus trip to Te Anau Downs with Fiordland Outdoors in Te Anau. Book return boat transfers from Te Anau Downs to Glade Wharf with **Fiordland Outdoors** (fiordlandoutdoors.co.nz) for adult/child $125/75, operating 1 November to the end of April. The boat leaves Te Anau Downs at 11.30am, returning there at 5pm; it leaves Glade Wharf again at 4pm. This gives you 3½ hours walking time. Outside of these dates, check what is available at the Fiordland National Park Visitor Centre in Te Anau.

Starting Point

Glade Wharf, at the head of Lake Te Anau, is the starting point for your walk.

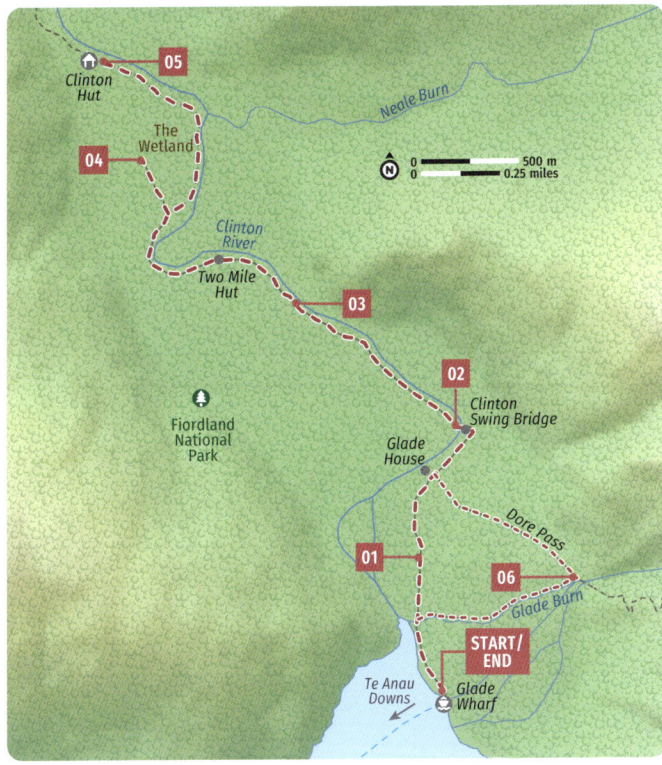

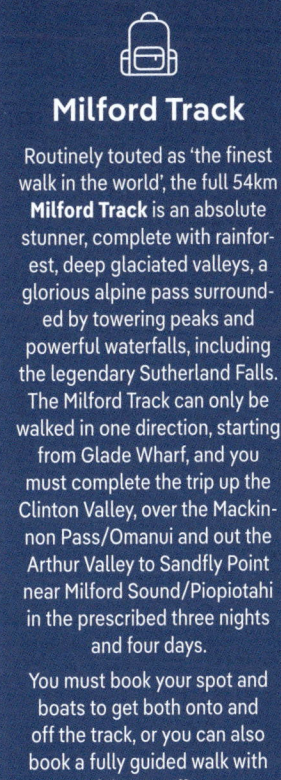

Milford Track

Routinely touted as 'the finest walk in the world', the full 54km **Milford Track** is an absolute stunner, complete with rainforest, deep glaciated valleys, a glorious alpine pass surrounded by towering peaks and powerful waterfalls, including the legendary Sutherland Falls. The Milford Track can only be walked in one direction, starting from Glade Wharf, and you must complete the trip up the Clinton Valley, over the Mackinnon Pass/Omanui and out the Arthur Valley to Sandfly Point near Milford Sound/Piopiotahi in the prescribed three nights and four days.

You must book your spot and boats to get both onto and off the track, or you can also book a fully guided walk with **Ultimate Hikes** (ultimatehikes.co.nz).

01 When you get off the boat at Glade Wharf, there's no need to rush as your only time target is to meet the boat's 4pm departure deadline back to Te Anau Downs (though it's a good idea to get back 20 minutes earlier than that). Everyone gets a photo with the Milford Track sign, just in from the wharf under the massive beech tree.

While it's only a 20-minute walk on what is essentially an unpaved vehicle track to get to **Glade House**, a private lodge for guests on the Ultimate Hikes guided walks package, it's a stunning introduction to the Clinton Valley, with incredibly green moss-draped **native forest** an indication of the increased levels of rainfall as you get nearer to the South Island's continental divide. While Glade House looks welcoming – there's a big 'Welcome' sign, it is a private lodge and not open to independent walkers or the public.

02 By this time, you'll probably have caught sight of the massive **swing bridge** over the Clinton River at the far end of Glade House's glade. High to the right is **Dore Pass**, which has an alpine track taking eight to 10 hours of hard hiking to connect Glade House in the Clinton Valley with the Milford Rd near Knobs Flat in the neighbouring Eglinton Valley. This is the only alternative to the boat for getting onto the Milford Track, though not many people use it. Walk down and cross the swing bridge, taking time to gaze into the clear Clinton River waters and look for trout and native eels. Your eyes will take time to adjust, so don't rush.

195

03 After climbing down off the swing bridge, the wide track follows the western side of the Clinton River through gorgeous **beech forest**, with ample opportunities to sit riverside and spot those elusive trout. Keen fishers are allowed to fly fish here, but you'll need to get a licence and talk to the DOC at the National Park Visitor Centre in Te Anau before you go.

New bits of track are at places where old sections have eroded into the river in times of heavy rain and flooding. The track is wide as packhorses were used to supply huts further up the valley until helicopters took over in the late 1970s. You'll pass the remains of Quintin McKinnon's original **Two Mile Hut** at the point where he could get no further up the river by boat; look for remnants of the old telephone line that linked huts before 'wireless' came into use in the valley. There is still no mobile phone coverage here.

04 A 15-minute signposted side track to **The Wetland** takes you onto a loop track to check out wetland flora and get spectacular views of the glacial carved valley. All the way along the track, you'll have the opportunity to spot birds such as friendly South Island bush robins, tomtits, fantails and bellbirds. Ahead, seeming to sit almost in the middle of the valley, is **The Sentinel**, an imposing peak in its own right. The full Milford Track heads up the valley to its left, continuing up to Mackinnon Pass/Omanui.

05 Shortly before Clinton Hut, where the Clinton River is joined by the Neale Burn, there is a lovely beach where it's possible to take a dip. **Clinton Hut** is on a side track just after a short climb that takes you above the river. This is a DOC-run hut and independent day walkers can use the excellent facilities – which will be especially welcome if it has been raining.

06 On the return trip, for a bit of an adventure off the main track: after you have crossed the swing bridge over the Clinton River, instead of following the track along the riverbank to pass Glade House, follow the obvious trail by the public toilet that heads straight

☕ Take a Break

There is nowhere to buy food and refreshments once you have left Te Anau. Make sure to buy picnic supplies before you leave town. There is a big **Fresh Choice Supermarket** in the middle of Te Anau, plus the **Wapiti Bakery & Cafe** is nearby with a decent selection of picnic goodies.

Swing bridge, Clinton River

ahead and into the forest. This track is the narrowest you'll have walked on all day and, after about 20 minutes of meandering and climbing through the forest, it will bring you to the **Glade Burn**, a refreshingly cold bouldery creek that makes a great spot for a rest.

Staying on the north side of the creek, head downhill through more bouldery terrain of lichen-covered rock for 10 to 15 minutes until you run into the main Milford Track that you walked along that morning. Turn left to reach Glade Wharf in another 10 to 15 minutes. Whatever you do, don't miss the boat!

Quintin McKinnon

As you wander the Te Anau waterfront, down near the Fiordland National Park Visitor Centre keep an eye out for the small bronze statue of Quintin McPherson McKinnon (1851–92), erected in 1988, 100 years after he and Ernest Mitchell were given credit for discovering the Mackinnon Pass/Omanui and establishing the Milford Track.

An adventuring Scotsman, McKinnon went on to become the Milford Track's first guide, improving the trail and taking parties of visitors by boat up to the north of the lake, walking up the Clinton Valley and over the Mackinnon Pass/Omanui to see the Sutherland Falls (580m). McKinnon was presumed drowned on Lake Te Anau in 1892 when his wrecked boat was discovered, though his body was never found.

53

Gertrude Saddle

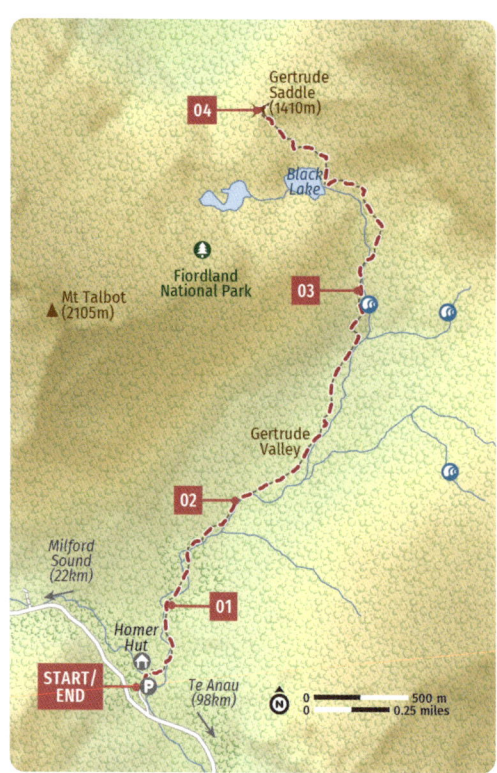

DURATION	DIFFICULTY	DISTANCE	START/END
4–6hrs	Hard	7km	Gertrude car park

TERRAIN	Easy valley walk; steep climb to saddle

Few ways of viewing Milford Sound/Piopiotahi include the solitude and sense of achievement that comes with standing atop Gertrude Saddle. This is a challenging but rewarding climb to a mountain pass, which can be shortened to a two-hour hike through the valley to the base of the climb and back. Walking in the glacial cirque that is the Gertrude Valley will itself provide plenty of memorable mountain scenes.

Getting Here

The trailhead is 98km from Te Anau along the Te Anau–Milford Hwy, just 2km before the Homer Tunnel. There is car parking here. It may be possible to arrange bus transport to the start of the hike – ask at Fiordland National Park Visitor Centre in Te Anau.

Starting Point

The track begins at the car park. Do not attempt this hike if it is or has been raining heavily.

01 From the car park, you'll be looking straight up the Gertrude Valley to the imposing wall of Barrier Peak – the saddle is tucked away in an unseen gap to the left of the wall, behind Mt Talbot, which rises directly along the left side of the valley. Cross the stream bed (usually dry), where the track begins, passing Homer Hut to the left and heading up the **valley**.

02 The stony trail stays close to the stream bed, and sometimes is in it, following orange-tipped poles. As the track nears the head of the valley with its enormous **wall of rock**,

Gertrude Saddle

Sound or Fiord?

As you gaze down on Milford Sound/Piopiotahi from the Gertrude Saddle, consider this: it is not actually a sound, but a fiord.

A sound is a valley carved by river action, later flooded by the sea, while a fiord is carved by glacial action, then flooded by the sea after the melting of the glacier. The 13 sounds of Fiordland National Park were misnamed by early explorers as sounds, though things were set right somewhat when the national park was created in 1952 as Fiordland NP. The word 'fiord' comes from Norwegian and is a loanword to New Zealand English. There are many other examples of NZ misnomers. The Mt Cook lily is in fact the world's largest buttercup.

it swings left, turning towards the obvious notch that will be your path up to the saddle.

03 Here, one hour from the car park, the poled route ends and a track continues, heading up to the left of the waterfall face (look for the cairns), beginning the **500m ascent** to Gertrude Saddle. The route crosses the first braid of the falls, then continues ascending a small ridge pinched between streams. After 15 minutes you'll come to a large rock wall, where the track swings right, crossing the main stream. Gertrude Saddle now becomes prominent above, with the track leading up to the shores of **Black Lake** and then directly up to the saddle. There are chains to assist on the ascent immediately below the lake and on the first bit of the climb just after it.

04 As you rise to **Gertrude Saddle** (1410m), shaped a little like a sagging rope strung between Barrier Knob and Mt Talbot, an extraordinary view awaits. The Darran Mountains rise like broken fingers, while it's difficult not to get excited by the glistening sight of Milford Sound/Piopiotahi pooled between a wide gap in the mountains. You can probably expect a visit from a kea on the saddle. Return to the car park along the same route, stepping carefully over the rocks on the descent.

 Take a Break

For a picnic on the walk, make sure to get supplies before leaving Te Anau. The closest place to the hike to head for refreshments is in Milford Sound/Piopiotahi at the **Discover Milford Sound Information Centre & Cafe**.

The 22km drive from the Gertrude car park through the Homer Tunnel and down through the Cleddau Valley out to Milford is one of the most spectacular drives in the world and should not be missed.

54

Lake Marian

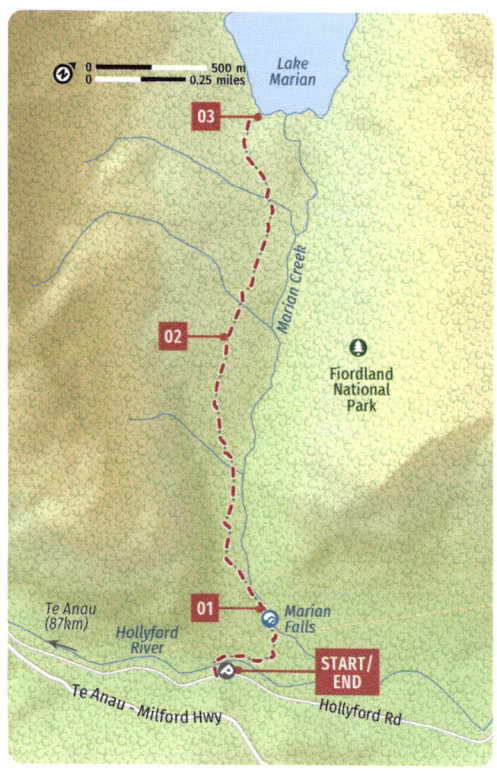

DURATION	DIFFICULTY	DISTANCE	START/END
3-4hrs	Moderate	6km	Lake Marian car park

TERRAIN	400m climb on rough track

Climb up through native forest into a hanging valley that once contained the head of a tributary glacier that flowed into the main Hollyford Glacier during the last ice age, 14,000 years ago. Just as rivers have tributaries, so do glaciers. This hanging valley's glacier has long gone though and the valley now holds gorgeous Lake Marian, surrounded by steep rock walls, perfect snowcapped peaks and endless photo opportunities.

Getting Here

The trailhead is 88km from Te Anau. Take the Te Anau–Milford Hwy for 87km, then turn right onto Hollyford Rd at Marian Corner. The car park is 1km down the gravel road on the left.

Starting Point

The track begins at the swing bridge over the Hollyford River at the Lake Marian car park.

 01 Cross the swing bridge, then head downriver for about 10 minutes, through pristine forest until you reach a spectacular series of rapids and waterfalls. This is **Marian Falls** on Marian Creek and the icy water is tumbling down out of Lake Marian, close to 400 vertical metres above you – and the target for your walk. The track climbs on a wooden boardwalk through this section, which is the DOC Lake Marian Falls short walk. The DOC advises that the track is a backcountry hike beyond this point and that walkers should be suitably prepared;

Lake Marian

The Hollyford Road

There's plenty of exploring to be done down the 18km deadend Hollyford Rd. You'll pass the former historic **Gunn's Camp**, mowed down by a landslide in 2020. The four- to eight-day Hollyford Track starts here, but the road also provides access to several spectacular day walks, including the **Hidden Falls Track**. The **Humboldt Falls Track** (30 minutes return) takes you to a viewing platform with views of the distant 275m-high cascade.

Lake Marian is gorgeous on a good day, but this walk should not be attempted in bad weather.

02 From here, while still easy to follow, the track steepens and becomes rocky, with tree roots and muddy sections, especially after it has been raining. There's a **stream crossing** that should not be attempted after heavy rain. Allow 1½ hours of steady climbing, then a final steepish spot over the moraine wall that blocked the valley and created Lake Marian.

03 On a good-weather day, this **alpine lake** is truly spectacular, hemmed in by steep mountain walls and surrounded by large boulders that have tumbled off the high peaks. When there's no wind, the snow-capped mountain reflections are hard to beat. Facing into the valley, Mt Lyttle (1899m) is high to your right, Mt Crosscut (2263m) is more or less dead ahead and Mt Christina (2474m) is high to your left. The track ends at the lake's edge, but it's also possible to do some careful exploring around the lake and further up the valley. Don't walk around the lake edge during winter and spring as this is avalanche country and avalanches don't give warnings.

Lake Marian was named by Surveyor-General EH Wilmot in 1889 after his cousin, Marian Lyttle.

Return to your car on the same track, being careful on the descent, especially if the track is slippery.

☕ Take a Break

Take picnic supplies from Te Anau for lunch at the lake. When you're back at your car drive to Milford and stop at **Discover Milford Sound Information Centre & Cafe** for refreshments. With good timing, it's possible to do this hike and take a cruise on Milford Sound/Piopiotahi on a day trip from Te Anau.

55

Key Summit

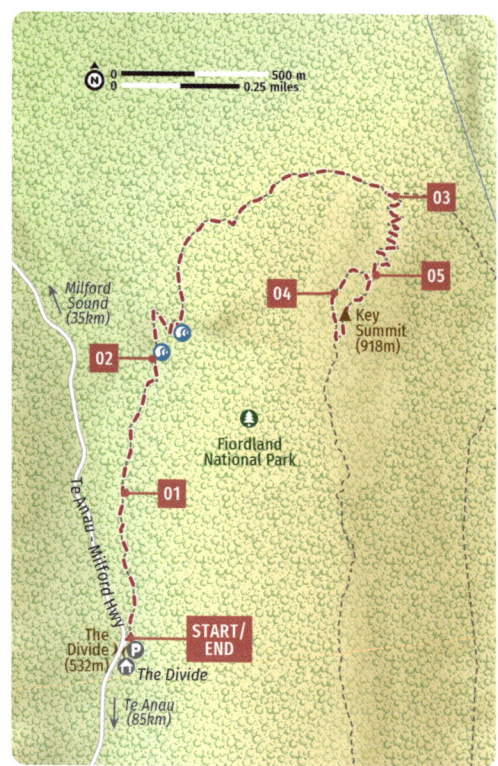

DURATION	DIFFICULTY	DISTANCE	START/END
3–4hrs	Moderate	7km	Divide car park
TERRAIN	Well-maintained track; 400m climb and descent		

This walk is at the western end of the well-known Routeburn Track, starting at The Divide (532m) on the Te Anau–Milford road. It offers a spectacular 360-degree panorama of Fiordland National Park when you get to Key Summit (918m), which is the bald summit and water divide sitting between three 'key' catchments: the Hollyford River flows west out to the Tasman Sea, the Greenstone River flows to Lake Wakatipu and eventually out east to the Pacific Ocean, and the Eglinton River flows to Lake Te Anau and onto the South Island's south coast west of Invercargill.

Getting Here
The Divide car park is 85km from Te Anau on the Te Anau–Milford road. Shuttle buses from Te Anau drop off and pick up here several times daily as The Divide is also the start or end for the full Routeburn Track and is on the road to Milford Sound/Piopiotahi.

Starting Point
The track starts at the top end of the car park, just above The Divide shelter. There are information panels here. Facilities include a shelter and public toilets.

01 Start out through moss-enshrouded forest in a gentle fashion along the lower western flank of Key Summit. It's easy walking to start, but you'll soon notice the steepness of the slopes both above and below, especially when you come across your first tree **avalanche scar**. There's very little soil on these slopes as the mountainsides were scraped bare by the glaciers, meaning that big trees are battling to hang on – many only remain by grabbing the roots of their neighbours. Big beeches outgrow their gripping power and, in times of strong wind and rain, avalanches of trees are common.

Best for

MOUNTAIN VIEWS

Routeburn Track

The 32km, three-day **Routeburn** is one of Aotearoa/New Zealand's best-known tracks, taking trampers over the Southern Alps' Main Divide as it links Fiordland and Mt Aspiring/Tititea National Parks. Much of it is through thick rainforest, where red, mountain and silver beech form the canopy, and ferns, mosses and fungi cover everything below like wall-to-wall shagpile carpet. The alpine sections are spectacular. Views from Harris Saddle (1255m) and the top of nearby Conical Hill take in waves breaking far to the west in Martins Bay, while the views from Key Summit, the target for this day walk, are breathtaking. The **Routeburn Track Day Walk** covers the eastern end of this iconic track.

Key Summit Track

02 Keep your eyes open for kākā, a brown cousin of the kea, the alpine parrot that lives at higher altitudes. Kākā are common around here, enjoying the berries of the native tree fuschia, the tree with the peeling bark. Pass a small **waterfall** and, before long, the track starts climbing more steeply and steadily with a number of switchbacks.

It will take an hour or so from The Divide to reach the clearly marked Key Summit turn-off.

03 From the **turn-off**, it will take 20 minutes to climb the zigzags up to the tree line and a scarred area that is devoid of large trees – the scene of an old tree avalanche. Just after a public toilet, you'll reach the start of the loop nature walk at the top. This is best walked clockwise and you'll reach the 918m **summit** a few minutes later. On a good day, you'll want to stick around for the views.

04 Continuing the **loop nature walk**, you'll find lookouts and a range of vegetation and information panels – low-growing beech trees, subalpine shrublands, alpine tarns and bogs. On the far side of the walk, look into the hanging valley that contains Lake Marian. Try to spot the rock-hugging South Island edelweiss.

05 Back at the start of the loop track, descend the **zigzags** and walk back to The Divide car park.

 Take a Break

Bring food for a picnic from Te Anau. The closest cafe is **Discover Milford Sound Information Centre & Cafe** at Milford Sound/Piopiotahi, 35km away.

56

Mavora Walkway

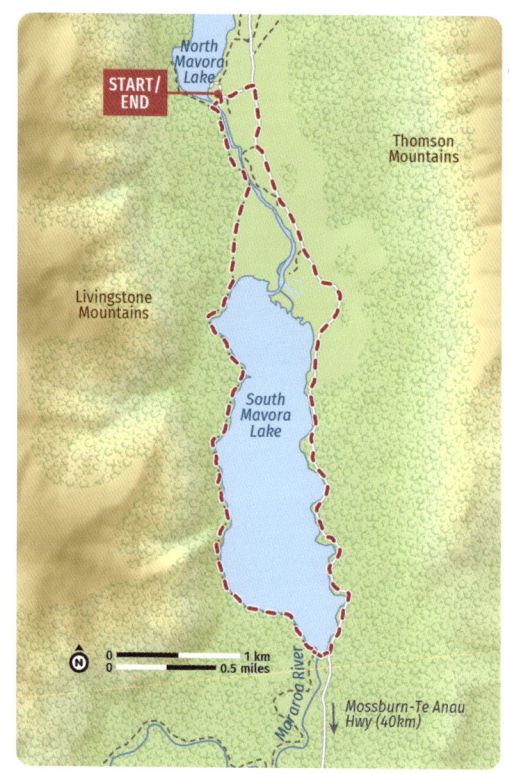

DURATION	DIFFICULTY	DISTANCE	START/END
4–5hrs	Easy	11km	Mararoa River swing bridge

TERRAIN	Easy walking on track and road

Officially the Mavora Lakes Conservation Park and part of the Te Wāhipounamu (Southwest New Zealand) World Heritage Area, the Mavora Lakes are an off-the-beaten-track gem, so spectacular that Peter Jackson used the valley when filming *Lord of the Rings*. Don't just race on by on the drive from Queenstown to Te Anau.

This loop involves circuiting South Mavora Lake, accessed from SW94 between Mossburn and Te Anau by turning off at either Centre Hill or Burwood Station and following gravel roads for around 40km north. Drive up into the narrow Mavora Valley, past South Mavora Lake, and park near the **swing bridge** that crosses the Mararoa River near the camping ground at the southern end of North Mavora Lake. There can be treefalls in the area that DOC may not have cleared, so be prepared to clamber.

Cross the swing bridge, then turn left (south) along the western side of the river. This side features a gorgeous **beech forest** and the track meanders south to **South Mavora Lake** and along its western edge, towered over by the Livingstone Mountains. After a couple of hours, the track will reach the Mararoa River outlet at the southern end of the lake. Cross back over east here on another swing bridge and walk out to the road you drove up earlier. This road has little traffic.

Walk north along the road, through the forest, back towards where you parked your car. About three-quarters of the way up South Mavora Lake, the forest peters out; continue through open grassland back to the camping ground at the southern end of **North Mavora Lake**. The narrow valley is squeezed between the Livingstone to the west and the Thomson range to the east.

Best for

OFF THE BEATEN PATH

THE SOUTH 56 MAVORA WALKWAY

South Mavora Lake

57

Brod Bay to Te Anau

DURATION	DIFFICULTY	DISTANCE	START/END
3–4hrs	Easy	8km	Te Anau waterfront

TERRAIN	Flat walk on a well-defined trail

This walk involves taking a boat from Te Anau township across Lake Te Anau to Brod Bay, then following the lakeside trail, which initially is part of the Kepler Track, back and around the southern end of Lake Te Anau to the town's waterfront. Along the way, the trail takes in impressive beech forest, the Lake Te Anau control gates, the Te Anau Bird Sanctuary and the Fiordland National Park Visitor Centre.

Getting Here

Take the **Kepler Water Taxi** (fiordlandoutdoors.co.nz) from the wharf on the Te Anau lakefront across to Brod Bay in 15 minutes. There are scheduled departures at 8.30am, 9.30am, 10.30am and 2.30pm April to October, and departures on demand May to September.

Starting Point

The Kepler Water Taxi will drop you on the beach at Brod Bay, across the lake in Fiordland National Park. The track is in the forest, just up from the beach.

01 Hop off the water taxi at **Brod Bay** and enjoy views of the southern end of Aotearoa/New Zealand's second-largest lake. You'll be walking all the way around, back to Te Anau. For those wanting a shorter forest-only walk, instead of taking the water taxi to Brod Bay, drive around to the start of the Kepler Track, park in the car park, then walk around to Brod Bay and back in two to three hours.

If you've taken the water taxi, the first 3km of your walk is on the **Kepler Track** through beautiful beech forest in Fiordland NP. The track is mostly flat, following, or close to, the lakeshore, and there

Best for

SPOTTING WILDLIFE

Lake Te Anau, Kepler Track

Kepler Track

This day walk covers the first part of the 60km, four-day **Kepler Track**, one of the Great Walks, opened in 1988 during NZ's centennial celebration of its national park system. It is one of the best-planned tracks in NZ: a loop beginning and ending near the control gates where the Waiau River heads out of the southern end of Lake Te Anau. The Kepler includes an all-day tramp across the tops, taking in incredible panoramas of Lake Te Anau, its South Fiord arm, the Jackson Peaks and the Kepler Mountains. Along the way, it traverses rocky ridges, tussock lands and peaceful beech forest. The Rainbow Reach to Shallow Bay walk covers a section of the Kepler Track near Lake Manapōuri.

are good opportunities for swimming and picnicking, either at Brod Bay or at **Dock Bay**.

02 You'll pass out of the national park at the Lake Te Anau **control gates**, which regulate water flows between the lakes Te Anau and Manapōuri for the West Arm hydroelectric power station. Look down the Waiau River, then all the way out to the South Island's south coast, west of Invercargill. This is also the start and end of the Kepler Track and you'll find a large car park with toilets just beyond the control gates.

03 The trail then follows the lakeshore below the Te Anau golf course before winding its way around to the **Te Anau Bird Sanctuary**. Here, you'll have the opportunity to spot a takahe, a flightless bird thought extinct for 50 years before its rediscovery near Te Anau in 1948. There are other birds, such as kākā, kākāriki and the ruru (morepork), a spotted owl, to be seen here. The path passes through the sanctuary.

04 Continue on the trail around to the **Fiordland National Park Visitor Centre**, which has outstanding displays and information on the country's largest national park. It will take another 10 minutes to walk back to the middle of town. Just past the visitor centre is a bronze statue of Quintin McKinnon, who discovered the Mackinnon Pass/Omanui and established the Milford Track in 1888.

Take a Break

Take picnic supplies from Te Anau to enjoy on the trail. Right at the end of your walk in the township, across from the waterfront, you'll find **The Moose**. This popular local watering hole offers pub food and liquid refreshments and is named in honour of the moose, a species that was introduced to Fiordland with around a dozen individuals from Canada in the early 1900s. None have been seen since 1952, but some locals still believe there's a moose or two out there.

58

Rainbow Reach to Shallow Bay

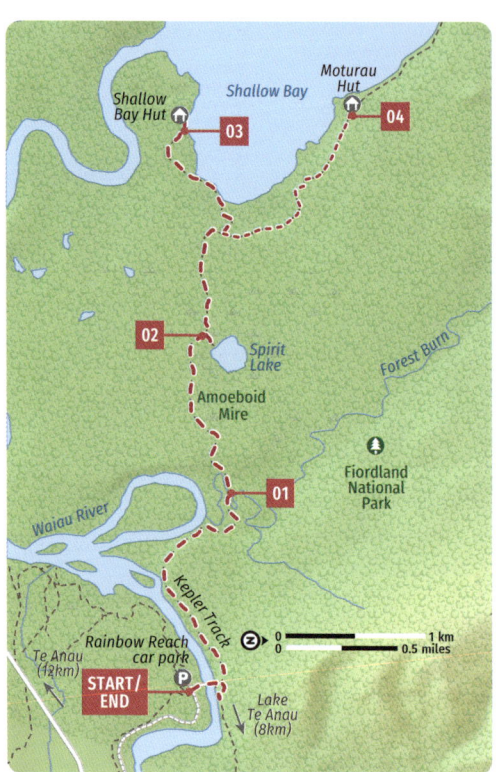

DURATION	DIFFICULTY	DISTANCE	START/END
3hrs	Easy	6km	Rainbow Reach car park

TERRAIN	Mostly flat; well-maintained track

An easy walk through native forest to a beautiful beach on the shores of Lake Manapōuri, this is a top walk for families and a superb taste of the Kepler Track. There's interesting flora plus the opportunity of a lake swim at Shallow Bay. The walk can be lengthened by 3½ hours to walk back to Lake Te Anau and the end of the Kepler Track.

Getting Here

The track begins at Rainbow Reach, 12km south of Te Anau on the Manapōuri–Te Anau Hwy. After 10.5km, turn right at the signposted road to get to Rainbow Reach car park in another 1.5km. There are shuttle buses to here from Te Anau during the November to April busy season.

Starting Point

From the car park, cross the swing bridge over the Waiau River to get onto the Kepler Track.

The Waiau is a popular fishing river, loaded with rainbow and brown trout, so keep your eyes open as you cross the **swing bridge**. When you're on the Kepler Track, it follows the river through mature beech forest, occasionally offering lovely river views until, after half an hour or so, you cross the **Forest Burn**, a small tributary of the Waiau, on a swing bridge.

After another 20 minutes or so, you'll reach the **Amoeboid Mire**, a wetland with an interesting short side track on boardwalk out to the **Spirit Lake** viewing platform, which has information panels. The wetland and lake are on a terrace that formed as the Manapōuri glacier melted.

Swing bridge, Kepler Track

Lake Manapōuri

The small town of Manapōuri, 20km south of Te Anau, is the jumping-off point for cruises to Doubtful Sound. It sits at the southeast corner of **Lake Manapōuri** – NZ's fifth-largest and second-deepest lake – which holds a special place in the history of the country's conservation movements.

In the late 1960s and early 1970s, determined conservationists mounted a successful 'Save Manapōuri' campaign against a scheme to raise the level of the lake by 30m as part of a hydroelectric power development. This was seen as a major win for conservationists – and with 34 islands, forested lakeshores and mountainous surrounds, Lake Manapōuri is arguably one of the most beautiful lakes in the country.

Expect wetland vegetation such as sphagnum moss, a wide variety of other mosses, wire rush and a range of herbs and shrubs. When there's no wind, the lake has great mountain reflections.

03 Back on the main track, 10 minutes after another section of boardwalk over part of the wetland, head left at the signed turn-off to **Shallow Bay**. You'll reach the beach 15 minutes later. Make sure to head around the pebbly beach and poke your nose into the DOC's tiny six-bed **Shallow Bay Hut** – and if it's warm, take a dip in the lake. This is a great spot for a picnic if you've brought supplies.

04 For some extra exploring, back at the junction, turn left to walk to the DOC's impressive 40-bed **Moturau Hut**, also close to the lake's foreshore, in another 20 minutes. This is where most Kepler walkers spend their last night before walking out to Lake Te Anau. If you came by shuttle and don't have a vehicle at Rainbow Reach car park, consider lengthening your walk by 3½ hours and following the **Kepler Track** all the way up the western side of the Waiau River to Lake Te Anau and the start/end of the Kepler Track. Otherwise, follow the trail back to the Rainbow Reach swing bridge and car park.

 Take a Break

Picnic supplies can be purchased in Te Anau or Manapōuri. When you have finished walking, head to **The Church** (facebook.com/manapouri.co.nz/) in Manapōuri; it's an 1885-built former Presbyterian Church that has been converted into a merry pub with exceptionally welcoming staff. This popular place serves up pub fare and refreshingly cold beer. Though there aren't a lot of options in Manapōuri, **Cathedral Cafe** is next door.

59

Ulva Island – Te Wharawhara Marine Reserve

DURATION	DIFFICULTY	DISTANCE	START/END
3hrs	Easy	6km	Post Office Bay

TERRAIN	Well-formed track, stepped in places

This predator-free island paradise, only a short boat ride from Stewart Island/Rakiura's Golden Bay wharf, was established as a bird sanctuary in 1922 and is a top spot to see lots of native Aotearoa/New Zealand bird species.

Covering only 267 hectares in Paterson Inlet/Whaka a Te Wera, Ulva Island/Te Wharawhara was declared rat-free in 1997 and was chosen as the site to release endangered tīeke (South Island saddlebacks). Today, the air is bristling with **birdsong**, which can be appreciated on walking tracks in the island's northwest.

The island is officially part of **Rakiura National Park** and is run as an 'open sanctuary' by the DOC with full public access. Taxi boats from Golden Bay Wharf drop visitors at the wharf at Ulva Island/Te Wharawhara's **Post Office Bay**, from where there are a number of good tracks.

We recommend a loop walk from Post Office Bay to Boulder Beach, West End Beach and back to Post Office Bay via **Sydney Cove**, taking around three hours. You'll find beautiful stands of rimu, miro, tōtara and rātā plus the chance to see birds such as the flightless weka, South Island kākā (parrot), kākāriki (parakeet), kererū (wood pigeon), korimako (bellbird), pīpipi (brown creeper), ngirungiru (tomtit), pīwakawaka (fantail), tūī and Stewart Island tokoeka (brown kiwi). Tīeke, mōhua (yellowhead), toutouwai (Stewart Island robin) and tītitipounamu (rifleman) have also been reintroduced to the island. This is a take-your-time-and-see-what-you-can-see type walk.

Rakiura National Park Visitor Centre has an *Ulva: Self-Guided Tour* pamphlet ($2), but to get the most out of an Ulva Island/Te Wharawhara visit, you may want to go on a tour with **Ulva's Guided Walks** (*ulva.co.nz*).

Best for

SPOTTING WILDLIFE

Weka, Ulva Island/Te Wharawhara

60
Port William/ Potirepo to Halfmoon Bay/Oban

Best for

COASTAL SCENERY

DURATION	DIFFICULTY	DISTANCE	START/END
4–5hrs	Easy–Moderate	12km	Port William/Halfmoon Bay/Oban

TERRAIN	Well-maintained track, stepped in places; road

Te Puka anchor stone chain-link sculpture (p214), Lee Bay

This lovely walk involves taking boat transport from Halfmoon Bay/Oban to Port William/Potirepo, then walking one-way back to Halfmoon Bay/Oban, firstly along the first section of the Rakiura Track, then along a road from the national park entrance at Lee Bay. Those wanting a shorter walk can miss the last 1½ hours or so by arranging shuttle transport from the national park entrance at Lee Bay back to Halfmoon Bay/Oban. A further option is to take a shuttle from Halfmoon Bay/Oban to the national park entrance at Lee Bay, walk to Māori Beach and back, then shuttle back to Halfmoon Bay/Oban.

Getting Here

Rakiura Charters & Water Taxi *(rakiuracharters.co.nz)* runs departures from Halfmoon Bay/Oban to Port William/Potirepo at 9am daily on demand, dropping you off in the morning so you can enjoy a leisurely walk back to town. Shuttles from Lee Bay to Halfmoon Bay/Oban cost $40 per group. A number of companies in Halfmoon Bay/Oban offer guided walks that include transportation on this first part of the Rakiura Track. Consider your options.

Starting Point

Enjoy the short, informative cruise to Port William/Potirepo wharf, where you'll start your hike.

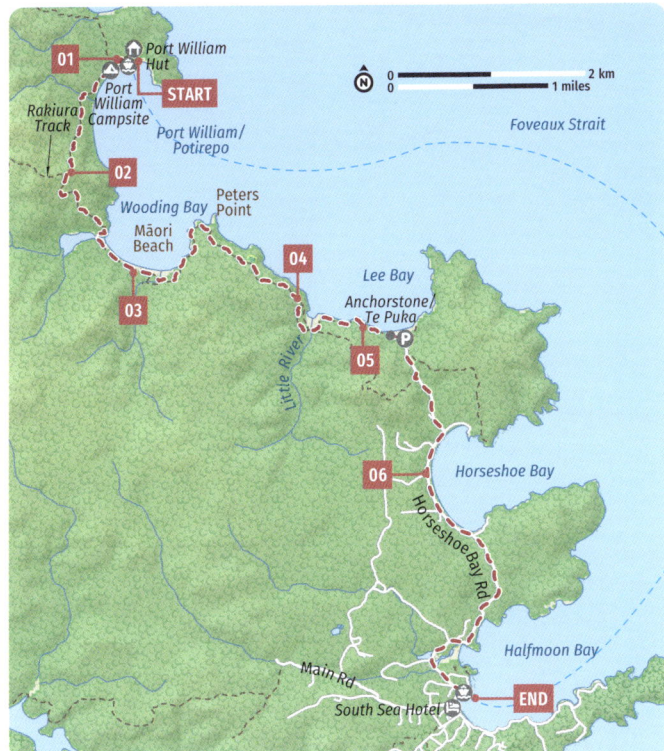

Rakiura Track

One of Aotearoa/New Zealand's Great Walks, the three-day **Rakiura Track** is a peaceful and leisurely loop that sidles around beautiful beaches before climbing over a 250m-high forested ridge and traversing the sheltered shores of Paterson Inlet/Whaka a Te Wera. It passes sites of historical interest, including Māori sites and sawmilling relics, and introduces many common sea and forest birds.

The Rakiura Track is 32km long, but adding in the road sections at either end bumps it up to 39km, conveniently forming a well-defined circuit from Halfmoon Bay/Oban. Being a Great Walk, it has been gravelled to eliminate most of the mud for which the island is infamous.

01 After getting off the boat at Port William/Potirepo wharf, do some exploring. Māori established a hunting camp or kāika at Port William/Potirepo, reached by outrigger canoe. This was the site of the early Māori settlement of Pā Whakataka. During the 1800s, its sheltered harbour was used by sealers, and later as a whaling base. A fishing village was set up here in the 1870s with immigrants from the Shetland and Orkney island groups of northern Scotland, but with no ready market for the fish, nor a guarantee that they would get title to the land they were clearing, the hardy but realistic immigrants soon abandoned Port William/Potirepo.

Eucalyptus trees are the most notable remains of the attempted European settlement. DOC's 24-bunk **Port William Hut** is here, plus a camping ground, both catering to Rakiura Track and Northwest Circuit Track walkers.

02 Follow the track around, just in from the beach, until it starts to climb. There are plenty of DOC-built steps for short climbs and descents before the track makes a steepish 120m climb up on a headland and meets the main **Rakiura Track** that runs over to **North Arm** after 45 minutes. You can take a 45-minute (return) side trip from here on the main track to see log haulers, huge machines used to drag giant trees from the depths of the gullies.

03 Back at the junction, follow signage for 'Māori Beach 45 minutes'. The track curls around and descends back down to sea level, where you'll cross a small estuary on a swing bridge and find yourself at the western end of **Māori Beach**. The track then is on the sand. Wander along this spectacular beach, which you might have all to yourself, to the eastern end, where you'll find a shelter and toilet.

☕ Take a Break

Take picnic supplies from Halfmoon Bay/Oban for a break while on the track. Halfmoon Bay/Oban is home to one of NZ's classic pubs, complete with stellar cod and chips, beer by the quart, a reliable restaurant and plenty of friendly banter in the public bar. The **South Sea Hotel** *(southseahotel.co.nz)* is great at any time of day (or night), and the Sunday-night quiz offers an unforgettable slice of island life. Basic rooms are available too, all within a stone's throw of the ferry terminal.

Māori Beach was a sawmilling community, populated from 1913 to 1931, with two sawmills and a school, but there's nothing here now apart from a rusting steam boiler and engine, plus a DOC campsite. It's hard to imagine that a community was thriving here only a century ago. This is a great spot for a picnic.

04 If the tide is low, cross the small stream and head up the track marked with a large orange triangle into the bush at the eastern end of the beach. If the tide is in and you can't cross the stream without getting your feet wet, follow the slightly longer 'high-tide route', which crosses the creek a bit further inland on a small footbridge and curls around to meet the 'low-tide route'. About 20 minutes further on, after rounding **Peters Point**, you'll come to a 'decision point' with signage. If the tide is out, head down steep steps to the beach, marvel at its beauty and meet the regular track at the footbridge. If the tide is in, continue on the main track as it heads inland and down to cross the **Little River estuary** on the footbridge.

05 Follow the track to Lee Bay with some gorgeous views down to hidden beaches well below the track. Eventually, you'll walk through the **Te Puka anchor stone** chain-link **sculpture** at Lee Bay, commissioned to commemorate the forming of Rakiura National Park when it was opened in 2002. The sculpture symbolises the Māori view that Stewart Island/Rakiura is anchored to the South Island, and a similar sculpture has been erected in Bluff, representing the other end of the chain. The car park is only a short amble from here.

06 If you haven't arranged a shuttle and are walking, it's 5km back to Halfmoon Bay/Oban. If you've had enough, there's mobile-phone coverage here and you could call **Aurora Cab Co** for a pick-up. Lee Bay Rd climbs up over a pass, then descends down to Horseshoe Bay Rd at beautiful **Horseshoe Bay**.

Head down onto the sand and follow the road around the bay. The road then makes a series of climbs and descents, passing **Butterfield Beach** before depositing you back in Halfmoon Bay/Oban, about 1½ hours after leaving the chain-link sculpture.

Footbridge, Little River estuary

Stewart Island/ Rakiura

Stewart Island's Māori name is Rakiura (Glowing Skies), and you only need to catch a glimpse of a spectacular blood-red sunset or the aurora australis to see why. According to myth, Aotearoa/New Zealand was hauled up from the ocean by Māui, who said, 'Let us go out of sight of land, far out in the open sea, and when we have quite lost sight of land, then let the anchor be dropped.' The North Island was the fish that Māui caught, the South Island his canoe and Rakiura was the anchor – Te Punga o te Waka o Māui. There is evidence that parts of Rakiura were occupied by moa (bird) hunters as early as the 13th century, while tītī (muttonbird) were, and still are, an important seasonal food source for southern Māori.

Also Try...

Lake Gunn Nature Walk

S WATSON/SHUTTERSTOCK

Catlins River

DURATION	DIFFICULTY	DISTANCE
5-6hrs	Easy	12km

In the Catlins Conservation Park of eastern Southland, the Catlins River Walk involves three sections of track that can be walked as one hike.

The full track includes lovely forest plus four wire-rope suspension bridges crossing the Catlins River with its many attractive waterfalls and rapids. There's the chance of seeing rare birds, such as the rifleman and mōhua, and at the Tawanui end of the track native mistletoe with its impressive scarlet flowers can be seen in December/January. The full walk involves hiking from The Wisp car park, 23km from the Catlins' main town of Owaka, to Tawanui campsite. The three shorter sections are The Wisp car park to Wallis Stream (one hour), Wallis Stream to Frank Stream (1½ to two hours) and Frank Stream to Tawanui Campsite (2½ to three hours).

Hidden Falls Track

DURATION	DIFFICULTY	DISTANCE
4-6hrs	Easy-Moderate	18km

Hike along the first section of the popular Hollyford Track to Sunshine Hut and 31m Hidden Falls.

The track follows the Hollyford River valley in Fiordland National Park from the end of the Lower Hollyford Rd, which turns off SH94 (Milford Rd) shortly after The Divide. While the full Hollyford Track runs 56km out to Martins Bay and the Tasman Sea, this is a relatively easy walk on the well-maintained track for 9km to Hidden Falls and back. At the road end, cross the swing bridge over Humboldt Creek and follow the old road to the start of the track, which initially sidles along bluffs, with swampland to the left. Sections of raised boardwalk cross areas prone to flooding. Just after Sunshine Hut, run by Hollyford Guided Walks, you'll find the swing bridge over Hidden Falls Creek and the photogenic falls.

Waituna Lagoon

Waituna Lagoon

DURATION	DIFFICULTY	DISTANCE
1½hrs	Easy	5km

There are good walking options around Waituna Lagoon, 40km southeast of Invercargill.

The wetlands loop track starts at the end of Waghorn Rd, initially on wheelchair-friendly boardwalking to a viewpoint. It then runs through manuka wetlands and past bog tarns on the northern side of the lagoon. It's also possible to walk along the spectacular, white quartz beach on the southern ocean side of the lagoon off Waituna Lagoon Rd. You can walk along the beach for 9km to where the lagoon opens to the sea.

Lake Gunn Nature Walk

DURATION	DIFFICULTY	DISTANCE
45mins	Easy	1.4km

This wheelchair-friendly loop through mature beech forest starts at Cascade Creek car park on the Milford Rd.

From the car park, 78km north of Te Anau, step straight into the moss-covered forest with its massive red beech trees, keeping your eye out for tomtits, riflemen and other forest birds. Turn right at the track junction and curl around with the track to a small beach at the southern end of Lake Gunn. The track follows the lake foreshore before turning back into the bush, to the track junction and the car park.

Arriving

Most international flights are to Auckland; there are also flights from Australia to Wellington, Christchurch or Queenstown and from San Francisco and Singapore to Christchurch. You'll need to clear customs on arrival before travelling domestically. New Zealand has extremely strict border rules so declare everything, including food: customs will check.

Aotearoa/New Zealand has tourist information centres at airports and i-Sites (tourist information points) in most towns and cities.

Travelling with Hiking Gear

As an island nation free of many international pests and diseases, New Zealand is vigilant about biosecurity. The New Zealand arrival form asks if you're carrying anything used for outdoor activities and Customs will check your gear, so declare it ahead of time.

Hikers, in particular, will need to remember to clean their tent, hiking poles, backpack, boots and other gear before they leave home so that not a leaf, seed or speck of mud remains. Pack these items at the top of your bag for easy access. Don't forget the base of tent poles.

If you need parts, patches or replacements, you can buy most of what you'll need at outdoor stores in New Zealand such as Macpac and Kathmandu, though if you require a specific European or American brand you'll probably be out of luck unless it's very widely available globally – check ahead if you're worried.

Airport to City Centre

	Auckland Airport	Wellington Airport	Christchurch Airport
BUS	$20/16	$11/5.50	$2
TAXI	$38/95	$40/60	$45/65
SHUTTLE	$35	$20	$25

WI-FI & SIM CARDS
Airports have free wi-fi, and you can get SIM cards or eSims there when you land. For hikers, Spark has the widest phone coverage in New Zealand. OneNZ offers satellite texting through Starlink.

VISAS
New Zealand has visa waiver agreements with more than 60 countries. Some travellers can use an NZeTA (electronic visa) without applying for a visa first. Get it at *nzeta. immigration.govt.nz* ($23; discounted to $17 through the free app).

CASH
Depending on your local bank rules and fees, it may pay to withdraw cash with purchases at most larger retailers, such as petrol stations and supermarkets. Carry smaller denominations, which smaller shops will appreciate.

TRANSPORT TO THE CITY
Look for an airport shuttle van or bus service when you arrive. New Zealand's public transport network is patchy at best and a shuttle shares the cost of transport between passengers.

Getting Around

TRANSPORT OPTIONS

Buses are common in larger towns and cities, and Auckland and Wellington have a limited train network. In smaller areas you'll be reliant on private car or taxi.

DRIVING INFO

New Zealand drives on the left. Pay attention at turns!

Don't drink and drive – one drink can exceed the limit.

One-way bridges are common. Follow the give-way arrows with caution.

Track Transport

Aotearoa/New Zealand is so well set up for tramping (hiking) that many tracks have transport services available that will shuttle you to the start and pick you up again at the end. Search online for your preferred track, as locals may run smaller services. The 'Tramping in New Zealand' Facebook page may also garner you a carshare with other walkers. The page is also handy to join for local information or questions about weather and track conditions.

Low-Carbon Travel

You can rent electric vehicles in Aotearoa/New Zealand from a number of companies, including Europcar, GO Rentals, Thrifty, evee and Budget. Check the range and charge facilities ahead of time as New Zealand does not have an extensive charging network.

Bus Lines

InterCity travels to all main centres and through most smaller ones. Its FlexiPass is an hours-based pass, which can include the InterIslander ferry between the North and South Islands, starting at 10 hours for $140. Book at *intercity.co.nz*.

Parking at Trailheads

You won't struggle for parking room at trailheads in Aotearoa/New Zealand, but take your valuables with you as break-ins do happen. Check ahead to see if you need a 4WD vehicle to access the beginning of some remote tracks.

Speed Limits

The speed limit is 100km/h on the open road, which drops to 80km/h or 60km/h outside of towns and cities, where the limit is usually 50km/h. Beware: speed cameras and lurking police cars abound.

TRAVEL COSTS

Car rental per day: $120 in high season

Approximate petrol cost per litre: $2.50

EV fast-charging cost: $10 per 100km

Bus ticket: Auckland–Kaitaia (6hrs 40mins) $120 return

FROM LEFT: RUSSELL HENDRY/GETTY IMAGES; CKTRAVELS.COM/SHUTTERSTOCK

Accommodation

HUTS

Aotearoa/New Zealand has an extensive, diverse network of more than 950 backcountry huts, administered by the Department of Conservation (DOC). These havens range from the modern palaces of the Great Walks to mice-invested hovels that are, at least, shelter. Some 250 more huts are managed privately and often accessible to visitors. A hut always makes an agreeable destination for a day walk.

HOW MUCH FOR A...

Night in a small-town holiday park cabin:
$80

Night in a standard DOC hut:
$10

Night in a rented family bach:
$160

Baches & Cribs

Kiwis call their holiday houses 'baches' in the north and 'cribs' in the south. Although taken over by flash holiday houses in more popular, beachy holiday destinations, there are still many humble baches around the country available to rent, stacked with bunk beds and bent frying pans. Try Airbnb, Bookabach, Holiday Houses or Bachcare for options.

Holiday Parks

A firm family favourite for generations, the Kiwi holiday or caravan park (campground) is a fun, relaxed accommodation option available in tourist destinations and on the outskirts of cities and even quite small towns. They are invariably safe, clean and affordable. Some offer cooking equipment in the kitchens, or to rent. A small cabin is usually a decent deal.

Campsites

Aotearoa/New Zealand is blessed with free or very cheap DOC campsites in some of the most beautiful locations on Earth. There are more than 300 options at beaches, in forests and on the shores of incredible lakes. The only downside will be the sandflies and the long-drop (pit toilets). Some are bookable so check ahead on *doc.govt.nz*. Take your rubbish with you.

HelpX & WWOOFing

If you're willing to exchange room and food for your sweat and muscle and have a valid work visa, HelpX and WWOOFing may work out well, and will at least provide an interesting Kiwi family experience. Food and board is provided for about five hours' work a day – offers vary. Your new friends may even be happy to ferry you about to trailheads. Visit *helpx.net* or *wwoof.nz*.

HUT ETIQUETTE

Rubbish and faeces are Kiwis' biggest outdoor bugbears, so pack out your rubbish with you, and dispose of faeces appropriately. That means in toilets or in a properly dug hole away from water. Building a cairn to cover your poo isn't good enough, and nor is leaving wet wipes behind. When you visit a hut, boots stay outside, and Kiwis will appreciate seeing you clean up their precious huts: prop up mattresses, wipe the bench, sweep the floor and replace firewood with deadfall. Always sign the hut book with your intentions for search and rescue.

Hiking

Gear Rental

It's always a good idea to at least rent a PLB (personal locator beacon) if you're going somewhere more remote; this will probably be available at an outdoors shop in a town, where you're also most likely to find gear rental available. Hotels and backpackers hostels in larger tourist destinations such as Tongariro National Park may also rent some gear such as crampons. Gearshop offers rental via delivery or in-store collection *(gearshophire.co.nz)*. PackBack *(packback.nz)* also offers gear rental delivery, as well as a full selection of food and other hiking bits and pieces. You may also have luck finding cheap gear on backpackers noticeboards or on the popular, if wordy, Facebook page: 'Hunting, Fishing, Camping, Tramping, Outdoors Buy/Sell/Trade New Zealand'.

TRAIL ETIQUETTE

Aotearoa/New Zealand has a high level of endemism, or native plants and animals, many of which are delicate and easily damaged. Stick to the formed tracks to help protect the surrounding landscape from stomping feet. Aotearoa/New Zealand tracks are also often, unfortunately, muddy. Yes, that means going straight through; avoid widening the track by trying to edge around it.

The most important aspect of trail etiquette is not to dump rubbish (watch out for the shiny corners of food wrappers). A gold star if you pick up what you find left by other hikers to dispose of in town.

Go to the toilet responsibly. A 'backcountry bidet' – a high-powered squirt top on a repurposed bottle – is a low-waste option compared to wads of toilet paper, or worse, wet wipes. On that note, some hut and track toilets are not the pit, composting variety but are high-powered variants which the waste is pumped out of at great expense. Pack out all rubbish, including sanitary waste.

Resources

Department of Conservation
doc.govt.nz
Invaluable for maps, booking, track conditions and updates.

'Tramping in New Zealand'
Facebook page
A know-it-all Kiwi will quickly answer your questions.

Wilderness Magazine
wildernessmag.co.nz
The popular magazine is an endless resource.

Health & Safe Travel

Drinking Water

Aotearoa/New Zealand doesn't have huge problems with polluted water, but giardia is a concern in the backcountry, so it's sensible to filter stream water. Even if a track seems very remote, there may be a dead goat leaching bacteria just around an upstream bend. Keep rivers clean of food scraps when you wash your picnic gear.

Wildfires

Although Aotearoa/New Zealand doesn't yet have the summer smoke problems of the US' Pacific Northwest, for example, wildfires are a very real risk in the summer months and a single spark can cause a runaway inferno. Mind your cigarette butts, or parking a hot vehicle on dry grass. Fires belong only in fireplaces.

Blisters

Try a variety of prevention methods to work out what is best for you; toe socks, thin socks, double socks. Hiker's Wool is a Kiwi solution to the problem; it is simply soft, washed sheep's wool sold in a plastic bag. You'll find it at outdoor stores. Wind it around potential hotspots and it'll weave itself into your sock.

Wasps, Mosquitos & Sandflies

Wasps have become a massive nuisance in some areas, such as Nelson Lakes National Park. If you are allergic, check ahead and consider avoiding some areas in warm months entirely. Meanwhile, mosquitos and sandflies have been ruining Aotearoa/New Zealand's best beauty spots since humans arrived. Try a local repellent recipe: Dettol (an antiseptic available from supermarkets) mixed with baby oil.

INSURANCE

You'll need insurance that covers any hiking mishaps such as gear loss. Unprepared hikers who are blasé about Aotearoa/New Zealand track and weather conditions are a search and rescue nuisance, so read up on your track. The no-fault ACC scheme will cover you for accident and injury medical care in Aotearoa/New Zealand.

IN CASE OF EMERGENCY

Police, ambulance and fire are all reachable on 111.

If you find an injured animal, ring the 24-hour DOC emergency hotline 0800 DOC HOT (0800 362 468).

FROM LEFT: UWE ARANAS/SHUTTERSTOCK, ADWO/SHUTTERSTOCK

Responsible Travel

Climate Change & Travel

Lonely Planet urges all travellers to engage with their travel carbon footprint, which will mainly come from air travel. While there often isn't an alternative, travellers can look to minimise the number of flights they take, opt for newer aircrafts and use cleaner ground transport, such as trains.

One proposed solution – purchasing carbon offsets – unfortunately does not cancel out the impact of individual flights. While most destinations will depend on air travel for the foreseeable future, for now, pursuing ground-based travel where possible is the best course of action.

The **UN Carbon Offset Calculator** shows how flying impacts a household's emissions

The **ICAO's carbon emissions calculator** allows visitors to analyse the CO_2 generated by point-to-point journeys

Resources

NZ Māori Tourism
maoritourism.co.nz
A searchable database of Māori experiences.

Tourism Industry Aotearoa
members.tia.org.nz/s/tsc-directory
Choose a sustainable tourism operator.

Rankers Camping
camping-nz.rankers.co.nz
Stay at approved camping spots so councils can dispose of waste.

MĀORI TOURISM

You'll come away enlightened after choosing a local Māori-led tourism initiative such as stargazing, guiding, a tour bus, or rafting; the *kōrero* (talk) you'll likely receive about the area will be extra illuminating.

'BIODEGRADABLE' PLASTICS

Only 'compostable' plastic items break down in the wild; 'biodegradable' plastic ends up as micro-plastics if not composted commercially. Ideally, carry reusables for items such as coffee, shopping bags and food.

TRUSTWORTHY GREEN LABELS

Eco Choice Aotearoa is the only official eco-label in Aotearoa/New Zealand, with independent verification and a life-cycle approach to products, from their raw materials to their ultimate demise.

223

Nuts & Bolts

CURRENCY: NEW ZEALAND DOLLAR $

GOOD TO KNOW

Time zone
New Zealand Daylight Time (GMT +13)

Country code
+64

Emergency number
111

Best Ways to Pay
Cash is welcome everywhere, as are debit card payments. Cash is particularly handy if you spot a roadside fruit or flower stall.

Card Payments
Credit cards and tap or Paywave methods, including your phone, generally incur a surcharge of up to 2.5% to cover bank fees.

Toilets
Trailheads usually have long-drop (outhouse) toilets, and they're easily findable in towns. Check Google Maps and *continence.org.nz/national-toilet-maps*.

Smoking
Smoking is banned everywhere indoors in Aotearoa/New Zealand, as well as in public spaces like parks and transit stations.

HOW MUCH FOR A...

Regular flat white coffee
$5

Service station meat pie
$7

Freeze-dried tramping meal
$15

Paperback book
$39

ELECTRICITY 230V/50HZ

Opening Hours
Expect shops to be open 9am to 5pm weekdays, with shorter hours on Saturdays. Aotearoa/New Zealand can be startlingly empty on a Sunday afternoon, but bustling on Saturday mornings.

TIPPING ETIQUETTE

Tipping is never expected; hospitality staff and other workers are guaranteed minimum wage. However, at cafes there is usually a jar at the till for spare change, and you may encounter the odd 'add tip' function on payment screens. Rewarding exceptional service will be appreciated – you'll be remembered forever!

By Difficulty

EASY

Arthur's Pass Walking Track 143
Blue Lake /Tikitapu 75
Blue Pools 189
Bob's Cove 176
Brod Bay to Te Anau 206
Cape Foulwind Walkway 161
Catlins River 216
Charming Creek
North Walkway 148
Cooks Cove Walkway 70
Harihari Coastal Walkway 160
Hooker Valley 138
Huka Falls to Aratiatia Rapids 74
Kaikōura Peninsula Walkway 126
Karangahake Gorge 42
Kawerau Track Loop 28
Lake Gunn Nature Walk 217
Lake Hayes 178
Lake Matheson 156
Long Beach 186
Mangawhai Cliffs Walkway 45
Mavora Walkway 204
Milford Track Day Walk 194
Monro Beach 158
Mueller Hut 140
Ōkārito Pack Track
& Coastal Walk 152
Ōpārara Basin 160
Point Elizabeth Walkway 161
Punakaiki-Pororari Loop 150
Rainbow Reach
to Shallow Bay 208
Rakaia Gorge Walkway 143
Ulva Island - Te Wharawhara
Marine Reserve 210
Waitonga Falls 74
Waituna Lagoon 217
Whirinaki Waterfall
Loop Track 62
Wilkies Pools 86

EASY – MODERATE

Diamond Lake &
Rocky Mountain 168
Hidden Falls Track 216
Lake Rere 188
Port William/Potirepo
to Halfmoon Bay/Oban 212
Queenstown Hill 189
Rob Roy Track 166
Sandymount & Sandfly Bay 184

MODERATE

GAbel Tasman Coast Track 116
Abel Tasman Day Walk 108
Bealey Spur 130
Bridle Path 142
Cape Brett Track 44
Coast to Coast Walkway 34
Godley Head/Awaroa 122
Green Hills &
Wharariki Beach 104
Kāpiti Island Summit 90
Kerikeri River 26
Key Summit 202
Lake Marian 200
Manawatū Gorge 88
Mt John (Ōtehīwai) 136
Ngā Tapuwae o Toi 64
Otari-Wilton's Bush loop 94
Paekākāriki Escarpment 92
Pupu Hydro Walkway 106
Queen Charlotte Day Walk 114
Queen Charlotte Track 116
Rainbow Mountain/Maunga
Kākaramea 58
Rangitoto Summit Loop 30
Routeburn Track Day Walk 180
Sawpit Gully 188
Sign of the Packhorse 124
Six Foot Track 45
Sunrise Track 98
Tama Lakes 56
Tarawera Trail 60
Te Ara Hura Day Walk 32
Te Mata Peak 72
Te Paki Coastal Track 24
Tongariro Alpine Crossing 50
Woolshed Creek Hut 132

MODERATE – HARD

Ben Lomond 172
Roys Peak 170

HARD

Alex Knob 154
Avalanche Peak 128
Castle Hill Peak 142
Gertrude Saddle 198
Heaphy Track 117
Kauaeranga Kauri Trail 40
Mt Holdsworth Jumbo Circuit 99
Mt Robert/Pourangahau
Circuit 112
Mt Ruapehu Crater Lake 75
Mt Taranaki Summit 98
Mueller Hut 140
Pouākai Crossing 80
Skyline Walkway 99
St Arnaud Range Track 117
Te Whara Track 44

225

Index

#ThatWanakaTree 171

A

Abel Tasman Coast Track 116
Abel Tasman Day Walk 108-11, **109**
accommodation 17, 220
    Canterbury 121
    Central North Island 49
    North, the 23
    Otago 165
    South, the 193
    Southern North Island 79
    Top of the South 103
    West Coast (South Island) 147
Ahukawakawa Swamp 82
airports 218
Alex Knob 154-5, **154**
ambulance 222
Aoraki/Mt Cook 138, 156
Aoraki/Mt Cook Village 141
Arrowtown 188
art galleries, *see* museums & galleries
Arthur's Pass 143
Arthur's Pass Walking Track 143
Auckland 22, 30, 32, 34, 41
Auckland Museum 38, 39
Auckland volcanic field 31
Avalanche Peak 128-9, 128

B

Bay of Islands 44
bays
    Anchorage Bay 110
    Apple Tree Bay 111
    Bark Bay 109
    Bendemeer Bay 178

> Walks 000
> **Map Pages 000**

    Boulder Bay 122-3
    Breeze Bay 123
    Brod Bay 206-7,
    Dock Bay 207
    Elfin Bay 188
    Enclosure Bay 33
    Glendhu Bay 169
    Golden Bay/Mohua 106
    Hawaiki Bay 61
    Horseshoe Bay 214
    Lee Bay 212, 214
    Martins Bay 203, 216
    Māwhitipana Bay 33
    Ngaio Bay 109
    Otarawairere Bay 66
    Owhanake Bay 32
    Post Office Bay 210
    Pukerua Bay 93
    Queenstown Bay 189
    Resolution Bay 115
    Sandfly Bay 184-5
    Schoolhouse Bay 115
    Shallow Bay 209
    Stillwell Bay 111
    Tauranga Bay 161
    Torrent Bay/Rākauroa 110
beaches 220
    Allans Beach 184
    Bob's Cove Beach 177
    Boulder Beach 210
    Butterfield Beach 214
    Farry's Beach 177
    Hekerua 33
    Hot Water Beach 60, 61
    Kāpiti Coast 91
    Lakes Hayes 178
    Little Oneroa Beach 33
    Long Beach 186
    Mangawhai Heads 45
    Māori Beach 213
    Medlands Beach 109
    Monro Beach 158
    Observation Beach 111
    Ōhope Beach 66
    Oneroa 33
    Onetahuti Beach 111
    Palm Beach 33
    Paraparaumu Beach 90
    Sandfly Bay 184-5
    Shallow Bay 209
    Te Werahi Beach 24
    Tolaga Bay Beach 70
    Twilight Beach/Paengarēhia 25
    West End Beach 210
    Wharariki Beach 104-5
Bealey Spur 130-1, **130**
Ben Lomond 172-5, **173**
bird-watching 12
    Adele Island/Motuareronui 111
    Farewell Spit 105
    Ōkārito Lagoon 153
    Ōkārito Pack Track 152
    Queen Charlotte Day Walk 114
    Ulva Island - Te Wharawhara Marine Reserve 210
blisters 222
Blue Lake 75
Blue Pools 189
Bob's Cove 176-7, **176**
books 19
Bridle Path 142
Brod Bay to Te Anau 206-7, **206**
buses 219

C

cable cars 75, 173
Campbell, John Logan 36
Canterbury 118-43, **118**
    accommodation 121
    climate 120
    festivals & events 121
    resources 121

seasonal travel 120-1
transport 121
Cape Brett Track 44
Cape Foulwind Walkway 161
Cape Maria van Diemen 25
Cape Reinga/Te Rerenga Wairua 25
Cape Saunders 184
Castle Hill Peak 142
Catlins Conservation Park 216
Catlins River 216
Centennial Walkway 39
Central North Island 46-75, **46**
  accommodation 49
  climate 48-9
  festivals & events 49
  resources 49
  transport 49
  travel seasons 48
Charming Creek North Walkway 148-9, **148**
Christchurch 120, 124, 142
Cleopatra's Pool 110
climate 16-17, 22
  Canterbury 120-1
  Central North Island 48-9
  North, the 22-3
  Otago 164-5
  South, the 192-3
  Southern North Island 78-9
  Top of the South 102
  West Coast 146-7
climate change 223
Coast to Coast Walkway 34-9, **35**
Cook, Captain James 70, 114
Cooks Cove Walkway 70-1, **70**
Coromandel Forest Park 40-1
Coromandel Peninsula 41
costs 219, 220, 224
country code 224
credit cards 224
cribs 220

D

debit cards 224
Diamond Lake & Rocky Mountain 168-9, **168**
digital payments 224
Dobson, Arthur 143
Dore Pass 195
driving 219
du Faur, Freda 138
Dunedin 165, 184
d'Urville, Jules Dumont 111

E

electricity 224
Emerald Pool 134
emergencies 222, 224
Enclosure Bay 33
etiquette 220, 221, 224
events, *see* festivals & events

F

festivals & events
  Canterbury 121
  Central North Island 49
  North, the 23
  Otago 165
  South, the 193
  Southern North Island 79
  Top of the South 103
West Coast (South Island) 147
fire services 222
Fox Glacier/Te Moeka o Tuawe 146-7
Franz Josef Glacier/Kā Roimata o Hine Hukatere 146
Freestone, Bruce 92
Furneaux Lodge 115

G

gardens, *see* parks & gardens
gear rental 221
Gertrude Saddle 198-9, **198**
glaciers
  Crow Glacier 129
  Franz Josef Glacier/Kā Roimata o Hine Hukatere 154
  Hollyford Glacier 200
  Mueller Glacier 140
  Rob Roy Glacier 167
Glenorchy 164, 180, 183
Godley Head/Awaroa 122-3, **122**
Green Hills & Wharariki Beach 104-5, **104**
Greymouth 161

H

Haast 147, 158
Halfmoon Bay/Oban 193
Harihari Coastal Walkway 160
Hauraki Gulf 28, 31-2
Havelock 115
Hawaiki Bay 61
health 222
Heaphy Track 117
Herangi Hill 25
Hidden Falls Track 216
highlights 8-15
Hika, Hongi 26
Hillary, Sir Edmund 141
history
  Blackburn Coal Mine 135
  Cook, Captain James 71
  Coromandel gold 43
  Gunn's Camp 201
  Treaty of Waitangi 65
  Wānaka Station 169
  White Island/Whakaari 68
  WWII 123
holiday parks 220
Hooker Valley 138-9, **138**
Horonuku Te Heuheu Tukino IV 51
Huka Falls to Aratiatia Rapids 74
hydroelectric power 87, 106

I

insects 222
insurance 222
Invercargill 192, 217

J

Johnsonville 99

K

Kaikōura 120, 126-7
Kaikōura Peninsula Walkway 126-7, **126**
Kāpiti Island Summit 90-1, **90**
Kapuni Loop Track 87
Kapu-te-Rangi 65
Karangahake Gorge 42-3, **42**
Karori 99
Kauaeranga Kauri Trail 40-1, **40**
kayaking 111
   Abel Tasman 111
   Queen Charlotte Drive 115
Kawerau Track Loop 28-9, **28**
Kea Point 140
Kenepuru Sound 116
Kepler Track 207
Kerikeri 22
Kerikeri River 26-7, **26**
Key Summit 202-3, **202**
Kōhī Point 66
Kohuamarua Bluff 153

L

Lake Gunn Nature Walk 217
Lake Hayes 178-9, **178**
Lake Marian 200-1, **200**
Lake Matheson 156-7, **156**
Lake Rere 188
lakes
   Black Lake 199
   Blue Lake 52, 54, 55, 75
   Blue/Tikitapu Lake 75
   Crater Lakes 58
   Diamond Lake 168-9
   Emerald Lakes 52
   Green (Rotokakahi) Lake 75
   Lake Gunn 217
   Lake Hayes 178-9, 188
   Lake Manapōuri 207, 209
   Lake Marian 201, 203
   Lake Matheson
     (Te Ara Kairaumati) 156
   Lake Moeraki 158
   Lake Pukaki 141
   Lake Rere 188
   Lake Rotoiti 113
   Lake Rotomahana 61
   Lake Tarawera 60-1
   Lake Te Anau 194-7, 202, 206-7
   Lake Tekapo (Takapō) 136
   Lake Wakatipu 172, 173, 174, 177, 178, 188, 189, 202
   Lake Wānaka 168-9
   Lake Wombat 154
   Lower Tama Lake 57
   Mavora Lakes 204
   Mt Ruapehu Crater Lake 75
   Mueller Lake 139
   North Mavora Lake 204
   Rotoiti 113
   Rotoroa 113
   Sealy Tarns 141
   South Mavora Lake 204
   Spirit Lake 208
   Tama Lakes 56-7
   Upper Tama Lake 56-7
Landsborough, Stuart 169
language 19
lighthouses 24
Little River estuary 214
Long Beach 186-7, **186**
Lye, Len 84
Lyttelton 142
Lyttleton Harbour/Whakaraupō 124

M

Mackinnon Pass/Omanui 195, 197
Manapōuri 209
Manawatū Gorge 88-9, **88**
Mangawhai Cliffs Walkway 45
Māori tourism 223
Marlborough Sounds 114, 115
Marsden, Rev Samuel 26
Martinborough 78
Mavora Walkway 204-5, **204**
Māwhitipana Bay 33
McKenzie Reserve 33
McKinnon, Quintin 197, 207
Melville Park 36
Milford Sound/Piopiotahi 195, 198, 199
Milford Track 195
Milford Track Day Walk 194-7, **195**
Mitchell, Ernest 197
Mitre Rocks 71
money 218, 224
Monro Beach 158-9, **158**
Moria Gate Arch 160
Motueka 102
mountain-biking 149, 173
mountains
   Alex Knob 154-5
   Aoraki/Mt Cook 139, 142, 156
   Avalanche Peak 128-9
   Ben Lomond 172, 173, 189
   Ben Lomond Saddle 174
   Bob's Knob 176, 177
   Castle Hill Peak 142
   Cecil Peak 189
   Foggy Peak 142
   Gertrude Saddle 198-9
   Godley Head/Awaroa 123
   Harris Saddle 203
   Jackson Peaks 207
   Kepler Mountains 207
   Key Summit 202, 203
   Mt Aspiring/Tititea 168, 172, 181
   Mt Bruce 131
   Mt Christina 201
   Mt Crosscut 201
   Mt Edward 137
   Mt Holdsworth 99
   Mt John (Ōtehīwail) 136
   Mt Lyttle 201
   Mt Maunganui 66
   Mt Ngauruhoe 50
   Mt Ollivier 141
   Mt Robert/Pourangahau 112
   Mt Rolleston 129
   Mt Ruapehu 74, 75
   Mt Sefton 139, 141

Walks 000
Map Pages 000, **000**

Mt Somers 133
Mt Stokes/Parorangi 115
Mt Talbot 198
Mt Taranaki 81, 86
Mt Tarawera 61
Mt Tasman 156
Mt Tongariro 50
Pinnacles 41
Rainbow Mountain/Maunga Kākaramea 58
Rocky Mountain 168-9
Roys Peak 169-70
Ruahine Range 98
Sandymount 184
Sentinel 196
Ship Cove Saddle 115
Somers Saddle 133
Tawa Saddle 115
Te Mata Peak 73
Te Tapu-nui 189
Tooth Peak 188
Tūteremoana 91
Two Thumbs Range 137
Walter Peak 189
movies 18
Mt Holdsworth Jumbo Circuit 99
Mt John Observatory 137
Mt John (Ōtehīwai) 136-7, **136**
Mt Robert/Pourangahau Circuit 112-13, **112**
Mt Ruapehu Crater Lake 75
Mt Taranaki Summit 98
Mueller Hut 140-1, **140**
museums & galleries
    Auckland Museum 38, 39
    Govett-Brewster 84
    Huia Lodge 36
    Puke Ariki 84
music 19, 35

N

Napier 49
national parks, *see* nature reserves, parks & gardens
nature reserves

Abel Tasman National Park 109
Arthur's Pass National Park 128, 130-1
Aspiring/Tititea National Park 203
Catlins Conservation Park 216
Diamond Lake Conservation Area 169
Egmont National Park 80
Farewell Spit 105
Fiordland National Park 192, 197, 198-203, 206-207
Kahurangi National Park 105, 106, 107
Lake Hayes Reserve 178
Long Beach Recreation Reserve 186
Mavora Lakes Conservation Park 204
McKenzie Reserve 33
Mt Aspiring/Tititea National Park 181
Nelson Lakes National Park 112-13, 117
Paparoa National Park 150
Rakiura National Park 210-13
Stack Conservation Area 171
Taranaki/Egmont National Park 80-3
Te Anau Bird Sanctuary 206, 207
Tongariro National Park 48, 51, 56
Waimarino 50
Nelson 102
New Plymouth 78, 80, 84
Ngā Tapuwae o Toi 64-9, **65**
North Island, *see* Central North Island; North, the; Southern North Island
North, the, 20-45, **20**
    accommodation 23
    climate 22-3
    festivals & events 23
    resources 23
    transport 23
    travel seasons 22-3

O

Oban 193
observatories 137
Ōhakune 74
Ōkārito Pack Track & Coastal Walk 152-3, **152**
One Tree Hill/Maungakiekie 35
Ōpārara Arch 160
Ōpārara Basin 160

opening hours 224
Otago 162-89, **162**
    accommodation 165
    climate 164
    festivals & events 165
    resources 165
    seasonal travel 164-5
    transport 165
Otago Peninsula 184
Otarawairere Bay 64, 66
Otari-Wilton's Bush loop 94-7, **94**
Owhanake Bay 32

P

Paekākāriki 91
Paekākāriki Escarpment 92-3, **92**
Pancake Rocks 150, 151
Paradise 183
Pari Pari 93
parking 219
parks & gardens
    Anzac Park 126
    Auckland Domain 39
    Cornwall Park 36
    Emily Place Reserve 39
    Jellicoe Park 35
    Otari-Wilton's Bush 95
    Wintergarden 39
Paterson Inlet/Whaka a Te Wera 213
payments 224
Pelorus Sound/Te Hoiere 115
Phoenix Bluff 182
Picton 103
Pinnacles Hut 41
planning
    climate 48-9, 78-9
    clothing 18-9
    highlights 8-15
plastics 223
podcasts 19
Point Elizabeth Walkway 161
police 222
Port William/Potirepo to Halfmoon Bay/Oban 212-13, **213**
Pouākai Crossing 80-5, **81**

229

Pouākai Tarns 82
Punakaiki-Pororari Loop 150-1, **150**
Pupu Hydro Walkway 106-7, **106**
Pūrākanui 186

Q

Queen Charlotte Day Walk 114-15, **114**
Queen Charlotte Sound/Tōtaranui 115, 116
Queen Charlotte Track 116
Queenstown 164, 172
Queenstown Hill 189

R

Rainbow Mountain/Maunga Kākaramea 58-9, **58**
Rainbow Reach to Shallow Bay 208-9, **208**
Rakaia Gorge Walkway 143
Rakiura Track 213
Rangitoto Summit Loop 30-1, **30**
Rapahoe 161
resources 221, 223
   Canterbury 121
   Central North Island 49
   North, the 23
   Otago 165
   Southern North Island 79
   South, the 193
   Top of the South 103
   West Coast 147
rivers
   Arrow River 188
   Billygoat Stream 41
   Bruce Stream 131
   Buller River 112
   Catlins River 216
   Clinton River 195, 196
   Eglinton River 202
   Emily Creek 182
   Falls River 109

> Walks000
> **Map Pages 000, 000**

   Forest Burn 208
   Frank Stream 216
   Glade Burn 197
   Green Hills Stream 104
   Greenstone River 188, 202
   Hidden Falls Creek 216
   Hollyford River 216
   Humboldt Creek 216
   Kapuni Stream 87
   Kauaeranga River 40, 41
   Kerikeri River 26
   Makarora River 189
   Manawatū River 88
   Mararoa River 204
   Matukituki River 168
   Minarapa Stream 81
   Morgan Stream 134
   Ngakawau River 149
   Ōpārara River 160
   Poerua River 160
   Pororari River 150-151
   Punakaiki River 150
   Rakaia River 143
   Rob Roy Stream 166
   Stocking Stream 139
   Stony River 82-85
   Torrent River 110
   Travers River 112
   Waiau River 207
   Waikato River 74
   Wairere Stream 56
   Wairua Stream 61
   Wallis Stream 216
   Wanganui River 160
   Webb Creek 40
   Whirinaki River 45, 62
   Woolshed Creek 133, 135
Rob Roy Track 166-167, **166**
Rotorua 48
Routeburn Track Day Walk 180-183, **181**
Roys Peak 170-171, **170**

S

safe travel 222
Sandfly Point 195

Sandy Bay 33
Sandymount & Sandfly Bay 184-185, **184**
Sawpit Gully 188
Scaife, Willis 171
seasonal travel 16-17
   Canterbury 120-1
   Central North Island 48-9
   North, the 22-3
   Otago 164-5
   Southern North Island 78-9
   South, the 192-3
   Top of the South 102-3
   West Coast 146-7
Seddonville 148, 149
Ship Cove/Meretoto 114, 116
Sign of the Packhorse 124-125, **124**
SIM cards 218
Six Foot Track 45
Skyline Walkway 99
smoking 224
Southern North Island 77-99
   accommodation 79
   climate 78-79
   festivals & events 79
   resources 79
   transport 79
   travel seasons 78-79
Southern North Island (m) 76
South Island, *see* Canterbury; Otago; South, the; Top of the South; West Coast
South, the 190-217, **190**
   accommodation 193
   climate 192-3
   festivals & events 193
   resources 193
   seasonal travel 192-3
   transport 193
speed limits 219
Split Apple Rock 109
sports grounds 36
springs 51, 55, 61
St Arnaud Range Track 117
Stewart Island/Rakiura 210-211
Stone Store 27
streams, *see* rivers

Sunrise Track 98
Sydney Cove 210

T

Tākaka 102
Tama Lakes 56-7, **56**
Taranaki/Egmont National Park 80-3
Tarawera Trail 60-1, **60**
Taupō 48
Te Anau 192, 206
Te Anau Downs 194, 195
Te Ara Hura Day Walk 32-3, **32**
Te Mata Peak 72-3, **72**
Te Paki Coastal Track 24-5, **24**
Te Wairoa 60
Te Whara Track 44
television 18
Thames 23
time zone 224
tipping 224
Tiritiri Matangi Island 28-9
toilets 224
Tongariro Alpine Crossing 50-5, **51**
Tongariro Northern Circuit 57
Top of the South 100-17, **100**
   accommodation 103
   climate 102-3
   festivals & events 103
   resources 103
   seasonal travel 102-3
   transport 103
Torrent Bay/Rākauroa 110
transport 219
   Canterbury 121
   Central North Island 49
   North, the 23
   Otago 165
   South, the 193
   Southern North Island 79
   Top of the South 103
   West Coast 147
travel to/from New Zealand 218
travel within New Zealand 219, *see also* individual regions
Troup Picnic Lawn 96
Twelve Mile Delta 177

U

Ulva Island - Te Wharawhara Marine Reserve 210-11, **210**
universities 39
University Clock Tower 39
Urquharts Bay 44

V

Viaduct Harbour 39
Victoria Battery 42
vineyards 33
visas 218
volcanoes
   Maungawhau/Mt Eden 36
   Mt Eden/Maungawhau 36
   Mt Ngauruhoe 50, 51, 52
   Mt Taranaki 81, 86, 98
   Mt Tongariro 50, 51
   Pouākai 81
   Rangitoto 31
   Tama Saddle 56, 57
   Te Maari 54

W

Waiorua 91
Waitonga Falls 74
Waituna Lagoon 217
Wānaka 164, 166, 189
water 222
waterfalls
   Bells Falls 81-4
   Bridal Veil Falls 143, 181
   Dawson Falls 87
   Devils Punchbowl Falls 129, 143
   Hidden Falls 216
   Huka Falls 74
   Ketetahi Falls 55
   Key Summit 203
   Mangatini Falls 148, 149
   Marian Falls 200
   Otari-Wilton's Bush 94
   Owharoa Falls 42
   Rainbow Falls 26
   Routeburn Falls 182
   Sutherland Falls 195
   Taranaki Falls 56, 57
   Twin Falls 169
   Wairere Falls 65
   Waitonga Falls 74
   Wharepuke Falls 26
   Whirinaki River 62
weather 16-17
Wellington 78, 79, 90, 99
West Coast (South Island) 144-61, **144**
   accommodation 147
   climate 146-7
   festivals & events 147
   resources 147
   transport 147
   travel seasons 146-7
Westport 146
Whakapapa Village 57
Whakatāne 64-7
Whatonga 88
Whirinaki Waterfall Loop Track 62-3, **62**
White Horse Hill 139
wi-fi 218
wildfires 222
Wilkies Pools 86-7, **86**
wineries 33
Woodville 88
Woolshed Creek Hut 132-5, **132**

THE WRITERS

Naomi Arnold
Naomi Arnold is an award-winning freelance journalist based in Nelson, NZ, who contributes to most national publications and international outlets including the Washington Post and the Guardian. Her memoir *Northbound* – about hiking the 3000km length of NZ – was published by HarperCollins in 2025. She's also author of acclaimed astronomy history *Southern Nights* and co-author of NZ conservation history *Force of Nature*.

Andrew Bain
Andrew Bain has a love of all things alpine, which regularly draws him across the Tasman Sea from his Australian home to the mountains of New Zealand. He is the author of Lonely Planet's *Hiking and Tramping in New Zealand*, and has an encyclopaedic list of South Island summits he still yearns to climb.
@bainonbike

Peter Dragicevich
Over the past 20 years, Peter's written well over 100 books for Lonely Planet on an oddly disparate collection of countries. New Zealand is home, though, and the opportunity to research the tracks featured in this book during the Southern Hemisphere summer made it one of his favourite assignments to date.

Craig McLachlan
A long-time Lonely Planet writer and Queenstown resident, Craig has been leading hiking tours around the south of Aotearoa for decades. He loves where he lives – and any chance to introduce the region's spectacular outdoor environment to international visitors. Check out *craigmclachlan.com*.

BEHIND THE SCENES

This book was researched and written by Naomi Arnold, Andrew Bain, Peter Dragicevich and Craig McLachlan. It was produced by the following:

Destination Editor Jessica Lockhart

Coordinating Editor Michael Mackenzie

Production Editor Jenni McCann

Book Designer Dermot Hegarty

Cartographer Mark Griffiths

Cover Design & Researcher Daisy Korpics

Assisting Editors Ronan Abayawickrema, Sofie Andersen, Alex Conroy, Karen Henderson, Melanie Dankel, Anne Mulvaney

ACKNOWLEDGMENTS

Digital Model Elevation Data Contains public sector information licensed under the Open Government Licence v3.0 website http://www.nationalarchives.gov.uk/doc/open-government-licence/version/3/

Cover photograph Mt Apsiring, South Island, Liz Carlson/Photographer